Theory/

This is a new and enlarged edition of Mark Fortier's very successful and widely used essential text for students. *Theory/Theatre* provides a unique and engaging introduction to literary theory as it relates to theatre and performance. Fortier lucidly examines current theoretical approaches, from semiotics and poststructuralism, through cultural materialism, postcolonial studies and feminist theory.

This new edition includes more detailed explanation of key ideas, new question sections at the end of each chapter to help the reader approach performances from specific theoretical perspectives, and an annotated further reading section and glossary.

Theory/Theatre is still the only study of its kind and is invaluable reading for beginning students and scholars of performance studies.

Mark Fortier is Associate Professor of English at the University of Winnipeg. He has published on Shakespeare, early modern literature, contemporary theatre, cultural studies and theory. He is co-editor of *Adaptations of Shakespeare* (Routledge 2000).

Theory/Theatre

An Introduction
Second Edition

Mark Fortier

LONDON AND NEW YORK

First published 1997
Second edition published 2002
by Routledge
2 Park Square, Milton Park, Abingdon, Oxon OX14 4RN

Simultaneously published in the USA and Canada
by Routledge
270 Madison Avenue, New York, NY 10016

Reprinted 2006 (twice)

Routledge is an imprint of the Taylor & Francis Group, an informa business

© 1997, 2002 Mark Fortier

Typeset in Joanna and ScalaSans by Taylor & Francis Books Ltd
Printed and bound in Great Britain by MPG Books Ltd, Bodmin, Cornwall

British Library Cataloguing in Publication Data
A catalogue record for this book is available from the British Library

Library of Congress Cataloging in Publication Data
A catalog record for this book has been requested

ISBN 10: 0–415–25436–1 (hbk)
ISBN 10: 0–415–25437–X (pbk)

ISBN 13: 978–0–415–25436–6 (hbk)
ISBN 13: 978–0–415–25437–3 (pbk)

CONTENTS

Acknowledgements

Rewriting a book you thought you'd finished years ago is an exhilarating experience – one of the rare instances in life when the benefits of hindsight can actually have a positive effect. I wish to thank Talia Rodgers at Routledge for initiating this process. Liz Thompson at Routledge took charge of editing this edition. Her own suggestions were invaluable, and her gathering and arranging of readers' responses to my first edition were amazingly helpful. The large number of readers she commissioned, as well as those who reviewed the first edition, have helped me immensely, and their suggestions have had an effect, in one way or another, on practically every page of this second edition. The University of Winnipeg provided various kinds of infrastructural support. Dorothy Hadfield prepared the index. Per Brask read the rewriting section by section and offered continuing and welcome encouragement. Debra Miller shared my pages and my life from start to finish. This edition is dedicated to her. Finally, I want to acknowledge and thank those who have used the first edition of this book and to offer them this new, expanded and improved version. I hope they will not be disappointed.

INTRODUCTION

WHY THIS BOOK?

Theory spoken here

Have you ever overheard an argument in which one person said to another, 'Don't psychoanalyse me'? Or have you heard someone on a popular television show use the word 'deconstruct'? Have you ever seen protesters shouting 'Down with patriarchy'? Or someone hesitate around an assertion by saying 'But that's just my reading of the situation'? It's unlikely that the two quarrellers were psychotherapists, the tv personality a graduate student, the protesters professors of feminist theory, or that the hesitant one knew much about reader-response, but they were all using words and ideas that have entered the popular vocabulary from cultural theory.

Cultural theory – the attempt to understand in a systematic way the nature of human cultural forms such as language, identity and art – began at least as far back as Ancient Greece, with Plato and Aristotle. Our own theoretical era, broadly conceived, began in the nineteenth century with such European philosophers as G.W.F. Hegel, Karl Marx and Friedrich Nietzsche; continued into the early twentieth century with Sigmund Freud, founder of psychoanalysis, and Ferdinand de Saussure, founder of semiology or semiotics; and then into the middle of this century with, among others, the Russian Mikhail Bakhtin, the Italian Marxist Antonio Gramsci, the German Walter Benjamin and the French feminist Simone de Beauvoir. But it is really since the 1960s that cultural theory, or just plain 'theory' as we now call it, has become a dominant force in academic and cultural environments. Deconstruction, feminism, post-colonialism, semiotics, queer theory, postmodernism and so forth, have come to define for many, at least in western academia, the most fruitful and appropriate ways of looking at culture, politics and society.

That theoretical vocabulary arises in everyday speech indicates how the ideas of cultural theory have in some measure entered into popular culture. On the other hand, however, people often use these words without having a very accurate or complex sense of what they mean. Nor has theory had a smooth and uncontested ride even within universities, where resistance to theory is nearly as strong as the insistence on theory. Theatre studies is a case in point.

Theatre is an area in which theory has had a powerful influence. There are learned journals rife with theoretical studies of theatre and many books that apply deconstruction, semiotics, psychoanalysis or some other theoretical perspective to various theatrical works. There is not, however, a book which systematically introduces theatre students to a broad range of theory and examines the application of theory to theatre. This book is intended to be such an introduction.

All disciplines where theory has encroached have offered a degree of resistance: for some, theory is too abstruse, too jargon-ridden, too divorced from practicality. Theory has often seemed too contemplative an activity to be more help than hindrance in such a practical pursuit as theatre. Theatre is not made in the mind or on the page. Moreover, much of the theory discussed in this book is often referred to, at least in literature departments, as 'literary theory'. Why should this be so? After all, this theory comes from a broad range of disciplines: philosophy, linguistics, psychoanalysis, political economics, history, anthropology and so forth. To call these theories literary theory is in large part a misrecognition. It is, however, a misrecognition which reveals something about a great deal of theory.

Much of the theory under discussion stresses the importance of language as the basis of human activity, as will be seen in the following chapters. Theories that are profoundly caught up in questions of language and writing have been more easily, more systematically and more fully applied to literature and other forms of writing than to art forms and cultural practices which emphasize the nonverbal. It becomes easy to think that activities involving writing are somehow at the heart of being human. Theorists of literature have appropriated language-based theories from other disciplines to such an extent that, for many working in theory and literature, all theory has become in effect literary theory. So it is designated, for instance, in the encyclopedias of Irena Makaryk (*Encyclopedia of Contemporary Literary Theory*) and Michael Groden and Martin Kreisworth (*The Johns Hopkins Guide to Literary Theory and Criticism*).

What happens to more or less nonverbal activities in the face of this emphasis on language and writing? Can literary theory do them justice? Many involved in theatre have been suspicious of this verbal predominance in theory. To treat everything as language or as dominated by language seems a distortion of the nature of theatre as rooted in the physical and the sensual, as much as it is in words and ideas.

Those who study theatre make a commonplace distinction between drama and theatre. Drama is most often written language, the words ascribed to the characters, which in the theatre are spoken by actors. As a written form, drama is easily appropriated by literary theory; it is understandable in the same general terms as fiction, poetry or any other form of letters. The affinity of drama and literature has produced a tendency for literary theory and literary studies to think of theatrical activity as drama rather than as theatre.

Unlike drama, theatre is not words on a page. Theatre is performance (though often the performance of a drama text) and entails not only words but space, actors, props, audience and the complex relations among these elements. Literary theory has often ignored all this. Moreover, if it doesn't reduce theatre to drama, literary theory is capable of making an even bolder gesture in which theatre is brought under the sway of language and writing in another way. Here theatre – bodies, lights, sounds – becomes a system of nonverbal signs, nonverbal language, nonverbal writing, yet dominated still by the predominance of language and letters as master-patterns for the workings of even the nonverbal. Theatre too is a literature. A big question remains: is theatre fully understandable when dominated by a linguistic model?

One side effect of literary theory's domination of theatre is that, despite the assimilation of drama into literary studies, and despite the attempt to see theatre as nonverbal literature, literary theory ignores those who have made the most profound contributions to a specific theory of theatre: drama and theatre belong to literary theory but theatre theorists do not. For instance, neither of the encyclopedias by Makaryk and Groden and Kreisworth has separate entries for Bertolt Brecht or Antonin Artaud. To anyone involved in theatre theory, these omissions are nothing short of shocking, as much as if Saussure, Freud or Derrida were absent. But shock gives way to speculation: Brecht and Artaud think about theatre in a way that is profoundly different from the way literary theory does, perhaps in a way that literary theory has trouble recognizing.

Given these concerns, to those in theatre with an entrenched antipathy to theory, my book is likely to be as much an affront as it is an introduction. In large measure this is unavoidable. Although my purpose is not to shove theory down anyone's throat (to use a Canadian turn of phrase), one of the key insights of much theory is that we cannot control how what we write or say will be taken by others – theatre people know this already in the way a performance is always inevitably different from the idea that began in someone's head. Those who are more open to theory, however, might see in this book not an attempt to conquer theatre under the flag of theory, but rather an attempt to create a place for dialogue, exploration and questioning.

For instance, one of the themes that runs throughout my discussion is the friction between language-based theory and the nonverbal aspects of theatre. For me, the point is not to reject language-based theory but to map the limits of its relevance with care and openness. Similarly, I think the relations between practice and reflection are not susceptible to easy dismissal. The word 'drama' comes from a word related to the Greek verb 'to do'; 'theatre', on the other hand, comes from a word related to the verb 'to see'. Theatre, of necessity, involves both doing and seeing, practice and contemplation. Who wants to see a performance with no thought behind it? Moreover, the word 'theory' comes from the same root as 'theatre'. Theatre and theory are both contemplative pursuits, although theatre has a practical and sensuous side which contemplation should not be allowed to overwhelm.

This book, therefore, seeks in the engagement of theory and theatre, questions to pose to each. Is theatre a kind of language, or, if not, how does it escape this master-pattern? If there is something about the theatre which is different from language, how does this reflect on the dominance of language and writing in theory's understanding of the world? What possible relations are there between thinking about theatre in theoretical terms and the practical act of making theatre? The resistance to theory offered by theatre, or put more benignly, the insistence that theatre have a voice in a true dialogue with theory, points to a second aspect of their relation. Theory can be applied to theatre, but in the other direction, theatre speaks back to theory. This is especially so in theatre pieces that themselves enact or induce complex thinking. Much of Shakespeare, for instance, is highly sophisticated reflection on theatre, culture and reality.

Suspicion about theory has come from surprising places in theatre studies. Bonnie Marranca, editor of *Performing Arts Journal*, which has been quite open to theoretical work, has recently questioned the use of theory in theatre studies. Although she rejects the separation of practice and production from thinking and reflection, she condemns what she sees as the knee-jerk and formulaic application of theory, a 'dogmatic corruption' of the openness that theory should entail (Marranca 1995: 65). In an introductory volume, some simplification is necessary. But I have not, I hope, written a dogmatic work. My summary of theories, issues and relations is put forward as a set of observations and explicit or implicit questions rather than as a set of conclusions. Theories produce variant and often contradictory ways of looking at issues; readers are encouraged to treat my accounts of theory and my readings of plays as provisional and revisable. On the largest scale, I am not arguing for any necessary relation between theory and theatre. Readers will work out the relation for themselves. Like Antonin Artaud, I would like 'not to define thoughts but *to cause thinking*' (Artaud 1958: 69).

The unique contribution of *Theory/Theatre* is to provide an introductory overview of current cultural theory as it might be applied to the study of theatre. In this particular combination of concerns, it stands alone. However, this does not mean that all other texts in the area can be ignored, and I encourage anyone interested in theory and theatre to read much more widely, using the suggestions for further reading set out at the end of this book.

Theory/Theatre is designed to introduce a wide spectrum of ideas that readers might pursue in more narrowly focused books, and in this way to complement existing publications. Primary texts in theory are of course invaluable, but, as the further reading section of this book will show, there are also many valuable anthologies of extracts from theoretical texts, introductions to theory or to specific aspects of theory, encyclo-pedias of theory and works which apply specific areas of cultural theory to the theatre.

Given the extensiveness of work in the fields of theory and theatre, this book takes advantage of its relative belatedness to look back on a field that has had time to take on a certain shape. From this vantage I have attempted to grasp theory as broadly as possible. Unlike many related studies, I am specifically con-cerned with theories that come from outside theatre; unlike other books listed, I have attempted to deal with theory in gen-eral. This book also differs from others in that I have focused on making it introductory; it is a book designed to be accessible to those engaging with the relations between theory and theatre for the first time.

WHICH THEORIES? WHICH THEATRE?

The theories introduced in this book all came to prominence in the last one hundred and fifty years or so and were chosen largely because they are theories still in wide use. Materialism as we know it came to the fore beginning with the work of Karl Marx in the second half of the nineteenth century. The first part of the twentieth century saw the rise of semiotics, psychoanalysis and phenomenology. The latter part of the twentieth century has brought forth reader-response, deconstruction, feminism and gender theory, postmodernism and post-colonialism. These theories have also been chosen because they each have something important to say about theatre.

This is not just a book about theory; nor is it only about theatre. On the most general level, I have organized the discussion of theory and the theatre not around schools of theory or the work of particular theorists but rather around issues related to the theatre; theories are discussed inasmuch as they focus on the specific issue under discussion. These issues are grouped under three large headings. Chapter 1 deals with the relations between the verbal and the nonverbal on the stage, with theatre as text and theatre as a live event. Issues of signification, representation, meaning, understanding, words and silence, the stage, life, body and voice are explored. Chapter 2 deals with the people involved in theatre, with subjectivity, agency, author, character, performer, audience and the collaborations which theatre entails among all those involved. Chapter 3 addresses theatre as an institution in the world and theatre's relations with the world outside the playhouse; here the issues include the historical, economic and political forces which tie theatre in a highly specific way to a particular time and place.

Within each of these chapters, I have chosen to deal with the specific theoretical schools which seem most appropriate to the issue under consideration. However, I have tailored my discussions of each theoretical school to the concerns of a particular chapter and ask the reader to remember that each school I discuss has a broader range of interests and applications than my structure enumerates. For instance, feminism is dealt with in Chapter 2, on subject and agency. Although much of feminism is about the effect of gender on subjectivity, feminism is also deeply concerned with the subject's relations with the world, and so could have been discussed in Chapter 3. Also, I have dealt with individual theorists under the rubric of particular schools of theory. This is less of a distortion for some theorists than for others: Freud is obviously a psychoanalytic thinker. Many theorists, however, have hybrid interests. Gayatri Chakravorty Spivak, discussed here under post-colonialism, combines in her work Marxism, deconstruction, feminism and post-colonialism. Julia Kristeva, discussed here under psychoanalytic theory, combines feminism, semiotics and psychoanalysis.

Given these caveats, each chapter is divided into three sections, each dealing with a particular theoretical movement. The theoretical movements I discuss are arranged in the following order. In Chapter 1, on language and life, I discuss semiotics, phenomenology and deconstruction. Among the theorists discussed in this chapter are Saussure, Charles Peirce, Martin Heidegger, Maurice Merleau-Ponty, Derrida and Paul de Man. In Chapter 2, on subjectivity, I discuss psychoanalytic theory, feminist and gender theory, including queer theory, and reader-response and reception theory. Among the theorists covered in Chapter 2 are Freud, Lacan, Kristeva, Virginia Woolf, Judith Fetterley, Jill Dolan, Adrienne Rich, Eve Kosofsky Sedgwick, Wolfgang Iser and Hans Robert Jauss. In Chapter 3, on theatre and the world, I discuss materialist theory, postmodernism and post-colonialism. Among the theorists in this chapter are Louis Althusser, Raymond Williams, Walter Benjamin, Michel Foucault, Fredric Jameson, Linda Hutcheon, Jean Baudrillard, Jean-François Lyotard, Edward Said, Spivak, Trinh T. Minh-Ha, Homi Bhabha and Augusto Boal. Within each section there is an attempt to give an overview of that movement, a discussion of particular theorists associated with that movement, particular critics who have applied this theory to the study of theatre, and an exploration of this theory in light of an application to particular works or questions of theatre.

Theory and theatre can have a number of different relationships. Theatre can sometimes be analogous or equivalent to theoretical reflection; this is how, for example, I position the relationship between phenomenology and Anton Chekhov, or deconstruction and Artaud or Herbert Blau. Closely related – sometimes interchangeable – are cases in which theatre enacts a theoretical position; here, for example, I would point to psychoanalytic theory and Hélène Cixous, feminist theory and Caryl Churchill's Cloud Nine, or post-colonialism and the projects of Augusto Boal. Moreover, theory can be used to explain and elucidate theatre in general or particular works of theatre; Derrida on representation and presence is an example of the first, my deconstructive reading of Jerzy Grotowski's Akropolis and postmodern reading of Anna Deavere Smith's Twilight: Los Angeles examples of the second. Finally, theatre can answer back to theory, calling presuppositions into question and exposing limitations and blindness; the theatrical 'desemiotics' which questions the assumption in semiotics that everything on stage has meaning, the exploration of the way Peter Brook's A Midsummer Night's Dream takes reader-response theory in complex new directions, or the way Shakespeare's theatre troubles the simpler pieties of materialist analysis are all examples of the confrontation of theory with theatre. Often, of course, several relations are at work at once: Hélène Cixous both enacts psychoanalytic theory and questions it from a feminist perspective. The most important point to make about this variety is that it would be fruitless and misleading to try and limit it, especially in an introductory volume that hopes to open up possibilities.

Earlier I drew a distinction between drama, as words on a page, and theatre, as enactment on stage. To this picture it is necessary to add the concept of performance. As Marvin Carlson points out in his book on performance, performance is a 'contested concept' with a variety of different, even contradictory meanings (Carlson 1996: 1). Performance widely conceived refers to any performative human activity – everything from murder trials and elections to religious and social rituals, to everyday acts, such as a high school English class or shaving in front of a mirror. Feminist theorists such as Judith Butler even see our sexual identities as performances. Everyday life is a performance in this sense. Performance in a narrow sense refers to certain recent developments in the performing arts, which Patrick Campbell, in his book *Analysing Performance*, sees as in a time of cultural flux, 'when the performing arts pose more questions than answers' (1996: 2). Campbell's book features 'essays on dance, music, drama and multi-media performance' (1996: 1). Carlson provides an even narrower focus on performance art, a kind of hybrid genre most common in the United States, including happenings, demonstrations, museum exhibits involving human participants and so forth, which are often autobiographical, rely little on a script, and highlight the human body (1996: 6–9). Performance artists in this sense who are discussed in this book include Carolee Schneemann, Annie Sprinkle and Coco Fusco.

Performance can also be a concept used in theatre – as one of the traditional performing arts – to encompass the entire theatrical experience. This is the way it is used in the following account from Richard Schechner:

> the drama is what the writer writes; the script is the interior map of a particular production; the theater is the specific set of gestures performed by the performers in any given performance; the performance is the whole event, including audience and performers (technicians, too, anyone who is there).
>
> (Schechner 1988: 85)

Performance as a concept in theatre, therefore, is the notion of theatre in its entirety. Colin Counsell uses the term performance in this theatrical context when he calls his introduction to twentieth-century theatre *Signs of Performance*. In theatre studies, therefore, drama, theatre and performance are related activities. One way of thinking of the relationship is to see drama as a part of theatre and theatre as a part of performance in the wide sense. Seeing this relationship points out the difficulty involved in trying to separate a concern with drama from, say, a concern with theatre. To discuss drama is to discuss a part of theatre. Those involved in theatre studies are rightly wary that those in literature studies tend to reduce theatre to drama. This does not mean that theatre studies can study only theatre and not drama. A full study of theatre must be open to words on the page. Moreover, a study of theatre which does not see its relation to performance in general has made an artificial and limiting distinction.

My subject, therefore, is theatre, but this will often entail regard for the drama text and understanding of the place of theatre in a wider field of performance, as well as occasional reference to performance art and performances in everyday life. To stray too far into performance, however, would be to lose focus, while to dwell too much on drama would reduce this study to the narrowly literary. Nevertheless, readers will note that dramatic elements play a large part in my discussion. This is in part because drama, as fixed and recordable, is the part of theatre most accessible to examination and analysis. Moreover, the drama text remains, especially in the western tradition, a seminal aspect of theatre.

The examples I have taken from theatre are guided by a desire to reach a broad, general audience, and by my own expertise and limitations. Although most of my examples are from Europe and the Americas, I also turn to Africa; although they are predominantly from the twentieth century, there are also examples from classical Greece and the Renaissance; although many of them are canonical, I have tried to present a broad range of examples, some of which are newer or marginal works that challenge the hegemony of canonical norms. Also, just as many theorists can be discussed under different theories, so can play-wrights and performances. Just because I deal with a play under a particular theory doesn't mean that that is the right or only way to look at it. In a few instances I have returned to an example under a new heading in order to stress this point. Ultimately, what I would like the reader to take away from this study is not a particular reading of a particular play or performance, but the skill to transfer theoretical understanding so that it can be applied in ever new situations.

Finally, at the end of the book I have provided a glossary of theoretical terms which appear in the text.

WHO IS SPEAKING?

One of the foremost insights that feminism, especially, has brought to theory is the need to articulate the position from which one speaks. Who one is (one's experience, biases and investments) is thought to have an inevitable effect on how one reasons. The actual importance of such a positioning is open to question: how exactly does any position authenticate, detract from or at least inform one's arguments? How necessary a bond is there between who we are and what we are able to think? At any rate, however, it has become naive to ignore the position from which one speaks.

To position myself in a personal history, I am a white, hetero-sexual male. Whatever privilege this affords has been joined with a personal and intellectual history of discomfort with this position. As to class, my life feels like a roller-coaster ride, and employment and financial security were a long time coming. If simple patterns are worth drawing, one might see this personal history of privilege, uncertainty and disappointment played out in this project in the self-confidence of the undertaking itself and the questioning and doubt that inform the examination.

One aspect of personal history worth mentioning is nationality. I am a Canadian. From a Canadian perspective, works by Americans or the English often seem blindly to take their Americanness or Englishness for granted. If I may be cranky for a moment, Canadians are familiar with American speakers who make the all too common mistake of beginning a remark with 'Here in the United States' when they happen to be speaking on Canadian soil, and with English academics who cross the Atlantic only to bandy about the minutiae of the English cultural scene as if we had all been at Oxbridge together. If nationality informs this study, it is in the way I try to leave open and unoccupied any sense of being at a centre which unintentionally marginalizes everyone from somewhere else. I have also tried to straddle the Atlantic, if not the Pacific, in terms of the theatrical examples I choose to work with and ask that readers take unfamiliar examples as an opportunity to expand their own horizons.

My horizons, however, remain limited and western. I don't know a great deal about the Far East and I feel it would be presumptuous to write as if I did. On the other hand, it would be irresponsible and even more jingoistic of me to leave non-western examples out of a work such as this completely. In a typically Canadian compromise, I have tried to include a modest number of references to the theatre of the developing world, without passing myself off as an expert in this material.

But one has an intellectual as well as a personal history, and often this intellectual history is at least as relevant to how one thinks as is where one comes from. Of the theories examined here, I am most invested, on the one hand, in the rigorous scepticism of deconstruction, and on the other in the historical and political insistence of materialist theory; somewhere, somehow, I also retain, especially as someone interested in theatre, an affinity with phenomenology's involvement in bringing the world to light for lived experience. I do not consider myself, however, a deconstructionist or a phenomenologist, and although I do consider myself a materialist, I do not cling to any dogmatic or even orthodox Marxism.

Despite having my own theoretical leanings, I want to stress that I have tried to hold on to a principle of pluralist openness in the following chapters. There is much doubt in recent politicized theory as to whether pluralism and neutrality are possible; accordingly, sometimes introductory works like this one are written from an openly partisan position: Terry Eagleton's Marxist *Literary Theory*, for instance. Such a strategy has its own strengths, including focus and candour. There do seem to be varying degrees of partisanship, however, and in many aspects of life we expect or hope that, despite their biases, people will attempt to retain some degree of neutrality. And so other works, Carlson's *Theories of the Theatre*, for instance, attempt to maintain a more or less open stance. Pluralism has its limits both in its viability and in its usefulness; but it has its strengths too, especially in a work that aims, as I have said, to be interrogative as well as introductory.

Since this is an interrogative work, one important reason for pluralism is to maintain a healthy scepticism and doubt. There are many things, theoretical and political, about which I remain, and perhaps will always remain, uncertain. Moreover, I distrust people who are too sure of themselves. I believe that a book which is open to uncertainty is truer to the questioning side of human reason and is a more trustworthy guide because of this.

It also seems to me important to maintain plurality and neutrality in an introductory work. Eagleton's introduction to literary theory is extremely engaging; however, it is hard to imagine that it would ever induce anyone to take up the study of phenomenology or any of the other movements that Eagleton ridicules or dismisses. In this book I extend introductions on the principle that the ideas presented are ones the reader might actually someday wish to know better. Otherwise, why bother with introductions at all?

Finally, it is a particular combination of interests of mine that has brought me to write this book. On the one hand, I am a questioning and sceptical fellow, and theory appeals to the part of me that seeks out intellectual rigour. On the other hand, like many people, I desire society, sensuality, passion and art, and theatre attracts me as a less solitary and more stimulating cultural form than many others. It is in bringing these two hands together that my personal proclivities, intellectual and artistic, come closest to completion. I like theory. I like theatre. Best of all, I think, is to unite them. That's like having your cake and thinking about it too.

1

THEATRE, LIFE AND LANGUAGE

Semiotics, Phenomenology and Deconstruction

There is no one theory in this book which takes precedence over the others. In the late stage of theoretical development we have reached at the beginning of the twenty-first century, all the theories I discuss have come to inform all the others: post-colonial theory and postmodernism are informed by materialism and vice versa, for instance; nor can one now understand language and semiotics without gender considerations. More and more, critics have come to work by combining elements from different theoretical traditions. But a book has to start somewhere and the three theories outlined in this chapter – semiotics, phenomenology and deconstruction – are good places to start for a number of reasons. First, they have been highly influential on theories developed in large part afterwards – a prominent feminist journal, for instance, is called *Signs*, which suggests its affiliation with semiotics. Second, these three theories attempt to get at something very basic about the human condition. In doing so, they perform what phenomenology calls 'bracketing': leaving some issues out of the analysis so that a focus on the fundamental can be maintained, which is not to say that the equally important bracketed issues do not have to be brought back into the analysis at a later point. If I want to contemplate my own existence, I may begin with what appears to be basic about my existence. Once I get my mind around that, I need to bring all the other aspects of my life into my reflections. Semiotics, phenomenology and deconstruction, therefore, attempt to elucidate something basic about the human: in the case of semiotics the way we communicate with signs, most pre-eminently language; phenomenology with what it means to have a living body and a consciousness; deconstruction with the misconceptions about language and ourselves that we inevitably bring to understanding the way things are.

These theories also allow us to understand some very basic aspects of theatre. On a fundamental level, much happens and many elements are at work on a theatrical stage: bodies, breathing, light, sound, movement, gestures, language, and the material accidents and details of existence. The range of such elements and their combinations are in many ways specific to theatre as an art form and cultural phenomenon. How is theatrical reality best understood? As life, embodiment, sensation, event, representation, meaning, a kind of writing? How does the nature of this reality limit the possibilities of theatre? What are the inescapable laws and fate of theatre? Different theoretical perspectives suggest different responses to these questions. In this chapter, three such perspectives – semiotics, phenomenology and deconstruction – are brought to bear upon the exploration of theatre as a specific and concrete reality.

1 SEMIOTICS

Saussure, Peirce and Barthes

Semiotics, or semiology, is the study of signs – those objects by which humans communicate meaning: words, images, behaviour, arrangements of many kinds, in which a meaning or idea is relayed by a corresponding manifestation we can perceive. If I stick my tongue out at you, which is something you can perceive, I am expressing my scorn, which is the idea my tongue makes manifest. There are signs in nature: oncoming cloud cover is often, though not always, a sign of rain; the falling leaves in autumn are a sign of the coming of winter. But there has to be a human to read these signs, and theatre semiotics is predominantly the study of signs that humans put on stage for others to interpret. The French theorist Patrice Pavis cites the French historian Michel Foucault and the Swiss linguist Ferdinand de Saussure (discussed more fully shortly) for definitions of semiotics. For Foucault it is 'the ensemble of knowledge and technical skills that enable us to perceive where signs might be, to define what constitutes them as signs and to understand the relationship between them and the laws governing their interaction'; for Saussure, it is 'A science that studies the life of signs' and demonstrates 'what signs consist of and what laws govern them' (Pavis 1982: 13). The theatre semioticians Elaine Aston and George Savona write, 'The usefulness of the approach lies in its potential to make us more aware of how drama and theatre *are made*' (1981: 5).

Semiotics is an important and trenchant place to begin an introduction to theory and theatre for a number of reasons. At least two are especially noteworthy. First, the study of signs and their meaning has been as important as any movement in twentieth-century cultural theory, informing developments in perhaps all subsequent areas of theoretical endeavour. Second, because of its emphasis on language over all else, and on signification over more visceral and physical activities and effects, semiotics as much as any theoretical movement has a problematic relationship to theatre and the understanding of theatre. Do light, sound and movement always have meaning? Isn't there a corporeality in theatre which is over and above the presentation of meaning?

Almost all semiological work in the twentieth century borrows basic tenets from Ferdinand de Saussure's *Course in General Linguistics*, collected and published shortly after Saussure's death, in 1916. Saussure defines the sign as having two parts: the signifier, which is the material phenomenon we are able to perceive – the sound of a word, such as 'hello'; the wave of a hand – and the signified, which is the concept invoked by the signifier – the idea of greeting, for instance (Saussure 1974: 66–7). For Saussure, language is the most characteristic semiotic system inasmuch as the relation between signifier and signified is most arbitrary (p. 68): 'tree', '*arbre*' and '*Baum*' have no necessary or essential connection to the idea of a tree – unlike, perhaps (human duplicity enters in here), the relation between a smile and the joy it expresses. Saussure is most interested in internal linguistics, that is, he is mainly concerned with language as a closed system of rules more or less unconnected to outside factors, to the world at large (pp. 20–1). In this regard, the signified is a concept and not a referent in the world – the idea of a tree rather than the tree itself. The real world does not impinge very much on Saussure's semiology. Neither, according to Saussure, do human beings think in a world as much as they do in language: 'our thought – apart from its expression in words – is only a shapeless and indistinct mass', and 'there are no pre-existing ideas, and nothing is distinct before the appearance of language' (pp. 111–12).

Because the linguistic signifier has no necessary connection to the signified concept or the real referent in the world, its significance is not grounded in anything very firm or positive. Words do not take their meanings from their relationship to ideas or things, but from their relationships with other words (p. 118), and these relationships are relationships of difference – 'tree' is tree because it isn't 'free' or 'thee' or 'trek'. Think of the deck of cards in the game of bridge: a jack only has value because it is less than a queen and more than a ten; without these relations it means nothing. This notion of difference, of a system without a transcendental or unified term to give it coherence, without a sameness by which everything is measured, is central to much theory after Saussure and plays itself out in other areas: the psychoanalytic subject as divided and different from itself; women as different from men or from each other; people of colour as different from and not reducible to standards of whiteness.

Saussure is interested in language not only as a closed semiotic system but also as an abstract system rather than as a system used by people in a changing world. He is more interested in *langue*, a particular language system (English, for example), than in *parole*, the individual use of language in spoken expression (p. 13), or, by extension, particular acts of discursive expression in writing. The difference between *langue* and *parole* is like the difference between the game of bridge in the abstract and a particular hand played in a particular match. Saussure is also more interested in the synchronic than in the diachronic aspects of language: in the abstract pattern of language as a system frozen in a moment of time rather than in history, change and event (pp. 101–2), the way, for instance, the English language has changed in the last 600 years.

The other founding figure of twentieth-century sign theory is the American Charles Peirce, who wrote in the later nineteenth century, although his work became very influential somewhat later. Peirce calls his field of study semiotics. He separates the sign (what Saussure calls the signifier) from the object, which is loosely what Saussure calls the signified, but a signified which can be in different situations a concept, a thing, or even another signifier. He works out a classification of signs which sees them not as monolithic in the arbitrariness of their relationship to the object but as related to the object in different ways and to different degrees. A symbol – a word, for example – has an arbitrary relation to its object. An index, however – a finger pointing to indicate direction, for instance – has a closer relation to its object; an icon – a photograph of someone or an actor playing a character – has a strong resemblance to its object. Despite these gradations, Peirce insists, much as does Saussure, that a sign stands for something which is not present (the photograph is not the person; the actor is not the character), thus reinforcing the absence and metaphysical hollowness that haunt all signification.

Peirce, unlike Saussure, is not so interested in sign systems apart from their deployment, and insists that a sign is always a sign for somebody – in fact, that interpretation is part of the sign itself. In this way, semiotics is made situational, activated only by people in actual situations. If a light turns red and there is no one there to see and obey it, does it still mean 'stop'? For Saussure, because the system is in place, yes; for Pierce, because interpreters are necessary to activate signs, no. Each act of interpretation begets another and leads to what Peirce calls 'unlimited semiosis', the endless play of meaning and regeneration of signs in time. This interest in interpretation and history makes Peirce's work quite different in emphasis from Saussure's (see Peirce 1991).

The writings of the French theorist Roland Barthes from the 1950s to the 1970s are so wide-ranging that they could be discussed under a number of different rubrics; however, for the present discussion, Barthes is important for his applications of semiotic analysis to specific cultural activities and for his application of semiotic analysis to nonverbal as well as verbal signification. Barthes' early work is much like Saussure's in its semiotic

principles, seeking abstract models behind certain areas of cultural production ('Introduction to the Structural Analysis of
Narratives') and imposing a linguistic semiological model on
nonverbal activity – for instance, *The Fashion System* is not concerned with clothing itself but with what is said about clothing;
politically Barthes begins with a sense of 'myth', which is a
semiological system whereby ideology (the dominant ideas and
practices of a culture) is sweepingly imposed on a society
through its images (a photo of a black French soldier saluting
the French flag signifies that French imperialism is good).
Barthes' applications, or readings, of cultural activities, or texts,
range from the minute analysis of literary texts (for example,
Honoré de Balzac's novella *Sarrasine* in S/Z [1974]) to the analysis
of forms of social discourse (the kinds of things lovers think and
say in *A Lover's Discourse* [1978]) to various popular icons (the face
of Greta Garbo, the Eiffel Tower [Barthes 1972b]), to systems of
representation in painting and music (1985b). These interests
eventually lead Barthes to question the relationship of language
to non-linguistic activity. In general, he begins with a rather
hegemonic view of language – for example, of *The Fashion System*,
he says, 'fashion in its complex form, which alone interests us,
exists only through discourse on fashion' (1985a: 44). 'Is Painting
a Language?' takes a slightly more open view of things. Late in his
career, Barthes is more open still to the specific texture of nonverbal phenomena – the 'grain of the voice' (1985b: 267–77).

Over his career, Barthes moves from a reliance on structure as
the imposition of an abstract model to an interest in structuration, which involves the specific and unique arrangements of
cultural material in any particular instance. This involves a number of revisions: the idea of myth is replaced by the more heterogeneous and complex notion of codes; an interest in politics
as imposition of 'the same old story' becomes an interest in the
political – the myriad forms that relations of power take in
everyday life (1985a: 218–20); work, as a fixed object to be

read, becomes text, open to the endless play of interpretation (1979: 73–81); the movement from the work to the text implies the death of the author as original guarantor of stable meaning and the rise of the reader as activator of *jouissance*, an orgasmic joy in the unbridled dissemination of meaning (1988: 167–72). Thus Barthes moves from an abstract, scientific posture to a rejection of science and abstraction for the sake of an immersion in the specific language of texts themselves (1985a: 212–14).

Theatre semiotics

Semiological studies of theatre have been undertaken by a great number of theorists. The American theorist Jean Alter notes that when she set out to write a study of semiotics and theatre in the late 1970s, within a short time the field 'was thoroughly mapped in several major studies and hundreds of articles' (Alter 1990: xi). A systematic and in many ways characteristic work of theatre semiotics is Keir Elam's *The Semiotics of Theatre and Drama* (1980). Elam displays the strong pattern-making bent of much semiological analysis, attempting to provide a coherent system capable of accounting for all significant activity of theatre and drama: smiles, gestures, tones of voice, blocking, music, light, character development and so forth. Elam quotes the Eastern European semiotician Jiri Veltrusky: 'All that is on the stage is a sign' (Elam 1980: 7). Similarly, the theatre theorist Erika Fischer-Lichte writes: 'Everything which humans produce is "significant" for themselves and each other, because humans in principle live "in a signifying world". ... Every sound, action, object, or custom ... involves the production of a meaning' (Fischer-Lichte 1992: 1). Elam presents elaborate charts to account for signification in the theatre and for the structures of signification in dramatic discourse: human emotions, for instance, can be reduced to a complex system of gestures and tones. Theatre becomes eminently analysable and understandable, eminently readable. The sensual and experiential thickness of theatre (as will be discussed in the next section on phenomenology) becomes for semiotics a density of signs, denser and more complex than many sign systems, but a sign system nonetheless.

Saussure is one of the founding figures in the theoretical movement known as structuralism, which purports to carry out a scientific and objective analysis of the basic abstract patterns that underlie and activate all cultural activities. Saussure inaugurated this abstraction in linguistics and the study of signs, and much semiological analysis, in theatre as elsewhere, continues in this mode of mapping abstract patterns. Many works of theatre semiotics, such as those of Elam and Aston and Savona, are full of graphs and charts which reduce theatrical activity to generalized structures which claim to see the big picture to which everything can be reduced. The French theatre semiologist Patrice Pavis has moved away from this attempt to grasp the big picture. A global systematization of theatrical signs is 'extremely problematic' (1982: 9), especially in the face of avant-garde theatre with a visceral distrust of meaning and signification (1981: 75–85). Although he does not reject the notion that semiology is in some way scientific, Pavis expresses 'a healthy state of suspicion about any universal model' (1982: 9). A more manageable task for semiotic analysis is to study moments of theatrical signification 'on the fly', as it were, in all their localized specificity, without attempting to account for meaning in theatre as a totality. Pavis sees semiology moving toward greater flexibility, an engagement with specifics and particulars, partly because any semiotic reading is governed by the 'reception of a given public under certain given conditions' (p. 17), away from abstraction which tends to smooth out all irregularities (p. 202). Semiology must be conducted amidst an 'anarchy of meanings' (pp. 204–5), a 'semiotic shipwreck' of 'the relativity of meanings' (p. 200).

Semiology must, therefore, be 'dynamic and provisional', a 'plural and open reading' (p. 204). In this way, the semiologist is not just a scientist but also 'an artist in disguise' (p. 206).

In his short collection of essays, *Theatre Semiotics*, the American Marvin Carlson stresses three concerns for the semiotic theory of theatre that he claims have been generally underdeveloped: the semiotic contributions of the audience to the meaning of a theatrical performance – in Peirce's terms, how the audience receives and interprets signs; the semiotics of the entire theatre experience – the 'appearance of the auditorium, the displays in the lobby, the information in the program, and countless other parts of the event as a whole'; and the iconic relationship of theatre to the life it represents (1990: xi–xviii). Carlson's interests open semiotic analysis of the theatre onto relations with other theoretical approaches: his concern with the audience onto reception theory; his concern with the total theatrical experience onto materialist analysis; his interest in life onto phenomenology. Thus, for Carlson, these complications make 'performance potentially one of the richest and most rewarding areas in the arts for exploring the interplay of society and culture' (p. 121).

Stage directions in Ibsen and Shaw

Let us consider how some of these issues can be addressed in a particular theatrical instance. An audience begins discerning theatrical signs the moment the play begins, as soon as the stage is unveiled, before anything happens or anyone speaks – which is to stress the importance of nonverbal signs in the theatre. And the signs to be interpreted will be of many kinds, calling on our interpretive abilities at a number of levels. We can see this if we look at the openings of two modernist masterpieces, Henrik Ibsen's *A Doll's House* and George Bernard Shaw's *Pygmalion*. Ibsen's play begins with the description of 'A comfortable room furnished inexpensively, but with taste' (1965: 147). Several notions

are being signified already. First, we realize we are in the realm
of realism, art which tries to mimic very closely the real world
around it. Here, we are in a house very much like a house in late
nineteenth-century Norway – there is, for instance, always mention of a stove to provide heat against the frigid climate in
Ibsen's stage directions (we are told that it is a winter's day). That
it is or looks like a real stove provides what Peirce would call an
iconic closeness to reality. The room is comfortable and tasteful –
signifying middle-class. That it is decorated inexpensively points
to the money problems that haunt the Helmer family. We are told
that a door leads to Helmer's study, the realm of masculine seri-
ousness which excludes the wife and mother Nora: we are being
shown how gender structures this household and others like it.
Nora enters with a porter and a maid. We must at this point be
able to distinguish class structures being shown to us. Aston and
Savona, in discussing the semiotics of stage directions, break the
discussion into two sections: one on the text, the other on performance. The text tells us that there is a porter and a maid, but
any performance must find ways – uniforms, gestures of defer-
ence – to indicate status to us. The porter carries in a Christmas
tree. Here we are in the realm of what Barthes calls the cultural
code (1974: 20), the knowledge that the culturally literate spectator brings to the play: one needs to know that a coniferous tree
in a house is a Christmas tree, part of the ritual associated with
that time of year, and not firewood or the idiosyncratic penchant
of a true individualist who just happens to like trees brought
indoors. That we recognize the tree as a Christmas tree also helps
us understand that it is a winter's day. That Nora is in charge of
the Christmas tree identifies her once again with the festive
rather than the serious and masculine aspects of the household.
The stage directions as text and performance provide us with all
this signification – and more – before a word has been spoken.

Shaw's *Pygmalion* begins in 'London at 11:15 p.m.' (1997: 826).
How would a performance signify this? How to show that we're

in London? Certain landmarks are represented on stage: 'the portico of St Paul's church (not Wren's cathedral but Inigo Jones's church in Covent Garden)'. Here cultural knowledge is important in order to recognize not only that we are in London, but at a particular place in London, although whether the spectator, as opposed to the reader, will think of Wren and Jones remains uncertain. How do we know the time? A clock, we are told, strikes the quarter hour. This is well and good, but how does the spectator, rather than the reader, know which quarter hour? Again, cultural literacy is called on: if we are in Covent Garden, we are in the theatre district, and if people are rushing about and cabs are moving in all directions (signified here by the sound of their whistles), then the theatre shows must have just finished: hence it is 11:15 – hence, also, the lady and her daughter in evening dress (which makes costume part of the signs at work). An audience in London in 1913 might get all this, but what about the rest of us? Do these signs still signify to a global audience in the twenty-first century? People are rushing about in the rain, we are told, 'except one man with his back turned to the rest, wholly preoccupied with a notebook in which he is writing'. Here we have what Barthes calls the hermeneutic code (1974: 19), which opens an enigma or question and stirs our curiosity. If we understand that this is the theatre district, we understand why everyone else is rushing about. But what about this exceptional fellow? He has his back to us, appearing secretive, so we wonder who he is. And what is he doing? He is writing in a notebook, but what is he writing and why? The play has signified these questions for us and can now go about the pressing job of answering them.

A few prickly questions to consider: although in these stage directions we see nonverbal signs at work, do we not, however, call on language when we interpret these nonverbal signs? At least in the kind of theatre practised by Ibsen and Shaw, doesn't what appears nonverbally on stage begin as words in the stage directions written in the drama text? Is performance merely a nonverbal translation of the text's words?

Brecht and Benjamin

For Barthes, writing on theatre, the work of Bertolt Brecht is 'exemplary' for a semiological theatre: 'For what Brechtian dramaturgy postulates is that today at least, the responsibility of a dramatic art is not so much to express reality as to signify it' (Barthes 1972a: 71, 74). Although Brecht's theory is not explicitly or directly influenced by semiotics, it is fairly easy to see what Barthes is getting at. Brecht's theatre is primarily concerned with conveying meaning and understanding rather than capturing a detailed illusion of reality. Throughout his theoretical work, Brecht stresses this aspect in a number of ways: his theatre is philosophical, scientific, intellectual, pedagogical (Brecht 1964: 14, 24, 26, 31). The purpose of theatre is to put the audience in a better position to understand the world around them, a world which, for Brecht and Barthes, is social and changeable. In this way, theatre involves 'a politics of the sign' (Barthes 1972a: 47). The social world and its meanings, like Saussure's signs, are arbitrary but not unmotivated: they construct hierarchies of power for the benefit of the few and hide from the many their ability to change things (Barthes writes of the 'demystification' of the status quo in Brecht's theatre [1972a: 34]). A sign, therefore, is a social sign, what Brecht calls a *gestus* and which Barthes defines as 'the external material expression of the social conflicts to which it bears witness' (1972a: 41) Imagine, for instance, being stopped for speeding by a member of the police. S/he approaches your car with an emotionless expression of authority and addresses you with a reserved, dominating correctness; you smile innocently, harmlessly and, sounding befuddled, address him/her deferentially as 'Officer': each of these artificial behaviours is a sign indicating the power relations and social roles at play.

Pavis insists, however, that *gestus* is not lifeless and abstract, not 'the reified image of a social relation' (1982: 48). For Brecht, as for Barthes, the generation of understanding and meaning is not an ascetic activity. Brecht writes of the 'pleasure of exploration' (1964: 204), of a sensuous rationalism rich in humour, which is the most appropriate and viable pleasure in a scientific age. He writes, 'Every art contributes to the greatest art of all, the art of living' (p. 277). But living is a social activity, and its art is not about making present but about making a different and better world.

Barthes focuses on costume as one type of social sign: 'The costume is nothing more than the second term [the signifier] of a relation which must constantly link the work's meaning [signified] to its "exteriority"' (1972a: 42); as such it must be constructed so as to aid in the reading of its social meaning. Pavis defines *gestus* as 'an intentional signal emitted by the actor … in order to indicate the character's social attitude and way of behaving', in order to indicate 'the relations among people' (1982: 41), between the citizen and the police officer, for instance. Each theatrical *gestus*, according to Barthes, should aim for clarity of argument, in the case of costume for 'a precise vestimentary code', and the sensuous qualities of a costume, its grain and texture, should be in the service of understanding, not sensuality. Wealth, for instance, is not to be signified by piling on random luxury – Rolex watches and Gucci loafers – but by presenting a careful and precise idea of privilege. Something as simple as a stylized top hat might do the trick. One could indicate a large set of social roles and relations using nothing but hats: a cowboy hat, an army helmet, a crown. Gestic costume, therefore, is, in Peirce's terms, more like an index than an icon: its purpose is less to look like reality than to point to it.

The social *gestus* does not arise from an identity, a phenomenological closeness to being and doing (my clothing is not the 'real me'); it is a role, one we agree or are forced to adopt, and importance is placed, in Brecht's theatre, on alienation or internal distance from social meaning. Brecht takes his model of acting from social life, from the 'Street Scene' in which someone demonstrates an event – an accident, for instance, or an assault – not by becoming the person or action represented but by demonstrating it objectively from without (1964: 121–9): think of a witness giving testimony at a trial. Theatrical action is made explicitly representation rather than identification, and the actor has a double role on stage as both character and actor/demonstrator (p. 194). Theatre may be, as Pavis asserts, 'the privileged domain of the icon' (quoted in Carlson 1993: 499), of signifiers with a close relationship to what they represent, but people and things on stage are not identical with what they represent: the stage chair is not the chair represented, although it may be a chair; the actor is not the character, although s/he is a human being.

There is a tension in Barthes' reading of Brecht between a structuralist desire for system and a provisional and inductive openness. On the one hand, Barthes writes, Brecht 'offers not only a body of work but also a strong, coherent, stable system' (1972a: 38); on the other, 'in Brecht's theater the Marxist elements always seem to be recreated. Basically, Brecht's greatness, and his solitude, is that he keeps inventing Marxism' (p. 74). Thus Brecht is interested in inductive science, in which answers are discovered in particular situations rather than imposed systematically from the outset. In a later work, Barthes argues that Brecht's theatre of discrete scenes means that there is 'no final meaning, nothing but projections, each of which possesses a sufficient demonstrative power' (p. 49). Nonetheless, for Barthes, Brecht's theatre effectively controls and limits signs and meanings:

> The costume is a kind of writing and has the ambiguity of writing, which is an instrument in the service of a purpose which transcends it; but if the writing is either too rich, too beautiful or too ugly, it can no longer be read and fails in its function.
>
> (1985b: 92)

Signs are instruments under human control; good theatre exercises this control in the service of understanding.

Semiotics, however, does not always take such an instrumentalist or functional view of the sign; nor does it necessarily believe that signification can be so controlled and limited. A different view of theatrical signification can be seen in an early work of Brecht's friend Walter Benjamin (discussed more fully in Chapter 3), *The Origin of German Tragic Drama* (1977). Benjamin discusses the German baroque *Trauerspiel*, or mourning play, which he aligns with Shakespeare's *Hamlet* against classical tragedy. The *Trauerspiel* is allegorical, so that characters and objects are the signifiers for a range of emblematic meanings. The allegory, however, is not tightly controlled, but gives onto the 'free play of significances' (1977: 175); the allegory is ambiguous, lacking in clarity and with a multiplicity of meanings (p. 177). (Anyone who reads much critical literature on *Hamlet*, for instance, will know that the significance of Hamlet's actions can be seen in any number of ways.) The individual character is dispersed in multiple significance (p. 193). Not only is this a theatre working in Peirce's 'unlimited semiosis', but also signs and allegory are not living expressions of human beings but an inhuman, mechanistic sign system with its own impetus. Humans are reduced to a function of signification, rather than, as in Brecht, signification to an instrument of human purpose. For this reason, the corpse is the 'pre-eminent emblematic property':

> the allegorization of the physis can only be carried through in all its vigour in respect of the corpse. And the characters of the Trauerspiele die, because it is only thus, as corpses, that they can enter into the homeland of the allegory.

> (1977: 217–18)

Like John F. Kennedy or Princess Diana, the allegorical character has a freer and wider significance in death than in life.

Barthes, in the 1950s, stresses the importance of Brecht 'for today', but he sees that there are a number of ways of reading Brecht, from the right and the left, and also differently within each camp (1972a: 72–3). This understanding raises another question for theatre semiotics: the role of the audience in generating meaning. Peirce posits each act of signification as becoming in turn a sign in a new signifying context. In this light, some theorists of semiotics and theatre – for example, in the work of Carlson noted earlier – have come to stress the importance of audience reception for signification; Pavis, for example, notes 'the general trend of theatre semiotics, reorienting its objectives in the light of a theory of reception' (Pavis 1987: 41; see Chapter 2 for more on reception and reader response). How is it possible, in this situation, to control meaning down the line? How is it possible, even for one performance, to control the multitude of meaning-making in a diverse theatrical audience? 'Unlimited semiosis' means not only the proliferation of meaning due to the nature of signs themselves, but also the proliferation of meaning among those who receive and generate signs. Brecht's theatre, as Barthes presents it, seems a very narrow, and perhaps impossible, example of signification in theatre, an example of control in the face of the infinite dispersal of significance.

Avant-garde theatre and desemiotics

Semiotics can be made to work fairly well with traditional or rationalist drama and theatre such as Ibsen's, Shaw's and Brecht's, and brings out a clear pattern of communication and meaning through verbal and nonverbal elements. Strikingly, however, the Italian theorist Marco de Marinis writes:

> Certainly, semiotics is of little use to an institutional theater which continues to conceive of and produce theatrical performance unreflectively (and commercially) simply as the illustration

of a dramatic text, without ever questioning itself, its categories or its mode of production.

(1993: 13)

The point here is that the use of semiotics on traditional theatre
can be too smooth, too pat, whereas de Marinis is more interested in the semiotics of avant-garde theatre, where analysis gets
more problematic, but potentially more interesting and intellectually challenging.

We can begin to explore the semiotics of avant-garde theatre
by looking at the ideas and strategies of the Italian playwright
and director Carmelo Bene. Bene, in conjunction with the French
philosopher Gilles Deleuze, has a project to disrupt the imposition of invariation and homogeneity, the domination of the text
over theatre, text being first the drama text that dictates the performance but also the performance text that functions as a systematic set of controls and limitations in the service of clarity
and reason. Bene wants to create a crisis or impasse, a disarticula-
tion whereby the performance would 'stop making text' (Bene
and Deleuze 1979: 89). This is accomplished by perpetual variation, turbulence and excess (p. 95) in light, sound, movement
and speech, whose purpose is not to clarify but to create a 'con-
gestion of signs' (Bene 1977: 67) and a breakdown in communication. Although the domination of the text over performance
is like the domination of *langue* over *parole* (Bene and Deleuze
1979: 97), of abstract and unchanging pattern over the concrete
and particular, for Bene *parole* is the enemy too, inasmuch as
words have fixed meanings. Bene wants the actor to sing incom-
prehensible words (1977: 78), to articulate like a troglodyte
(Bene and Deleuze 1979: 15), so as to become not a source of
meaning but a disruptively 'intolerable presence' (p. 10).

Is it true, however, that everything on the stage, even in traditional theatre, is a sign, controlled or otherwise? Are there
aspects of theatrical reality that are in excess of signification?

In 1987 there was a production of Shakespeare's *Measure for Measure* at the Young Vic in London. For this production the stage was a square constructed of shiny black tiles in the centre of the audience. As people entered, there were stagehands to make sure that they did not walk across the stage to get to their seats, since the shiny platform caught every dusty shoe print. By the end of the night, however, the actors had transformed that polished pristine space into a smudged grey record of their every movement. Were these shoe prints theatrical signs? If so, what did they mean? One might see in them echoes of the inevitable corruption that haunts Vienna in the play. One might fault the director for allowing such wayward signifying noise to disrupt the clarity of the production. One might ignore them, as one ignores the idiosyncrasies of, for example, any particular stop sign, its dents and chipped paint. A perhaps inescapable drive of semiotics is to make of something a sign or otherwise exclude it from consideration. Aloysius van Kesteren, for example, from a highly scientific and rationalist semiotic perspective, calls for 'disinfecting' the discipline of 'non-analytical dirt' (Carlson 1993: 518). But what if non-analytical dirt is part of what is there on the stage or in the theatre? Shakespeare's original audience stood on earth rich in hazelnut shells and apple cores. This was part of their experience, as was the shifting light and shade of a London afternoon. But the hazelnuts and the clouds didn't necessarily mean anything. In his essay on Gilles Deleuze, Michel Foucault (both discussed more fully in later parts of this book) approves of Deleuze's philosophical interest in 'the dirt under the fingernails of Platonism' (Foucault 1977: 168). Not all, or all that is interesting, in theatre is allegory, understanding or sign. In reaction to the encroachment of semiotics, Jean-François Lyotard has called for a 'generalized desemiotics' (Pavis 1981: 84), which would see theatre as energy and event rather than as signification. Like phenomenology, desemiotics is interested in the sensuous reality of theatre, but its drives are much more libidinous and visceral than phenomenology's contemplative relationship with the world.

If there is a politics of the sign (as in Brecht's *gestus*), there is also a politics of desemiotics. For instance, the German playwright Heiner Müller, ambivalent disciple of Brecht, writes of the 'rebellion of the body against ideas', or 'the thrusting on stage of bodies and their conflict with ideas' (Müller 1982: 65), specifically the bodies of oppressed groups against the hegemonic and oppressive ideas of western male culture. Unlike Brecht, Müller does not see in Enlightenment rationalist values a history of liberation, but rather a long history of intellectualized injustice through the hegemony of the word. Irrationality, disorder and the senses promise more political liberation than does the strict control of meaning. But perhaps the fostering of western injustice and oppression is too great a guilt to lay at the feet of semiotics; conversely, a generalized desemiotics runs the risk of intellectual impoverishment: what richness is there in a theatre voided of meaning? Besides, the choice may be a phantom one. Ultimately, it is no easier to escape signs than it is to reduce all physical and theatrical reality to signification alone.

QUESTIONS ONE MIGHT ASK OF A PLAY OR PERFORMANCE

How do nonverbal elements such as light, sound, space and movement signify in any particular play or performance? In performance are these nonverbal signifiers reducible to their verbal significance?

What actions and gestures do actors in a particular performance use, over and above the words they speak, to indicate character? Can you analyse the semiotics of costume in any particular performance?

How open to different readings are the signs of any play or performance? Could all members of a particular audience be expected to read the signs in the same way? Do you and your peers agree on the meaning of particular signs? Are there significant elements in a play or performance which seem particularly hard to pin down to an agreed-upon meaning?

What elements of a performance escape a sense of being meaningful? Do some aspects of production have their impact from just being there, or just affecting us physically or emotionally? Do music and light, for instance, always have meaning in the way words and ideas do?

2 PHENOMENOLOGY

A theoretical approach extremely different from – if not diametrically opposed to – semiotics is that taken by phenomenology. The theatre phenomenologist Bert O. States, for instance, argues that 'The problem with semiotics is that in addressing theater as a system of codes it necessarily dissects the perceptual impression theater makes on the spectator' (1985: 13). That is, in tending to the analytic, scientific and abstract, semiotics misses how theatre feels to us. Thus, phenomenology's task is to 'keep [...] the life in theater'. Another theatre phenomenologist, Stanton B. Garner Jr, sees phenomenology's aims as:

> to redirect attention from the world as it is conceived by the abstracting, 'scientific' gaze (the objective world) to the world as it appears or discloses itself to the perceiving subject (the phenomenal world); to pursue the thing as it is given to consciousness in direct experience; to return perception to the fullness of its encounter with its environment.
>
> (1994: 2)

But what exactly is phenomenology? Phenomenology is a philosophical movement which began in Germany early in the twentieth century and eventually spread into France. Among its leading figures are the German philosophers Edmund Husserl (1964) and Martin Heidegger and the French philosophers Maurice Merleau-Ponty and Jean-Paul Sartre. Phenomenology is not concerned with the world as it exists in itself but with how the world appears (as phenomena) to the humans who encounter it. We have all heard the philosophical question whether a tree makes a sound if it falls in the forest and there's no one there to hear it. Phenomenology is not concerned with such a situation. It focuses on the way the tree appears to those who *are* there to witness it: the way the leaves turn in the light; their rustling in the wind; the coolness of the shade; the way it feels when you knock up against the trunk; the way the tree's growth and seasonal changes mark out periods of one's life; the uses of its wood, burning in a fire or hewn into art.

Phenomenology is concerned with what it is like for human beings to be alive in the world around them and how they perceive that world. Human perception has a number of aspects. First, humans have bodies with senses. Garner quotes the French phenomenologist Maurice Merleau-Ponty, who writes, 'To perceive is to render oneself present to something through the body' (p. 27) and refers to our 'lived bodiliness' (1994: 28). Aside, most strikingly, from late nineteenth- and early twentieth-century experiments with marionettes in place of people, as in the theatre of Maurice Maeterlinck (Carlson 1993: 295–6), theatre has most often worked with living actors on stage. The body is the actor's instrument. Garner writes, '[T]heatrical space is phenomenal space, governed by the body and its spatial concerns' (1994: 4). Theatre is live theatre, or in the clarion call of the 1960s' experimental theatre of Julian Beck, 'The Living Theatre'. Moreover, in a manner different from literary or pictorial arts, theatre has a special relationship with the presentation of lived experience to the spectator. Theatre appears to the spectator's senses as something to be seen and heard, and, less often, as something to be touched, tasted and smelled. The sensory effects of theatre are central to phenomenological concerns. Furthermore, lived bodiliness can be seen in the ways that theatre sometimes works through sensory channels for extreme effects. In the 1970s, for instance, performance artist Gina Pane subjected herself on stage to self-laceration (Battock and Nickas 1984: 326). In the 1990s, the Toronto theatre company DNA, in a play called Sick, which dealt with the experience of AIDS, used the senses to impart to the audience a feeling analogous to illness: a tape loop repeated over and over at ear-splitting volume a short musical crescendo. After several minutes the audience member was inside the monotonous discomfort of the experience as the sick person is inside his or her pain. When the music suddenly stopped, the inescapable difference between sickness and relief was made physically present.

Phenomenology is also concerned, however, with the way humans think and act in the world. To be human is to have a sense of time, memory and intention. Inasmuch as a play is driven by the interior projects of its characters – how they carry within what has happened to them in the past, how they feel in the present and how they work towards a future they intend for themselves – all theatre engages with what it means to be conscious in and of time. Samuel Beckett's short play *Act Without Words* I begins as follows:

Desert. Dazzling light.
　The man is flung backwards on stage from right wing. He falls, gets up immediately, dusts himself off, turns aside, reflects.
　Whistle from right wing.
　He reflects, goes out right.
　Immediately flung back on stage he falls, gets up immediately, dusts himself off, turns aside, reflects.
　Whistle from left wing.
　He reflects, goes out left.

Immediately flung back on stage he falls, gets up immediately, dusts himself, turns aside, reflects.

Whistle from left wing.

He reflects, goes toward left wing, hesitates, thinks better of it, halts, turns aside, reflects.

(1984: 43)

Here in miniature is the phenomenological condition: a human being encountering the environment with the body, attempting to act in or against that environment, reflecting on the situation, and revising future actions in light of what has already taken place.

Alice Rayner uses a phenomenological approach – although she also relies on Jacques Derrida (see the section on Post-structuralism and Deconstruction) and Jacques Lacan (see the section on Psychoanalytic Theory) – to study action in theatre and drama. She attempts to get at the 'thickness' of action, its 'phenomenal complexity' (1994: 4): our circumstances are rarely as simple as they are in Beckett's play: we are often in more complex environments than Beckett's desert; our motivations are more complicated than following a whistle off stage; our acts do have words. Rayner uses the conventional distinction between drama and theatre to pinpoint two aspects of action: giving shape and making visible. For Rayner, action itself is a larger potential field or medium which theatre actualizes in particular circumstances; works of dramatic art, however, are also 'ways of seeing' which allow us to think through our relation to action and reality (p. 10).

Phenomenological concerns focus, in a way that sets them apart from much recent literary and cultural theory, not so much on the social subject as on the individual consciousness, conceived in part as autonomous of social forces and capable of insight and reflection. Language is a concern of phenomenology inasmuch as language affects an individual's engagement with the world, but language is thought of more as an instrument for getting at truth than as a force for unavoidable confusion. Language isn't, in the phrase of Fredric Jameson, a prison-house, but rather a way of seeing and doing. Especially in the work of Merleau-Ponty (Merleau-Ponty 1962), there is an emphasis on the manifestation of the world to the body and its senses that is absent in many language-based theories, such as semiotics and deconstruction. Phenomenology's primary concern is with the engagement in lived experience between the individual consciousness and reality, which manifests itself not as a series of linguistic signs but as sensory and mental phenomena – the 'world' is what we encounter in perception and reflection, while the 'earth' is things as they may be in themselves outside human perception (the tree falling in the uninhabited forest). In this way, the emphasis is on the presence or 'unconcealing' of the world for consciousness rather than its disappearance into language, and therefore on the interplay with the real rather than on its inevitable deferral. There is less interest in the specifics of history as developed in materialist thought than in an at once more general and more personal idea of time; time comes to us first and foremost as an individual lifetime.

Nonetheless, phenomenology takes account of the fact that to be in the world is to encounter other people, and part of our awareness is an awareness that others perceive us, judge us and set limits for us. Jean-Paul Sartre's phenomenology is concerned with how we act in light of others who are watching us, who force us to see ourselves in less than the idealized light in which we might otherwise want to see ourselves: as it is put so tersely at the end of Sartre's play No Exit: 'Hell is – other people' (1989: 45). In Sartre's play each character constructs and defends a flattering myth about him or herself, while the other characters see through this myth and undermine it. Sick, the play mentioned above, made the audience aware of its condition of being watched in a number of striking ways. Members of the audience were hand-picked to enter the theatre at different times; everyone had to wait until recognized by the authoritarian and judgemental ushers. At one point in the play, individual actors sat down beside particular people in the audience and, looking directly at them, graphically described the symptoms of various diseases. These techniques tended to make the spectator uncomfortably aware of being the object of someone else's attention.

Phenomenologists often posit the possibility of a more authentic way for humans to exist in the world, one which brings them in fuller touch with things and themselves and which ultimately gives access to truth and even a spiritual realm. Following the German phenomenologist Martin Heidegger, States argues that the work of art creates a spiritual presence or truth (1985: 2); fights the battle between what is holy and what unholy; and discloses 'a different kind of *here* than we "usually tend to be" in' (p. 4). For Heidegger, the work of art has a special relation to truth (Heidegger 1975). Unlike objects of utility or our day-to-day existence, works of art endure without being used up, passed by or cast aside. They provide access, not to things in themselves, but to a privileged relation, of reflection and understanding, with the world, a relation usually concealed in day-to-day human activity. How much of yesterday, for instance, do you actually remember experiencing: did you hear the different kinds of birds distinctively singing, feel the heat or coldness on your skin, were you struck with wonder by events around you, or did you eat, open doors, walk down the street without even realizing – because of the routines you were caught up in – that you were doing these things? States notes the way certain beings on stage – clocks, chairs, children, animals – refuse to be strictly tied to, utilized for, representation and illusion: dogs bark when they're not supposed to; a gun when fired may fail to discharge (1985: 31–3); in *Monster in a Box* Spalding Gray tells of a young boy actor vomiting during a performance of the final act of Thornton Wilder's *Our Town* (Gray 1992b: 69–70). In these moments we are reminded that theatre works with vitality, corporeality — in short, life. Its primary accomplishment is not to represent the world but to be part of it, to effect a 'transaction between consciousness and the thickness of existence' (States 1992: 378). Given day-to-day forces which rob us of our being present in our lives, the theatre must disclose to us both our presences and our absences, but rather than deny the possibility of presence, as in much contemporary theory, States wishes to make it paramount.

Phenomenology is concerned with truth, no matter how mediated, provisional and revisable. However, although phenomenology posits the possibility of an authentic or fully human relation to the world, it is not naively rosy about such a relation coming about — the world is as often concealed as unconcealed, or unconcealed in counterproductive ways. Heidegger traces a history in which 'the way of technology' has progressed at the expense of a more poetic engagement with truth. Technology has turned the world, and humans themselves, into a 'standing reserve' in which everything and everyone is instrumental, a means to be used up or laid waste, rather than a fully present end in themselves (Heidegger 1977: 3–35). For Sartre, humans bring nothingness to their consciousness of the world, and this sets them apart from things in themselves as 'not myself'. This gives radical freedom but also alienation and anguish in our relationship to things. As a way of avoiding the difficult responsibilities of life, we tend to act in bad faith, hiding the truth from ourselves rather than seeking it out (Sartre 1966). The reading of Heidegger in the work of the Italian theorist of postmodernism, Gianni Vattimo, provides a fusion of phenomenology with post-structuralist thought in which our perception of particular phenomena or beings goes hand in hand with the recognition of the absence of Being, the full presence which no particular being can entail; phenomenology becomes the awareness of the absence of this Being. In this reading, works of art are privileged instances of endurance in time, an endurance always accompanied by death, loss of origin, loss of self. The endurance of art reminds us that life is short; the presence of a single work of art reminds us of everything else that is passing or missing. Phenomena still reveal truth, but it is 'weak' truth, riddled with absence and adrift in time (Vattimo 1988). Garner sees phenomenology as revealing in theatre not only the presence of appearances but also 'dys-appearance' (1994: 32–3) in which '[i]nvaded on all sides by an irremediable absence, [the body's] very presence to itself is no longer secure' (p. 29). Phenomenology and phenomenological theatre, therefore, not only search out a fully present human existence but also the failure to achieve this existence, which is more often than not the condition in which we live.

In a very powerful critique of the 'traditional, unreflective assumptions' that our culture has about live performance, the performance theorist Philip Auslander attacks

> attempts to explicate the value of 'liveness' [by] invoking clichés and mystifications like 'the magic of live theatre', the 'energy' that supposedly exists between performers and events in a live event, and the 'community' that live performance is often said to create among performers and spectators.
>
> (1999: 2)

Auslander traces the complex ways that media and reproduction have come to affect live performance, and argues not only that almost all live performances now incorporate the technology of reproduction, such as television and sound recording (p. 158), but that live performances are not in essence different from such mediatized forms (p. 159). This argument brings Heidegger's way of technology to a point where the possibility of an unfettered liveness is no longer open. We can no longer be 'live' in an essential and authentic way.

Phenomenology has come under attack in much recent criticism as essentialist (positing basic truths about human existence that come before the social conventions that – critics of phenomenology argue – are the real source of understanding and values), and Heidegger, like the deconstructionist Paul de Man, has a very troubled reputation as a Nazi sympathizer. Terry Eagleton gives a particularly dismissive reading of phenomenology from a Marxist perspective (1983: 54–66). Nevertheless, phenomenology does treat lived experience in a compelling way that is different from other theoretical perspectives. Bonnie Marranca and Gautam Dasgupta, editors of *Conversations on Art and Performance*, argue that artists continue to be motivated by what could be seen as phenomenological concerns in opposition to the scepticism and objectivism of much cultural theory – 'the force of inner necessity that compels artists to search for an authenticity rooted in emotional need' (1999: xii):

> Often overlooked in contemporary culture is precisely that condition [artists] so eloquently speak to: the role of art as spiritual discipline.... And, what cannot be overstated is the very real conflict between the desire of artists to make work that reflects their attachment to the world, even to make visionary works, at the same time that many of them have abandoned the moral imperatives of previous art making.... A certain amount of demythologizing of art and artists is necessary, but to ignore the special grace of artistic vision is to trivialize the entire realm of human endeavor.
>
> (p. xiii)

Taken with a healthy scepticism, phenomenology can be aligned with more political perspectives also interested in embodiment and experience. Judith Butler, for instance, uses phenomenology in a feminist context. She traces the French feminist Simone de Beauvoir's assertion that 'one is not born, but *becomes* a woman' back to Merleau-Ponty's idea that 'the body in its sexual being' is 'an historical idea' rather than a 'natural species' (1990: 270–1). Becoming a woman happens through the acts that the body repeats under social pressures: how one carries oneself, how one dresses, how one speaks and feels. Butler writes, 'phenomenology shares with feminist analysis a commitment to grounding theory in lived experience, and in revealing the way in which the world is produced through the constituting acts of subjective experience' (p. 273). Unlike some phenomenologists, Butler argues that there is no essential human identity before bodily acts fashion it: we are a product of our social embodiment, which means changing how the body acts can change who we are. The particulars of women's bodies are used in much feminist performance art. Beginning in the 1960s, the American performance artist Carolee Schneeman used her body in a 'celebration of flesh' (1997: 63). In a performance piece called *Interior Scroll* she explored her own 'vulvic space' in 'a total reversal and reinterpretation of myth and symbol' around the female body. This piece entailed her slowly pulling a scroll from her vagina on which she had written a male critic's attack on her work as too personal. She writes, 'I thought of the vagina in many ways – physically, conceptually: as a sculptural form, an architectural referent, the source of sacred knowledge, ecstasy, birth passage, transformation' (p. 234). The performance artist and sex-trade worker Annie Sprinkle has invited members of the audience to examine her cervix through a speculum, thus, among other things, undermining the traditional masculine eroticization of female genitalia (Campbell 1996: 284–5).

Krapp's Last Tape; Stanislavski and Chekhov

Stanton Garner focuses on the late plays of Samuel Beckett in his phenomenological analysis of theatre, and one can see many of the concerns of phenomenology in a play such as Beckett's *Krapp's*

Last Tape. In this play we see before anything else the old man Krapp mechanically take his aged body with its '[l]aborious walk' (Beckett 1984: 55) through his repeated, routine actions. On the one hand, Krapp is a broken-down automaton, caught in thoughtless habits; on the other hand, it is often in frailties and ailments that the reality of the body is brought home, as in Krapp's chronic constipation, his near-sightedness and hardness of hearing. Eventually Krapp begins listening to a tape he made on his birthday thirty years before. What do we make of this tape? Is it the way of technology taking him away from bodily presence? Or does it create a presence, if not a liveness, for Krapp's past in a way that pure recollection lacks? But then, if it makes Krapp's past voice present, it cannot overcome the distance and alienation Krapp in the present feels towards that voice. In large part the presence of the voice from the past only heightens its difference – in inflection and attitude – from the voice in the present.

Krapp's tapes bring the dimesion of time to the forefront of his life. They act as a memory aid and a spur to recollection and reflection on his lifetime, past, present and future (in Krapp's diminishing world the future figures less and less prominently). As his life has changed, however, some things have remained constant: his constipation, his drinking, his 'less ... engrossing sexual life' (p. 58). His life has featured an alienated yet insistent relationship with others: Bianca, his mother, Fanny – indeed, it is the moment of lying with Bianca as they broke off their relationship that he dwells on in the tape from thirty years before. In the past, his inner life swings spiritually between 'profound gloom and indigence' and the memorable night 'when suddenly I saw the whole thing. The vision at last' (p. 60). In the present, no longer at all interested in visions, Krapp wavers between the desire to end and the desire to 'be again' (p. 63) and live his life all over. At any rate, his life has been an unhappy attempt at 'separating the grain from the husks', the grain being 'those things worth having when all the dust has – when all my dust has settled' (p. 57). In Beckett's pessimistic universe, it's not clear that Krapp has ever had a firm grasp of the grain. Krapp is not a phenomenological success story. As Garner suggests, however, Krapp, like other Beckett characters, clings to life even as it diminishes: 'On the threshold of the body's disappearance into nothingness or its reversion to pure matter, there are stirrings still' (Garner 1994: 37).

What can be seen as phenomenological concerns also figure prominently in the work of Constantin Stanislavski, the Russian director and inventor of perhaps the most influential theory of acting in the twentieth century (his 'system' profoundly influenced, for instance, American 'method' acting). Stanislavski's autobiographical My Life in Art reveals a phenomenological bent in its very title. 'My' speaks to the importance of individual experience and consciousness in the theatrical pursuit – the autobiographical form itself points to the importance of the individual life. 'Life', as in a phenomenological sense of fully engaged consciousness – what Stanislavski calls 'THE SUPER-CONSCIOUS THROUGH THE CONSCIOUS' (Stanislavski 1948: 483) – is of paramount importance to Stanislavski, but such life is most available 'in Art', in living theatre.

When true theatre is taking place (and this is the goal of Stanislavski's new method of acting), 'the actor passes from the plane of actual reality into the plane of another life' (p. 466); the actor creates life and 'the feeling of truth' (p. 467), incarnates the human spirit (p. 565) to the point of forgetting that he or she is on stage (p. 464). This process Stanislavski calls 'living over' a part (p. 462). Stanislavski calls for a 'new beginning' (p. 483) in this way, to set against 'the outworn theatrical stencil' (p. 332) of wooden, lifeless repetition and routine of traditional 'mechanical' acting, which leaves the actor in a 'spiritual torpor' that corrupts 'his soul, his body, and his roles' (Magarshack 1992: 222). In this way the stage becomes 'the ground of a battle between life and death' (Stanislavski 1948: 334). The tools of Stanislavski's system – as opposed to the standing reserve of traditional actor's tricks – include a 'well-trained attention' (Magarshack 1992: 239), akin to the careful 'heeding' or listening phenomenologists call for in our relation to the world and ourselves, and 'emotional memory', 'the memory that resides in the actor's feelings and is brought to the surface of his consciousness by his five senses' (p. 252). It is in part by invoking this emotional memory that an actor comes to live over a role rather than merely going through the motions provided by traditional training. Moreover, acting of this kind involves 'communion' between actors and between actors and audience (Counsell 1996: 43).

Unfortunately, although he writes of 'the Eternal in art' (Stanislavski 1948: 535), Stanislavski is saddled with an art form which has a distinctive relationship to time: 'a work of art born on the stage lives only for a moment, and no matter how beautiful it may be it cannot be commanded to stay with us' (p. 570). This is why a study of theatre such as this one of my own must always invoke references to performances long gone, which makes the study of theatre different from the study of literary or pictorial arts – as Stanislavksi says, 'the theatre cannot give the beginner such results as the library and the museum give to the writer and the artist' (p. 570). The art of the actor is to recreate, which is not the same as repetition: repetition if mechanical is lifeless; repetition of a moment of truth is impossible. 'Nature is unkind to man and rarely gives him what he needs in life', Stanislavski writes (p. 566). He compares himself to Tantalus – 'I tried to reach something that forever escaped me' (p. 327) – or to a gold seeker who spends a lifetime to find a few precious grains. Theatre does not often match actual achievements to the loftiness of its goals.

Unlike the work of art phenomenology often invokes, theatre doesn't endure; but in this way it has a special elegiac relation to life, in which the past is gone and death awaits. As each performance slips away, so does each life and each person's knowledge and experience. Stanislavski writes, 'I cannot will to my heirs my labors, my quests, my losses, my joys and my disappointments', and:

> nothing can fix and pass on to our descendants those inner paths of feeling, that conscious road to the gates of the unconscious, which, and which alone, are the true foundation of the art of the theatre. This is the sphere of living tradition.
>
> (pp. 571–2)

Stanislavski's most famous work was with the Moscow Art Theatre on the plays of the late nineteenth-century Russian playwright Anton Chekhov. In Chekhov's plays we can see phenomenological concerns much like Stanislavski's played out, with more subtlety than in Stanislavski's often broad enthusiasms, on the level of theme and subject matter: time, action, the impact of others, the emptiness of the day-to-day, the longing for a fuller life. Chekhov's characters long for a rich and complete existence – a real life – in the face of a life which they find empty, dull, indeed lifeless. They are driven by a pessimistic phenomenological longing.

Chekhov's plays have often been treated as naturalistic works immersed in the mundane details of Russian provincial life at the end of the nineteenth century. For Stanislavski, however, the plays addressed central concerns of art and theatre. Similarly, in 1959 the Polish director Jerzy Grotowski (discussed more fully later in this chapter) produced a very abstract Uncle Vanya shorn of realistic detail, which concentrated on the distinction between alienation and convention on the one hand and spontaneity and life on the other, thus dwelling on the play's 'universal' meaning in 'a pure and aloof world of ideas' (Osinski 1986: 27–30). Moreover, Louis Malle's 1995 film of André Gregory's production of the play, *Vanya on 42nd Street*, although it featured a traditionally realistic approach to acting as identification with a specific character, was set in an empty theatre with no invocation of provincial Russia. Most striking was the way the actors were filmed as they eased into and out of their roles, so that the interplay between acting and non-acting was rendered problematic – at what precise moment and in what precise way do actors become or cease to be a character? It is not necessary, however, to reduce or add to Chekhov's plays in order to bring out their philosophical interests – indeed, from a phenomenological perspective, their very specific details of Russian provincial life constitute the complex sensuous particulars, the 'thickness' of these characters' lives.

Chekhov's plays are filled with characters who feel they haven't lived, whose lives have been a kind of death. Masha begins *The Seagull* 'in mourning for my life' (Chekhov 1982: 74). Sorin says, 'Twenty-eight years I've worked for the Department of Justice, but I haven't lived yet, haven't experienced anything – that's what it comes to' (pp. 92–3). The two very different writers in the play, Treplev and Trigorin, are united in a similar sentiment: Treplev says, 'It's as if someone had banged a nail into my brain, damn it – and damn the selfishness that seems to suck my blood like a vampire' (p. 97), and Trigorin, 'I seem to see life and learning vanishing into the distance, while I lag more and more behind' (p. 100). In *Uncle Vanya*, Helen is 'bored to death' (p. 161), while Astrov says, 'As for my own private life, well, heaven knows there's absolutely nothing good about that' (p. 154). Vanya himself exclaims:

> Day and night my thoughts choke me, haunt me with the spectre of a life hopelessly wasted. I've never lived. My past life has been thrown away on stupid trivialities and the present is so futile, it appals me.

(p. 149)

Such feelings are expressed over and over again, in a special relation to time and repetition. *Uncle Vanya* begins with Astrov, worn out by ten years of labour 'from morning to night with never a moment's peace' (p. 133) and ends with Sonya forecasting 'a long succession of days and endless evenings' (p. 187). In between is Vanya, who has been 'cooped up in this place like a mole' for twenty-five years (p. 173) and wonders how he will fill the time he has left to live (p. 180). Bogged down in overwork or idleness, Chekhov's characters exist in a state of Heideggerian 'standing reserve', like the district forests – such a concern of Astrov – disappearing before the forces of utility and waste.

As in Sartre's *No Exit*, the unhappiness of Chekhov's characters comes in large measure from their relationships with others, from how others appear to feel about them. They want others to love or respect them, but that rarely happens. Helen does not love Vanya as he thinks he needs her to; Vanya refuses to give Serebryakov, the retired professor, the respect and honour the professor's self-esteem requires. Love and honour exist as goals in this world, but they are almost always directed in ways that make people less or no happier than they otherwise would be. Moreover, Chekhov's characters are often reduced to a set of routine behaviours, lost in unreflective responses at odds with an open life attuned to new possibilities. The knee-jerk reactions of the actress Irena Arkadin in *The Seagull*, for instance, are telegraphed to us by her son Treplev two acts before we witness them: 'She's stingy too. She has seventy thousand roubles in the bank in Odessa, I know that for a fact. But you ask her to lend you some and you'll have her in tears' (p. 76). Others – and through them the audience – are aware of her actions in a way she herself is not.

In *The Seagull*, Sorin imagines a short novel called *The Man Who Wanted*, and lifelessness in Chekhov is tied to a longing for the fullness of existence: 'One wants to live, even at sixty', Sorin says (p. 92). Vanya longs 'to wake up some fine, clear morning feel-

ing as if you'd started living again, as if the past was all forgotten, gone like a puff of smoke' (p. 180). People search for this
new life in love affairs which always disappoint, in exciting
locales such as Moscow or Genoa, where 'You share its life, enter
into its spirit and begin to think there really could be such a
thing as a World Spirit' (p. 118), in a nostalgia which forgets the
discontents of the past. At the end of Uncle Vanya, Sonya seeks
peace only in the afterlife, when 'We shall see all the evils of this
life, all our own sufferings, vanish in the flood of mercy which
will fill the whole world' (p. 187).

The most telling projection of life and happiness in Chekhov
is into a distant human future. In Uncle Vanya, it is Astrov who
thinks in these terms: 'Those who live a century or two after us
and despise us for leading lives so stupid and tasteless, perhaps
they'll find a way to be happy, but as for us –' (p. 180) and pro-
jecting even more distantly, 'if man is happy a thousand years
from now I'll have done a bit towards it myself' (p. 143). Visions
of human happiness, of life fulfilled, remain compelling, but
only through deferral; what endures in life is a radical postpone-
ment of living, a profound failure very understandable from a
phenomenological perspective.

The Seagull begins with a theatre experiment at odds with the
usual tenor of Chekhov's theatre: Treplev's drama of the 'World
Spirit', which attempts to 'show life neither as it is nor as it
ought to be, but as we see it in our dreams' (p. 79). Treplev
rejects conventional theatre for 'a new kind of theatre' (p. 76) in
which souls will be united in a unified work of art. Stanislavski
sees Treplev as a talented artist, 'with the soul of Chekhov and a
true comprehension of art', set against the stencil of conventional realism represented by 'the worthless Trigorin'
(Stanislavski 1948: 355). Chekhov's play, however, is much more
ambivalent than this. For a start, Treplev's play is set – taking
Chekhov's usual projections to extremes – 200,000 years in the
future. But even then life has not triumphed: 'that will only

come about after a long, long succession of millennia, when Moon, bright Sirius and Earth shall gradually have turned to dust. Until then there shall be horror upon horror' (p. 82). The distant future looks much like the present, only worse. Also, the play is framed by the failure of Treplev's work, its interruption in act one and its empty stage, 'bare and ugly as a skeleton' (p. 114) at the end. Finally, if Treplev's play is true theatre, what of Chekhov elsewhere, always mixing in the here-and-now bathos with pathos, both ridiculous and compelling? *The Seagull* is neither Treplev nor Trigorin; it hollows out both dream and convention, promising fulfilment only as something that has not arrived and is not likely to. In this way, the phenomenology of Chekhov's theatre is like that of Vattimo, with the power of a weak truth and the presence only of deferral.

Artaud, Nietzsche, theatre anthropology

Beckett, Stanislavski and Chekhov were not phenomenologists; nor were they influenced by phenomenology. The concerns of their work, however, are elucidated by a phenomenological perspective. This holds true for other work, not strictly speaking phenomenological, that shows similar concerns, especially with the truth of lived experience and the place of living theatre in human spirituality and ritual.

The mid-twentieth-century French theatre theorist Antonin Artaud has been extremely influential on subsequent work in the theatre with his call for a 'theatre of cruelty'. Cruelty in this context means a rigorous and relentless disruption of comfortable and limiting norms and habits both in society and theatre, a disruption which is driven by an understanding which resonates with the concerns of phenomenology. For a start, Artaud's project is motivated by a painful dissatisfaction with mechanized and secularized modern life. Artaud writes of:

the age of confusion in which we live, an age filled with blas-
phemies and with the phosphorescent gleams of an infinite
denial, an age in which all values, artistic as well as moral,
seem to be dissolving into an abyss that nothing in any previous age of the mind can give any idea of.

(Artaud 1988: 159)

This is an age 'in which we see at last the reign of all the fake
manufactured products, / of all the vile synthetic substitutes / in
which beautiful real nature has no part' (p. 556). This sounds like
a phenomenologist attack on a society in which technological
efficiency has eradicated the sacred, nature, fully lived experience
and the work of art – in this society theatre, for instance, can do
nothing but prostitute itself (Artaud 1958: 89), rather than help
'to rediscover an idea of sacred theater' (Artaud 1988: 276).

The theatre Artaud longs for is deeply connected with life – it
is 'the true spectacle of life' (1958: 12), indeed 'must make itself
the equal of life' (p. 116). He writes, 'With this theater, in short,
we reestablish communication with life instead of cutting ourselves off from it' (1988: 157). The life in question is a kind of
essence of human existence, 'where lives drink at their source'
(1958: 146), and this theatre would constitute 'the creation of a
reality, the unprecedented eruption of a world' (1988: 155),
which would wreak havoc with the mundane reality we know.

Artaud's theatre would work in part by remaking the body,
first of the actor, then of the spectator, into something much
more sensitive and open than it is now, a 'fine Nerve Meter'
(p. 86), which would deliver us from the 'automatic reactions'
(p. 571) which society and technology have instilled in us. This
theatre, however, is not just about visceral reactions – just as
phenomenology is a philosophy of the body, Artaud's theatre is to
be a 'drama of high intellectual importance' (1958: 33), which
would not 'separate the mind from the body nor the senses from
the intelligence' (p. 86). Moreover, as noted above, Artaud has in

mind 'the idea of a sacred theater', an 'archetypal, primitive theater' (p. 50), 'the essential drama, the one at the root of all the Great Mysteries' (p. 51), 'spiritualized gold' (p. 52). Artaud imagines a theatre, therefore, which would release the body, the mind, the soul, into a pure and profound existence at deepest odds with the social status quo. This is a very tall order, which we will see put to question in the next section of this chapter.

Artaud is not the only thinker to relate theatre to the sacred, to religion and ritual. The German philosopher Friedrich Nietzsche, near the end of the nineteenth century, argued in *The Birth of Tragedy* that Greek classical tragedy arose out of ecstatic, intoxicated cult activities surrounding the god Dionysus in tension with more sober dream visions associated with Apollo. Tragedy gave access to the 'higher truth, the perfection of these states in contrast to the incompletely intelligible everyday world' (1967: 35). Approaches such as Nietzsche's point the way towards theatre anthropology, the study of the basic place and uses of theatre in human social and religious practices. The performance theorist Richard Schechner begins his book on performance theory with a discussion of anthropologists' study of Greek tragedy:

> For the last hundred years or more, Greek tragedy has been understood as an outgrowth of rites celebrated annually at the Festival of Dionysus. Those rites have been investigated both in their relation to the God Dionysus and in their relation to the primitive religion of the Greeks. The result is a conception of Greek tragedy which is very different from that which prevailed from the Renaissance into the eighteenth century. The Renaissance humanists and their successors saw it in 'civilized' and rational terms; in our time we see much of its form and meaning is due to its primitive source, and to the religious festival of which it was a part.
>
> (1988: 1)

Similarly, the theatre anthropologist Eugenio Barba sees the genesis of his studies in his Catholic Italian childhood, in its 'culture of faith' (Barba 1995: 1):

> There is a boy in a warm place full of people singing, fragrant odours, vivid colours. In front of him, high up, is a statue wrapped in a purple cloth. Suddenly, while bells ring, the smell of incense becomes more pungent and the singing swells, the purple cloth is pulled down revealing a risen Christ.
>
> This is how Easter was celebrated in Gallipoli, the village in southern Italy where I spent my childhood. I was deeply religious. It was a pleasure to the senses to go to church, to find myself in an atmosphere of darkness and candlelight, shadows and gilt stucco, perfumes, flowers and people engrossed in prayer.

There is, therefore, from this point of view, an affiliation between religious ritual and theatre, an affiliation not only in its sacredness but in its sensuous performance, all of which can be related to phenomenological concerns.

Schechner and Barba note, however, that this is not the whole story. For Schechner, theatre is not pure ritual but also 'entertainment', which is a much less pious idea. For Barba, the culture of faith is followed by 'the culture of corrosion' (p. 3), as innocence and faith are lost in experience of the world. Theatre is thus agnostic, questioning and disruptive as much as it is orthodox and religious. *Paradoja del teatro, según esta teoría*

QUESTIONS ONE MIGHT ASK OF A PLAY OR PERFORMANCE

Does the play or performance highlight the bodies of the actors or the bodily responses of the audience in any special way? If so, to what purpose or point?

Does the play or performance make special use of its essence as a live experience? How does any use it makes of technology enter into this?

Does the play or performance invoke the ideas of memory or time? Does it invoke the idea of a lifetime? Does it try to bring the characters or audience into some kind of communication with nature?

Does the play or performance criticize or attack anything about society and its norms which stands in the way of a full and satisfying human experience? Does the play or performance suggest that a fuller and more satisfying human experience is possible? If so, what would it be like?

3 POST-STRUCTURALISM AND DECONSTRUCTION

Structuralism, as discussed in the section on semiotics, works systematically and scientifically to analyse the abstract patterns on which various cultural activities are supposedly based. The French structuralist anthropologist Claude Lévi-Strauss, for instance, analyses the Oedipus myth as patterned on very general ideas about kinship relations (Scholes 1974: 69–74). Post-structuralism, arising in the 1960s and 1970s, calls the premises of structuralism into question: is a scientific understanding of culture possible? Are abstraction, pattern and system the best way of looking at culture, or is it composed of fragmentary, singular and peculiar elements that call for more ad hoc analysis? Post-structuralists are often less interested in unified and systematically arranged works of art, which lend themselves easily to structuralist and highly coherent readings, than they are in quirky, off-balanced, incomplete or ambiguous works.

A play such as Elizabeth Cary's seventeenth-century *The Tragedy of Mariam*, for instance (discussed also in the section on feminist theory), lends itself to a post-structuralist approach. Cary was an independent-minded woman oppressed by a patriarchal husband, family and society. Her play concerns the oppression of a similarly independent main character. The play, however, features three strikingly different female characters: Mariam, the virtuous and independent protagonist; the villainous and independent Salome; Graphina, virtuous and subordinate in spirit. How are we to judge these three women, with their overlapping combinations of qualities? Salome and Graphina, opposites in every way, survive, while the complex Mariam is beheaded. Mariam is often unsure herself how to judge her own actions. Salome, though obviously a villain, speaks forcefully on behalf of women, in order 'To show my sex the way to freedom's door' (Cerasano and Wynne-Davies 1996: 53); her virtuous husband, on the other hand, gives speeches that are passionately misogynist. Moreover, the last word in every act of the play is given to the chorus. The tradition from Greek tragedy is to listen to the chorus as if its pronouncements have a privileged relationship to the truth. Here, however, the chorus condemns Mariam but not Salome, often seeming to misconstrue the events that have just taken place. And yet are we meant simply to dismiss the chorus's pronouncements? There is nothing in the play that explicitly points us in that direction. Is this a play that celebrates or condemns female independence? What kind of play is it if it somehow does both at once? We are left, as the critic Margaret W. Ferguson argues, to puzzle out why 'the play's ideological statement is so mixed, so contradictory' (Ferguson 1991: 226). The puzzling, the mixed and the contradictory – these are the qualities that excite the post-structuralist.

Post-structuralism and deconstruction (defined more fully shortly) question not only the premises of structuralism and its approach to interpreting works of art and culture but also, more broadly, the basic certainties and assurances of western ways of thinking that date back to classical Greece. In the late nineteenth century, the German philosopher Friedrich Nietzsche, whose *The Birth of Tragedy* was discussed in the previous section, performed a critique of western philosophy that has been of great influence on more recent theorists of post-structuralism and deconstruction. Nietzsche is a key figure in what the phenomenologist Paul Ricoeur calls 'the school of suspicion' (Ricoeur 1970: 32). The objects of Nietzsche's suspicion are 'truth' (which he regularly puts in quotation marks), God and religion, and language. Truth and religion are, for Nietzsche, ridiculous illusions, usually in the service of forces that seek to restrain human freedom and creativity. Language, however, is a problem only inasmuch as we think we can get at the 'truth' with it, or conversely, that it hides the 'truth' from us. If we accept language as a play of appearances rather than a force for truth, since '[i]t is no more than a moral prejudice that truth is worth more than mere appearance' (Nietzsche 1966: 46), we can be quite happy with it, free in the play of words rather than tied by them to a restrictive 'truth'. Not only language but the world can never be anything but appearance, because it is always intelligible only from a perspective informed by our drives, our creative 'will to power'. The world is always a fiction or vision we create for our own ends. To think this way is to open up 'a philosophy of the future': Nietzsche thinks we are on the 'threshold' of a new era (Nietzsche 1966: 44), although that new era will be two centuries in the making (Nietzsche 1964: 209). In this new era, philosophers will be 'free spirits', freed from metaphysical and moral illusions, who will be 'suspicious at long last of all thinking' (Nietzsche 1966: 46), of all claims to truth and moralistic restraint.

In the last section I touched upon Nietzsche's view of theatre as seen in his *Birth of Tragedy*, but the philosophical position put forward here, which is to be found in Nietzsche's later work, is in part a conscious refutation of his earlier work on Greek tragedy. In this later work Nietzsche launches a spirited attack on the deluded piety he sees in such works of culture as Richard

Wagner's opera *Parsifal*, the espousal of asceticism and Christianity in which calls forth from Nietzsche the strongest suspicion and condemnation (Nietzsche 1964: 121–7).

Derrida and deconstruction

Roland Barthes' later work, discussed under semiotics, with its movement away from system, abstract model and scientific principles, can be taken as post-structuralist, but nothing has marked the advent of post-structuralist thought as distinctly as the work of the French/North African theorist Jacques Derrida, beginning in the mid-1960s with the manifesto-like 'Structure, Sign and Play in the Discourse of the Human Sciences' (Derrida 1978: 278–93). Derrida argues that structuralism is caught up in many of the philosophical assumptions it sets itself against; that this is necessarily so for any discourse in the western tradition (the metaphysical tradition that believes in such abstract notions as truth, being and oneness); that there is no easy escape from this; that the unravelling of these assumptions must be slow and painstaking and opens up on a free play of signification that always already underlies any meaning and yet that all discourses, even those critical of philosophical certainty, tend in part to want to arrest. That's a mouthful and a great deal for anybody to get his or her mind around. Deconstruction is an extremely difficult theoretical position to understand, not only because its ideas are complex and often counter-intuitive, but also because it is often expressed – especially by Derrida – in extremely difficult language. But these difficulties are part of deconstruction's integrity and rigour, and to ignore them would be to fashion a very simplistic version of deconstruction. Without doing that, let us try and see if we can get a rudimentary grasp of this highly sophisticated theory.

Structuralism, which in its day was taken as a profound questioning of traditional western thought, is taken by Derrida actually to be in support of just those ways of thought (more on these in a moment). This must be true, according to deconstructive thought, of all critique of western thought that arises from within western thought: it will inevitably be bound up with that which it questions (this is also true of deconstruction itself). Semiotics and phenomenology are similarly compromised: semiotics stresses the fundamental connection of language to speech in a way that undermines its insistence on the inherently arbitrary nature of the sign; phenomenology rejects metaphysical truths in favour of phenomena and appearance only to insist on the truth to be discovered in human consciousness and lived experience. In each of these cases, the theory contradicts itself and brings back some naive assumption it has attempted to dispel. In a certain way, deconstruction takes theories such as structuralism, semiotics and phenomenology to their logical conclusions, even if the conclusions suggested differ from many of the tenets these theories suggest to themselves.

Why is it so difficult or impossible for theories critical of western thought to escape these complicities and contradictions? To answer this we need to begin by understanding the nature of language, or to be more exact, writing, or more exact still, what Derrida calls 'arche-writing'. Derrida is involved in what he calls 'grammatology', which is the study of the necessary effects of writing on any text (Derrida 1976). Writing here means not only actual writing in all its forms but 'arche-writing', a process which underlies not only written but spoken language as well as thought, self and any activity taken to be text. And for Derrida, 'there is nothing outside the text'. This famous dictum has been taken in many ways, all of which are partly implied; for the present purposes, the following quotation, from a discussion of apartheid and South Africa, may serve as gloss:

> I found it necessary to recast the concept of text by generalizing it almost without limit, in any case without present or perceptible limit, without any limit that is. That's why there is nothing

'*beyond* the text'. That's why South Africa and *apartheid* are, like you and me, part of this general text, which is not to say it can be read the way one reads a book.

(Derrida 1986: 165)

Everything – or at least everything humans deal with – is, for Derrida, text, that is, having the properties of arche-writing.

What are some of the characteristics of writing and textuality? For Saussure, difference is the relationship between signifiers, and Derrida takes difference to be at the heart of writing. He rewrites '*difference*' as '*différance*', meaning difference and deferral: nothing, no word, idea, text or subject, is what it was intended to be; nothing is identical with itself; the moment something is thought, said, written or intended, it becomes a trace of itself, no longer itself, no longer present; in this way, meaning, truth, identity, presence are always deferred and never arrive. Similarly, Derrida is involved in the undermining of any search for origins, for an earlier moment when thoughts, words, self and truth were identical and present to one another, when writing had access to the real and the truth. In this regard he also undertakes a critique of logocentrism, the belief that spoken language has more integrity than writing and that in speaking the separation of speaker and language is somehow avoided. The critique of the primacy of speech goes with a critique of presence, immediacy in all its forms, which entails not only an undermining of metaphysics but also of phenomenology's interest in the truth-seeking encounter between consciousness and reality. That is, maybe the dissatisfaction with everyday life and consciousness and the longing for a fuller existence that characterize phenomenology are the products of arche-writing: we can never be fully present, but we long to be. Thus, phenomenology's values are reversed: lack of presence and truth is the real thing; the desire for full presence and truth is the illusion in which we are trapped.

The belief in origins, logocentrism, truth, unity, identity, presence – these are the linchpins of western metaphysical thought. Therefore, there is a basic contradiction between the nature of the arche-writing we are all part of and the assumptions that have guided western thinking. Just as no writing, even western metaphysics, can escape from the nature of writing, writing in the western tradition cannot escape falling into the metaphysical assumptions from which it comes. This is why even theories critical of western thought such as semiotics and phenomenology – even deconstruction – end up falling back into the metaphysics they are questioning. It is hard, for instance, to talk about *différance* and arche-writing without calling them the truth or origin. Derrida says *différance* is originary but not in the traditional metaphysical sense of an original moment of unity and presence, and so he puts 'originary' in quotation marks (Derrida 1992: 113).

The free play inherent in writing means that categorizations, identities, unities arising inevitably in western language and thought are always undermined by slippage. Systems of genre, for instance (Derrida 1980b), are ultimately untenable and undone by the uncontrollability and excess that are part of any writing. Even a classicist such as Shakespeare's contemporary Ben Jonson, very caught up in rigorous modes of categorization and decorum, will have an impossible job keeping strict differences of genre under control: note how, for example, his famous comedies *Volpone* and *The Alchemist* have basic similarities to his less famous tragedy *Sejanus*: in each play a pair of scoundrels and con men attempt to dupe the public; in each play the two scoundrels fall out, compete against each other and come to somewhat different ends, of relative failure or success. In fact, *The Alchemist* and *Sejanus* are perhaps more closely parallel than either is to *Volpone* in this regard, inasmuch as each features an ending in which one scoundrel clearly falls, while the other struts his success (whereas in *Volpone* both are punished). The law of genre,

disputes genre

according to Derrida, is the need to impose a textual order which, in text and writing, cannot possibly be maintained.

There is no easy escape from these predicaments, and we find ourselves caught in a double bind. We can't escape to metaphysics because metaphysics is an impossible illusion, and we can't easily go forward into the world of free play because we are so caught up in a tradition of thinking over 2,000 years old. If any movement in that direction is to be made it will have to be slow and painstaking – deconstructing the world one text at a time. Derrida's theory should properly be called grammatology, but his work is called deconstruction, which is a reading process whereby the hidden and unacknowledged metaphysical assumptions (of truth, presence, identity, essence and so forth) and complicities of any particular text are unravelled from within and in the text's own terms. Deconstruction proceeds by an emphasis on the reading of particular texts, as opposed to general models, and from radical suspicion about the philosophic or scientific integrity possible in any piece of writing.

The verb 'to deconstruct' is now used loosely to apply to any critique of another's position, but Derrida means something more specific and rigorous. Deconstruction is not done from a smug position above the idea being deconstructed; rather, it takes its object seriously, from within, pushing to the limits where writing inevitably begins to contradict itself. Derrida is at his best when he works through the ideas of great western philosophers and others he, at least in part, admires; he is at his worst, petulant and dismissive, when he attacks those he does not respect (for example, in Derrida 1986).

Stephen Bonnycastle, in his introduction to theory, In Search of Authority, writes that deconstruction is only useful as a way of resisting oppressive authority and is not 'very satisfying on its own' (Bonnycastle 1996: 112). In other words, deconstruction is something you only use against your enemies or opponents, to challenge their positions, and not something one needs to bring to one's own beliefs, since, one assumes, they don't need it and it doesn't provide positive and meaningful answers. Deconstruction, however, is not interested in being satisfying if that means providing pat truths to live by; but Nietzsche, as we have seen, argues that suspicion provides its own kind of joyousness and freedom. Moreover, because of the basic characteristics of writing and 'arche-writing', everything is open to deconstruction, not just works that parade their authoritarianism in obviously distasteful ways. For example, David Henry Hwang's M. Butterfly (discussed more fully in the section on post-colonialism), which is itself an explicit attempt to deconstruct the racist and sexist ideas in Puccini's opera Madame Butterfly, has as its climax a moment when a character strips to reveal the naked truth of his sexual identity. This moment, however, is followed by another character, a western male, having seen this naked truth, dressing as an Asian woman. Is he simply deluded? Is he ignoring the naked truth? Is he falling back into oppressive ways of thinking and behaving? Yes, but on the other hand isn't there something naive and oppressive in assuming that the truth about anyone can be read off his or her naked body? Isn't it the oppression under attack in the play that assumes because a person is Asian or a woman he or she must be one way and one way only? The play seems to need to come to its naked truth, but ultimately cannot escape a sense that identity is not a naked truth but appearance and role-playing. M. Butterfly remains caught in this tension in a way that unsettles both the forms of oppression it attacks and the possibilities of liberation it points toward. For deconstruction that is a necessary and healthy – if not a satisfying or easy – tension to be caught in.

Derrida's painstaking suspicion of truth claims also result in an extreme care and hesitance about coming to conclusions on intellectual, ethical and political questions. He asserts:

> And if I speak so often of the incalculable and the undecidable it's not out of a simple predilection for play nor in order to neu-

tralize decision: on the contrary, I believe there is no responsibility, no ethico-political decision, that must not pass through
the proofs of the incalculable or the undecidable.

(Derrida 1991: 108)

Although Derrida says, 'history is not the last word, the final key,
of reading', and that he is 'suspicious of the traditional concepts
of history' (Derrida 1980a: 22), his notion of writing as iterable,
that is, as always displaced from its first situation into new and
unforeseen circumstances (think of the way plays from the past
are always being remounted in places, times, and circumstances
far different from where they began), introduces the play of history into Derrida's analysis. Although he is not interested in the
particulars of history – his usual unit of temporal analysis is the
western epoch since the Greeks – his work entails a study of
the conditions of historicity itself as endless iterability (Derrida
1988: 1–23). Related to iterability are Derrida's interests in
translation and the inevitable differences that occur from one language or semiotic system or context to another (Derrida 1985).

Nevertheless, Derrida does foresee the advent of a great historical change. Like Nietzsche, he announces the coming of a
future civilization, an epoch which will undo all the patterns of
our own, but announces it only 'at a distance of a few centuries'
(Derrida 1976: 8).

Aspects of deconstruction are also enacted relentlessly in the
work of the Belgian/American theorist Paul de Man. De Man
argues for a radical separation of language and nature: in any
understanding of the world, there is the imposition of linguistic
and rhetorical structures which have nothing to do with the natural objects under examination (de Man 1984). When we think
and write about the world, it is writing we see, not the world.
Similarly, de Man radically separates human intention and language: language performs its rhetorical operations ultimately
independent of human agency (de Man 1986). Language does its

thing and says what it tends to say, not what we want it to say. Nevertheless, while language is separate from nature and human intention, its rhetorical structures unite all forms of writing: philosophy, as well as poetry, is caught in misleading tropes which get in the way of the possibility of clear thinking, while poetry, as well as philosophy, is capable of deconstructing its own rhetorical blindness from within (de Man 1979); this deconstruction slowly and never completely leads toward a critical awareness of this blindness, which is the undoing, as well as the most accomplished form, of the Enlightenment belief in rational understanding.

One of many critiques of this way of thinking can be found in the work of Jürgen Habermas, who is associated with the Frankfurt School of 'Critical Theory', founded in the first part of the twentieth century by Theodor Adorno and Max Horkheimer. Habermas argues that enlightenment and reason must work toward an 'ideal speech situation' in which all distortions of ideology, institution, power and rhetoric have been understood and set aside, so that rational exchange of truth can take place unhampered (Habermas 1979). On the one hand, the ideal speech situation is a utopian idea which post-structuralist and deconstructive thought would take as an illusion and an impossibility; on the other hand, the assumption of the possibility of some rational exchange underlies even the relations of Derrida and de Man with their readers.

Deconstruction has been applied to theatre in the United States by Gerald Rabkin and Elinor Fuchs in the 1980s. Rabkin uses a variety of post-structuralist thinkers, most prominently Barthes and Derrida, to deconstruct authorial control and the stability of the written text in theatre, which give way to the 'dispersion, discontinuity and dissemination' (Rabkin 1983: 51) of open interpretation, especially in the hands of radical directors and troupes. What authors and playwrights intend passes; what endures is their writing iterated and reactivated in new contexts. Fuchs, like Philip Auslander more recently in his critique of 'liveness' (discussed in the section on phenomenology), takes aim at the aura of theatrical presence that is often associated with live actors on stage and 'the theatrical enterprise of spontaneous speech with its logocentric claims to origination, authority, authenticity' (Fuchs 1985: 172). In the place of speech and presence she posits a 'theatre of Absence' which 'disperses the center, displaces the Subject, destabilizes meaning' (165). Stratos E. Constantinidis has attempted to systematize deconstruction as an analytical method derived from a 'skepticism which questions all kinds of interpretation' (Constantinidis 1993: 291), especially around issues of authoritative consciousness and has brought his somewhat idiosyncratic analysis to bear on a wide range of theatrical figures, from Stanislavski to the American playwright Sam Shepard.

Artaud

The most careful and exacting deconstructive work on theatre, however, has been done by Derrida himself. Derrida might well have chosen Chekhov as an exemplary object or model of theatre and deconstruction; as noted, like Chekhov and Nietzsche, Derrida announces the coming of a future civilization 'at a distance of a few centuries' (1976: 8). Inasmuch as deconstruction is in part an unravelling of phenomenological assumptions from within, Chekhov and Derrida partake of a common project. Be that as it may, Derrida has chosen to do his major study of the theatre in two very dense essays on the work of Antonin Artaud (discussed in the section on phenomenology): 'La Parole soufflée' (which means, among other things, the stolen or spirited away word or speech) and 'The Theater of Cruelty and the Closure of Representation' (Derrida 1978: 169–95, 232–50).

Artaud's work combines a radical semiotics and a radical phenomenology. For Artaud, there is a 'rupture between things and words, between things and the ideas and signs that are their representation' (Artaud 1958: 7), but this gap is to be overcome in a language of living signs:

> The objects, the props, even the scenery which will appear on the stage will have to be understood in an immediate sense, without transposition; they will have to be taken not for what they represent but for what they really are.
>
> (Artaud 1988: 160)

In a theatre of unalienated signs, in which the arbitrariness and conventionality of social signification have given way to visceral and intellectual presence, we will be 'like victims burnt at the stake, signaling through the flames' (Artaud 1958: 13).

Artaud's language is laced with images of pain and cruelty. In part this arises from a phenomenological sense of having been separated from self or life: 'I am a man who has lost his life and who is seeking by every means to restore it to its place' (Artaud 1988: 110). Such restoration calls for drastic measures: 'The theater like the plague is a crisis which is resolved by death or cure' (Artaud 1958: 31). What is necessary in the theatre is 'the creation of a reality, the unprecedented eruption of a world' (Artaud 1988: 155). 'Theater must make itself the equal of life' – moreover it must take us 'where lives drink at their source' (Artaud 1958: 116, 146). Such a theatre takes us beyond the standing reserve of all social limitations and utility to 'an immediate gratuitousness provoking acts without use or profit' (p. 24).

One thrust of Derrida's reading of Artaud is to reveal the necessary paradoxes and contradictions in such thinking: signs by their very nature are arbitrary representations and not the presence of what really is; there is no source or origin of life where human existence does not involve separation from itself. In 'La Parole soufflée' Derrida argues that the living closeness of language, thought and self that Artaud envisions ultimately returns to the need for perfection in a fixed written text, which Artaud adamantly rejects elsewhere as the imposition of death and repetition; in 'The Theater of Cruelty and the Closure of Representation', Artaud's attempt to close and put an end to representation and get to living reality is seen to be inextricably bound up with the closure of representation in another sense: representation as the limit and unpassable horizon of possibility in the theatre.

This is not to say, however, that Derrida believes Artaud to have been a particularly careless thinker. On the contrary, according to Derrida, Artaud has gone further than anyone – 'perhaps even Nietzsche' (Derrida 1978: 327) – in unravelling western metaphysical thought from within, and he has done this by being more faithful to metaphysics than it is to itself (p. 183). Artaud is to western metaphysics as Dorothy is to the wizard in *The Wizard of Oz*: it is because Dorothy takes the wizard's promises seriously, because she takes him at his word, that she exposes the deception at work. Derrida's interest is in the margins and liminal areas of thinking where opposites share an entanglement, and he sees Artaud as working at the limits of western thought where there is an infinitely close complicity between metaphysics and difference, between error and truth, a complicity only made apparent by work at the limits. No one, for instance, has made as much of the limiting (or enabling) effects of language on thought, discussed by de Man, as has Artaud. Artaud writes:

> All writing is garbage. People who come out of nowhere to try and put into words any part of what goes on in their minds are pigs ...
>
> (Artaud 1988: 85)

and:

> I am truly LOCALIZED by my terms, I mean that I do not recognize them as valid in my thought. I am truly paralyzed by my

> terms, by a series of terminations. And however ELSEWHERE
> my thought may be at these moments, I have no choice but to
> bring it out through these terms, however contradictory to
> itself, however parallel, however ambiguous they may be, or pay
> the penalty of no longer being able to think.
>
> (p. 83)

Thus for Derrida, Artaud's writings are 'more a system of critiques *shaking the entirety* of Occidental history than a treatise on theatrical practice' (Derrida 1978: 235).

One reason that Artaud's writings are not so much a treatise on theatrical practice is because of Artaud's close connection with impossibility. For Derrida, the complicity between metaphysics and Artaud's theatre of cruelty is a 'fatal complicity', inescapable and insurmountable, which 'obeys a law': 'The transgression of metaphysics through the "thought" which, Artaud tells us, has not yet begun, always risks returning to metaphysics' (p. 194), even though Artaud's ultimate purpose is the destruction of western civilization and thought and the advent of a new epoch. Thus there is no way to create a theatre beyond representation or with signs fully present to themselves. Derrida demonstrates this by asking, 'Under what conditions can a theater today legitimately invoke Artaud's name?' (p. 234). By a lengthy process of elimination, Derrida concludes that no theatre can be what Artaud proposes: 'There is no theater in the world today which fulfills Artaud's desire. And there would be no exception to be made for the attempts made by Artaud himself' (p. 248).

Certainly there is a discrepancy between Artaud's theoretical proposals and what he himself was able to achieve in practice. Derrida's categorical relegation of theatre of cruelty to impossibility, however, leaves us with the complex problem of exemplarity in Artaud. Artaud often succumbs to the impossibility delineated by Derrida: 'Theater is the one thing in the world most impossible to save' (Artaud 1988: 155), he writes, and asks, 'But who has drunk at the sources of life?' (Artaud 1958: 146). And yet Artaud is always finding examples of the kind of theatre he is proposing: August Strindberg's *The Dream Play*, Balinese theatre, Vincent Van Gogh's paintings, the Marx Brothers' *Animal Crackers* and *Monkey Business*, Jean-Louis Barrault's mime. It may be that the proliferation of examples is a compulsive response to Artaud's inability to make the theatre of cruelty a reality, but it might also be that, if we set our sights, as Artaud often does, below the absolute, it becomes possible to find intimations of the kind of theatre he is searching for. In Strindberg's play, for example, Artaud sees 'a new spiritual order given to the ordinary objects and things of life' (Artaud 1988: 164); in the Marx Brothers' films, he sees 'an exercise in intellectual freedom in which the unconscious of each of the characters, repressed by conventions and habits, avenges itself and us at the same time' (Artaud 1958: 143). While Sophocles' *Oedipus Rex* presents incest and rape in refined and indirect language 'as if he were speaking beside the point' (p. 75), John Ford's *'Tis a Pity She's a Whore* presents incest as absolute freedom and absolute danger in a way that advances us into 'an endless vertigo' (p. 29). Towards the end of his life, Artaud sees in the radio broadcast of his own play *To Have Done with the Judgment of God* 'a small-scale model for what I want to do in the *Theater of cruelty*' (Artaud 1988: 577). But it is on this small scale of theatrical practice that Derrida fails to address Artaud's project. Artaud sees himself labouring 'at the incandescent edges of the future' (Artaud 1958: 51), neither mired in an impossible present nor fully arrived in a time yet to come. For all his torment, Artaud is much more optimistic – naively so – in his forecasting of the advent of the future than either Chekhov or Derrida: 'I shall be understood in ten years', he writes (Artaud 1988: 86).

The absoluteness of Derrida's concerns also undermines the carefulness of his reading of Artaud's politics. At its most sensitive and sophisticated, deconstruction brings an unrelenting interrogation to politics and decision-making. At its most cavalier, it jumps to the conclusion that political progress is impossible. In a note to 'La Parole soufflée', most egregiously, Derrida draws a connection between Artaud's anal retentiveness – his mourning of the loss of self in loss of the faeces – and Karl Marx's articulation of the alienation of the worker from his or her labour (p. 325). Derrida sees the connection as arising from a necessary metaphysics of alienation. But such a connection rides roughshod over important differences. For Marx, of course, workers are not alienated because they defecate, or even because their labour is separated from themselves and externalized as work on the material world, but because of relations of production which rob and exploit them – externalization is not the same thing as alienation. Derrida leaves the significance of the connection he draws undeveloped, but this connection runs the risk of casting Marxist politics into fatality and impossibility. Derrida's connection implies that there can be no political liberation as long as human beings have anuses; Artaud may possibly have believed that, but Marx, his followers, and many uncommitted to his thinking, have believed otherwise.

le acusa de simplicación

Jerzy Grotowski and Herbert Blau

A very different approach to Artaud from Derrida's can be found in the theorizing and theatre of the Polish director Jerzy Grotowski. Grotowski sees theatre as 'entering the age of Artaud' (Grotowski 1975: 85), but the task is to find concrete ways of carrying out aspects of what Artaud suggests – 'his idea of salvation through theatre' (p. 93), for instance – while realizing that 'it is impossible to carry out his proposals' (p. 86) and rejecting what he sees as Artaud's sickness and imprecision. Grotowski works in 'confrontation' with Artaud, not as an obedient follower but as an adapter, taking up and remaking whatever is compelling and useful. What he adds to Artaud's project is a sense that acting and theatre are particularly disciplined and rigorous undertakings (in this thinking Grotowski is influenced by Stanislavski). In this way, Grotowski is able to take up a precise and particular task without the generalized sense of impossibility that Derrida brings to his reading of Artaud.

Grotowski's theatre takes place in the conjunction of opposites: spontaneity and precision, spirituality and physical rigour, theatre as both new testament and laboratory. Derrida's essays on Artaud make several references to the 'eve' of our own epoch or of an epoch to come. Deconstruction is interested in the 'eve' because it is a time when a new age has been announced but has not yet arrived and because it marks a marginal or liminal state when one thing is in the process of turning into its opposite – as Artaud's work is both the closing down and the inescapable enclosure of representation and metaphysics. Perhaps no 'eve' so plays with margins and opposites as does the Saturday before Easter, the eve of the resurrection. Stanislavski, long before Grotowski, uses Easter as a recurring motif in his work for moments when theatre is reborn, but resurrection's eve takes on a rich and deconstructive meaning in Grotowski's play *Akropolis*, which was filmed in 1968 for American television.

The Canadian theorist Northrop Frye, in his last book, discusses the importance of epitaphs for deconstruction. He writes:

> The most primitive form of visual poetry is the epitaph, which manifests Derrida's principle of *différance* very clearly. The epitaph typically says: stop and look at me; I'm dead and you're alive (difference), but you'll soon be dead too (deferral).
>
> (Frye 1990: 69)

But the relation of life and death on resurrection's eve is more complicated than this. One of the things deconstruction does is to complicate the relations between binary oppositions – often metaphysical pairs, such as truth and falsehood, good and evil, in which the terms are taken to be completely distinct and in which one term (truth, good) is valued over the other (falsehood, evil). Deconstruction tends to show how these oppositions are much too simple. Consider for a moment the kinds of personal and social performances involving costume and identity that happen on Halloween. Gender roles, traditionally taken as a clear binary opposition between masculine and feminine, can become complicated, for instance. Common, in big, western cities, are men dressing in drag. There is a male body in a feminine costume, but which is the real identity? The costume denies that the male body, with whatever traditional norms of masculinity associated with it, is the real self. On the other hand, the feminine costume as drag costume means what it means because it is culturally displaced onto a male body. On a woman's body it would more readily indicate traditional femininity and gender roles. The role being expressed in drag happens in the relation between the male body and the feminine costume, neither of which is a true identity in itself.

More relevant to the discussion of Grotowski's *Akropolis* is the binary opposition between life and death, also often enacted on Halloween (and central – as in Auslander and Fuchs – to notions of live or living theatre as opposed to the dead letter or dead writing). Imagine someone in a skeleton costume. The costume is innocuous inasmuch as it is mere fantasy of dead bones over a living body of flesh. But, of course, there is a skeleton beneath that living flesh. Just as the skeleton is a costume over the flesh, the flesh is a costume over the skeleton. Flesh dies and reveals the skeleton, as if the skeleton is the death to come that is already inside the living flesh. The skeleton costume is both innocuous – the person is not really dead – and tellingly macabre – death is already there inside, and someday it will be revealed behind the façade of the flesh. In a related and reversed way, on the eve of the resurrection Christ is dead and death rules the world, but soon Christ will rise from the dead and live again. He has died only so he can rise. Is Easter Saturday a time of life or death, or both? What if the resurrection, like the new age for Derrida or Chekhov, is indefinitely postponed? It is in such a complex matrix that *Akropolis* is set. The play is based on an earlier work by Stanislaw Wyspianski, in which biblical characters depicted in a cathedral come to life on the night before the resurrection. Grotowski transposes the action to Auschwitz and the characters to prisoners about to enter the ovens. The simple belief in eternal life or the progress of civilization is replaced by an intertwining of life and death: the acropolis, the height of western civilization, is equally the necropolis, the death camp, the cemetery of civilization. At the end of the play the actors, singing a Christmas carol at the top of their lungs, enter the oven in search of God and salvation.

In its staging, the play mixes the presence of bodies and life with the presence of death. The actors exhibit superlative physical power and presence, in extreme control of facial, gestural and vocal expression. There is a radical sense of their disciplined and focused presence as bodies acting. The biblical characters who come to life in Wyspianski's original, however, have been replaced by the lifeless fetish objects of the concentration camp: Christ is a headless rag doll; Rachel is a stove pipe; the hair of the dead is a strip of gauze or plastic – signifiers radically alienated from what they represent. Even the bodies of the living actors are tormented, twisted and shorn of their identities. As much as the play presents life, it presents life's absence. In making the spirit of the concentration camp live again, it recreates death and alienation, deferring resurrection on resurrection's eve and presenting rebirth as incineration and absence.

Deconstructive ideas are explicitly at work in the theatre and theory of the American Herbert Blau, who often refers to Derrida and deconstruction in his writing. What Blau draws from Derrida and elsewhere is a carefulness in working through complicity and illusion in theatre and theory, which are seen, in a manner reminiscent of de Man's interlacing of poetry and philosophy, as interrelated activities. Theatre is 'blooded abstraction' (Blau 1982a: xiii) and 'metaphysics of the flesh' (Blau 1981: 83), while theory combines a performative impulse with an intellectualized anti-theatrical prejudice (Blau 1987b: xvii) that values ideas over representations. Thus, Elsinore, Blau's adaptation of Hamlet, is labelled an 'analytic scenario', while Crooked Eclipses, his adaptation of Shakespeare's sonnets, is a 'theatrical essay'.

Blau's theatrical and theoretical work involves the 'sounding' of the subtle distinctions and the vertigo of seeming and truth in any attempt to clarify and understand the human and theatrical condition: 'the unremitting meticulousness of the thinking through of illusion' (Blau 1983: 460). This involves Blau in many of the conundrums mapped out by deconstruction. Is theatre, for instance, a place of presence or what Blau calls 'ghosting'? The idea of immediate and unmediated presence is an illusion (Blau 1987b: 164) and the body is always ghosted with words (Blau 1982b: 224) – indeed performance seems written even when there is no text (Blau 1987b: 171). However, it would be equally illusory to think of the actor as entirely absent. The actor, like every human being, is a thinking body performing blooded thought. As an actor says in Elsinore, 'I saw my body...and how I couldn't get out of it' (Blau 1981: 61). In this inescapable struggle between blood and thought, theatre enacts the problem of western metaphysics (Blau 1983: 457) – the inextricable difficulty of thinking through the relationship between ideas and bodies: we are both, but we can never clearly work through how they relate.

Intellectually, Blau combines relentless suspicion and unremitting commitment, both of which he sees in Shakespeare. Hamlet, for instance, presents thought so dense it 'feels, structurally, like brain damage' (Blau 1982b: 169). Here we are given a sense of deconstruction's hopelessness vis-à-vis the human capacity to see clearly past illusion to the heart of things. In this way, Blau's thought and theatre resemble the thought of de Man. On the other hand, a key moment in *Crooked Eclipses* involves the actor Ellen, 'kneeling, speaking simply to somebody in the audience', speaking the sonnet 'Let me not to the marriage of true minds / Admit impediments' (Blau, *Crooked Eclipses*: 26). Here, no matter how circumscribed by illusion, is the enactment of a moment of ideal communication like that envisioned by Habermas.

Blau's politics are equally conflicted. He sees 'a virtually irremediable split between art and politics' (Blau 1987a: 68). And yet he remains 'messianic about the theater … in it to create the possibility of a valid public life, to save the world in fact' (Blau 1982b: 31, 1987b: 205); if reality makes that seem impossible, then Blau will work for change despite the forces of reality.

QUESTIONS ONE MIGHT ASK OF A PLAY OR PERFORMANCE

Is the play or performance attempting to espouse or relying on some truth, idea or position? Are there ways in which it undermines its own arguments? If so, is this simply shoddy thinking or writing or a necessary dilemma, intentional or otherwise, in working through that truth or idea?

What systems of categorization and opposition are being relied upon in the play or performance: distinctions of genre, good and evil, truth and falsehood? Can these be deconstructed?

Can you come to the play or performance with an attitude of suspicion? What does that do to your enjoyment of it? Is there a different kind of enjoyment that comes from suspicion?

Can you deconstruct a play or performance that you deeply appreciate and respect? Is this a negative thing to do? How do you feel about the play or performance afterwards?

Is an attitude of suspicion of any use for an actor or director? What kind of play or performance would it produce?

In this chapter, through semiotics, phenomenology and deconstruction, we have asked if there is a fundamental reality to theatre, what Stanislavski calls the laws of nature that lie behind theatre, or Derrida calls the necessity that underlies all textuality. Is there an essence to theatre? Is it a sign, lived experience or text? Does theatre have a multiple reality, so that it is sign, lived experience, word and body, absence and presence, and much more, all at once? How can we articulate the connections and inevitable contradictions between different ways of thinking about the nature of theatre?

Second, if we were to come to some understanding or conclusion about this reality, where does this leave the theatre artist? Is the reality of theatre such as to arrest all work in a necessary fate, to defeat the possibility of many, if not all, theatrical projects? Or is there space, in the interstices of overlapping realities, to make theatre happen, no matter how incompletely and momentarily? What do the great laws and necessities of theatre mean for the specific performances of theatre artists in the world? Does theatrical reality create a limiting necessity or a space of structured possibility?

These are some of the questions we are left with in the face of theories which try to explain the nature of theatre. Such theories may clarify the theatrical predicament and hone our questioning, but they will not make such questions go away.

Finally, this chapter for the most part has dealt with theatre as a closed system set apart from other concerns and activities. As I said in the introduction, this does not imply that semiotics, phenomenology and deconstruction have nothing to say about theatre in relation to these other concerns and activities – quite the contrary. Nor do I wish to imply that theatre can ever be completely set apart from the rest of life and society. As I mention at the beginning of this chapter, there is a procedure in phenomenology called 'bracketing', whereby certain concerns are bracketed or set aside so that consideration can focus on a more limited set of questions. In this chapter I have, in effect, bracketed off concerns of subjectivity and the social sphere discussed more fully in the next two chapters. A full discussion of Chekhov, for instance (one of many possible examples), would need to examine the historical and social, as well as the phenomenological, grounds of disappointment, and a full discussion of Artaud would need to discuss his anti-Americanism and anti-imperialism and, in consequence, his affinity with post-colonial thought.

2

SUBJECTIVITY AND THEATRE

Psychoanalytic, Gender and Reader-Response Theory

In the section on phenomenology in Chapter 1, I discussed the living body of the human being as it exists in theatrical activity. But whose body are we talking about? There are any number of human beings involved in specific capacities in making theatre. In drama, there are the author, the reader and, in a fictional sense, the characters; in theatre, there are the director, the actors, the technicians and the audience. We can add the drama or theatre critic to this mix. If we think collectively or relationally of all those involved, then we need to consider each human being not only in his or her particular role but as part of a complex whole. And we can posit this whole in larger or smaller ways: from a whole society or cultural formation to those in attendance at one theatre on one particular occasion.

Much recent theory has focused on two specific terms to understand who human beings are and what they do. The first term is 'subject', and it implies (most specifically in the work of the Marxist theorist Louis Althusser) two contradictory qualities. First, we are subjected in the sense of moulded, fashioned, made to someone or something else's orders, whether that someone or something else is the father or patriarch in psychoanalysis and feminism or capital in Marxism. To be a subject, therefore, is to be something other than free or autonomous, something other than self-created or independent of others. But subject also implies, in grammar or liberal political theory, a doer, capable of independent action and self-direction. To some degree, the first sense of subject gives the lie to the second, or at least indicates its profound limitations. But does our subjectedness completely limit our subjective freedom? The second important term is 'agent', that which has power to act or effect something, and in many ways the idea of the agent is tied up with the idea of the subject in the second sense. The idea of agency, however, has tried to avoid some of the naivety in the idea of the autonomous individual. The agent can only act in its position as subjected and therefore has only very limited power and autonomy. Also, given our subjection to others, it may be that our fullest agency is as part of a group, which gives us necessary direction and support, rather than on our own (see Althusser 1971; Smith 1988).

In this chapter I have chosen to focus on three theoretical movements in order to explore questions of subjectivity and agency as they apply to those involved in making theatre. The first theoretical movement is psychoanalytic theory, which attempts to understand the human mind – how human beings become the way they are and why they act in the ways they do. The second movement is gender theory, which includes feminist theory as well as gay and lesbian theory and what has most recently come to be called queer theory. Like much psychoanalytic theory, gender theory stresses the importance of sexuality in human identity, but it often takes a more contestatory and liberatory stance toward the possibility of making ourselves over in new and more satisfying ways. Finally, I look at reception or reader-response theory. In running reception and reader-response theory together, I am doing a disservice to sophisticated and somewhat distinct theoretical approaches; I do this because there is something to be gained for theatre studies in thinking of these two schools as part of one large concern: the mapping of those involved in making cultural significance. In the reading of a book, it might be said, there is an interchange between only two subjects: author and reader. A more sophisticated and historicized reception theory would note that book publishers, teachers, critics and many others haunt this interchange. In the theatre, however, it is much more apparent that what happens is the responsibility of many human forces: a director who cuts or shapes a scene; an actor who flubs a line or gives an idiosyncratic reading; an audience that laughs or doesn't laugh; a critic whose bad review effectively shuts down a production and fixes its failure in the public record.

Once again, a few caveats are in order before we begin. As in Chapter 1, the three theoretical approaches chosen do not exhaust the exploration of the issues at hand. Phenomenology, for instance, or materialist theory have much to say about the human subject. Nor should it be assumed that feminism, for instance, only speaks to the concerns of subjectivity raised in this chapter. Also, my discussion at the beginning of the section on reception theory points out the complex intersections with other theories which make any theory of reception possible. Such intersections must at times retreat into the background, but they should not be forgotten.

1 PSYCHOANALYTIC THEORY

Freud

Psychoanalytic theory is concerned with the way that the minds or psyches of human beings are formulated and how that affects what we think, feel and do. The first and most important name in psychoanalytic theory is Sigmund Freud, an Austrian medical doctor who wrote in the first part of the twentieth century. As the critic Elizabeth Wright says in her recent reappraisal of psychoanalytic criticism:

> On the one hand, over the last ten years there has been a spate of virulent and visible attacks on psychoanalysis, and Freud in particular; on the other hand, paradoxically, studies informed by psychoanalysis have burgeoned and thrived in academic situations. The political status of psychoanalysis is thus a controversial issue with broad implications.
>
> (Wright 1998: 1)

Anyone coming to psychoanalysis should therefore keep in mind both the controversial status of psychoanalysis and the importance and prominence of Freud in cultural thinking over the last hundred years.

Freud's work is far-ranging and detailed (see Freud 1953–66), but we can extract a number of important basic principles. First, as its name implies, psychoanalysis presents ideas about the nature and structure of the human mind or psyche, which is not the brain with all its physical characteristics, but our mental condition and development. For Freud, the psyche is constructed; the psyche is segmented; the psyche is gendered. The constructedness of the human psyche is seen in the stages of development that it undergoes (oral, anal, genital; pre-oedipal, oedipal – the stages of our sexual fixations from infancy to adulthood, as Freud maps them), as well as in the range of normal and 'aberrant' outcomes that are possible for psychic development (heterosexual, homosexual, bisexual; neurotic, psychotic, etc.): human minds are not so much born as made and can be formed in a number of ways, depending on circumstances.

The segmentation of the psyche is seen in various topologies or mappings Freud proposes over the course of his career, such as the division of the psyche into superego (conscience), ego (consciousness) and id (unconscious drives). We are like a dog drooling before dainties on a coffee table: the superego is the master which forbids the dog to take; the id is the drooling desire; the ego is that part of the dog caught between desire and denial. There is also, for Freud, the separation of the conscious and the vast unconscious, so that the bulk of our thoughts, of our psychic forces, like the bulk of an iceberg, lies below the surface of our awareness: the human psyche is not one entity fully present to itself as consciousness but rather a divided and largely unknowable complex: we are not who we are aware of being; we are motivated and driven by parts of our minds that we are not conscious of. Finally, for Freud, all psychic development is gendered, and since sexuality plays such an important part in our mental development, the psychic difference between men and women is fundamental: males (are allowed to) develop differently from females; the presence or absence of the penis allows for the development of very different identities and ways of being in the world. These differences are controlled and organized by the 'oedipal' patterns whereby we are slotted into various sexual and familial roles as father, mother, son and daughter. Basically, we all have to learn to renounce our primary sexual attachment to our mothers and, under the stern eyes of our fathers and the superego they instil within us, learn to fix our sexual interests on a socially acceptable substitute – in the simplest case, the boy finds a girl who is 'just like mom', but definitely not mom.

Like the drooling dog, the human being is driven by a set of basic desires most of which are socially unacceptable, at least until brought into some kind of regulation. Our sexual desires are regulated by the oedipal developments just alluded to. Art, for Freud, is the product of another kind of regulation of basic drives: artists sublimate their basic instincts, suppressing their base and anti-social energies and desires and, through 'sublimation', allow them to re-emerge in a more idealized and socially acceptable form. Psychoanalytic study of an artist's life, therefore, is likely to reveal the origins of sublime masterpieces in personal and unpleasant psychological histories. Late in his career, in *Beyond the Pleasure Principle*, Freud posits a drive deeper than the 'pleasure principle', the life-affirming, if selfish, drive that leads the dog in us to want the dainties. This is the death drive, a desire for stillness and stasis, a desire to escape and end all the wanting and hankering after pleasure that excite and enervate us.

Much of the nature of the psyche as constructed, segmented and gendered is not immediately apparent. Our consciousness does not think of itself as constructed, or as one small element of a psyche we don't really know. Moreover, the truth about our drives and the way the superego frustrates them is unsavoury. Neither we nor society like to acknowledge such things. All this inaccessible reality about our psychic life can only be apprehended — like the workings of the unconscious — indirectly, through careful analysis of such phenomena as dreams, which are, according to Freud, the royal road to the unconscious. In dreams we let things out (albeit in disguise) that we can't admit to when we're awake. Much of Freud's work maps ways of uncovering the psyche's hidden truths. In dreams, for instance — and by extension in other of our creations — the manifest content (the literal, surface meaning of the dream) needs to be seen through to get at the latent content (the hidden or disguised meaning, what the dream is really meant to show). Freud's theory is, therefore, also a theory of interpretation, based on the idea that the psychic truth is by its very nature something we attempt to hide under more obvious but misleading messages.

Freud's best-known contribution to dramatic criticism is his analysis in his *Interpretation of Dreams* of the Oedipus complex at work in Sophocles' *Oedipus Rex* and Shakespeare's *Hamlet*. Freud's reading of Sophocles' play is pretty straightforward:

> If *Oedipus Rex* is capable of moving a modern reader or play-goer no less powerfully than it moved the contemporary Greeks, the only possible explanation is that the effect of the Greek tragedy does not depend upon the conflict between fate and human will, but upon the peculiar nature of the material by which this conflict is revealed.... [Oedipus's] fate moves us only because it might have been our own, because the oracle laid upon us before our birth the very curse which rested upon him. It may well be that we were all destined to direct our first sexual impulses toward our mothers, and our first impulses of hatred and violence toward our fathers.... As the poet brings the guilt of Oedipus to light by his investigation, he forces us to become aware of our own inner selves, in which the same impulses are still extant, even though they are suppressed.
>
> (Freud 1974: 828–9)

The play's power arises from our own primal impulses of love and hatred toward our parents. Similarly, about *Hamlet*, Freud writes:

> The play is based upon Hamlet's hesitation in accomplishing the task of revenge assigned to him; the play does not give the cause or the motive of this hesitation.... Here the explanation offers itself that it is the peculiar nature of the task. Hamlet is able to do anything but take vengeance upon the man who did away with his father and has taken his father's place with his mother – the man who shows him in realization the repressed desires of his own childhood. The loathing which should have driven him to revenge is thus replaced by self-reproach, by conscientious scruples, which tell him that he himself is no better than the murderer whom he is required to punish.
>
> (p. 830)

Of course, very few admit to, or are untroubled by, their own oedipal desires. Because they cause us guilt and trauma, we repress them. Even these great works of drama, which do so much toward revealing oedipal desires, work by various levels of repression. In Sophocles the psychological reality is hidden under a disingenuous story about fate and the gods; in Shakespeare we don't even get an actual acting out of the oedipal desires – Hamlet neither kills his father nor sleeps with his mother. Rather we see these desires 'only through the inhibitory effects which proceed from' them (p. 830): we see the way these desires keep him from taking revenge upon his uncle. Art, therefore, like the patient in psychoanalysis, demands a 'hyper-interpretation' (p. 831), which allows us to read what is really going on behind the repression and obfuscation.

Ultimately, Sophocles and Shakespeare could not show oedipal truths directly because these plays arise from their own psychological histories of desire and repression. Of *Hamlet*, Freud writes: 'the drama was composed immediately after the death of Shakespeare's father (1601) – that is to say, when he was still mourning the loss, and during a revival, as we may fairly assume, of his own childish feelings in respect of his father' (p. 831). For Freud, psychoanalytic study of the play and its characters leads to psychoanalytic study of the author.

From Freud's analysis, we can see that his psychoanalysis has dealt with art and literature, including drama, mainly in three ways. The first is to use the art to psychoanalyse the artist, as if the art were a symptomatic document like a dream or a slip of the tongue. Freud uses this approach in making associations between Shakespeare's life and the writing of *Hamlet*. The second approach psychoanalyses the characters in order to draw out compelling examples of psychic mechanisms and patterns at work – Oedipus and Hamlet become primary examples of the Oedipus complex. The third approach brings psychoanalysis to bear on a cultural formation or institution; for example, Freud suggests that Greek society and theatre could only deal with oedipal truths by hiding them behind misleading religious allegory, while by Shakespeare's time society and theatre couldn't even present oedipal actions directly, as the Greeks had done – as if the psychic history of western society is a history of increasing repression. In each of these modes of analysis, interpretation demands that we read past the manifest content of the author's life, the character's actions, the society's practices, to get at the hidden latent content, which tells the real story. In the analysis of Hamlet's character, for instance, we must see past the surface, manifest hesitation to see the unconscious, hidden, true reasons why Hamlet cannot kill his uncle.

Jacques Lacan

Freud has had many followers, but the one who has had the most impact on contemporary cultural theory is Jacques Lacan, a French psychoanalyst who wrote mainly in the second half of the twentieth century. Lacan's work is gathered in a number of English collections, including Écrits (1977b) and The Four Fundamental Concepts of Psycho-Analysis (1978).

Following semiotic and linguistic theory (discussed in Chapter 1), Lacan stresses the importance of language for the human psyche. The unconscious – the seat of our deepest drives and desires – is in Lacan's formulation structured as a language (Lacan 1970: 188). Freud sees dreams and the unconscious working through condensation (a simple object in a dream is loaded with multiple significance) and displacement (rather than expressing something directly, the dream refers to something associated with the thing to be expressed). Lacan sees that condensation and displacement, the mechanisms whereby associations work in the unconscious, are equivalent to metaphor and metonymy, concepts in the linguistic theory of Roman Jakobson that explain how associations are made in language. Our unconscious minds, that is to say, have the characteristics of a language – in fact, the human subject is nothing more than the chain of signifiers suggested by the unconscious to the conscious mind: the human psyche becomes for all intents and purposes a linguistic entity.

Because our subjectivity exists in language, Lacan distances our mental life from the 'real' – the actual world, the way things really are. The subject lives inescapably in a mental world, not a real one. We can live in the mental world in one of two registers: the imaginary or the symbolic. The imaginary is an inflexible and delusory state associated with infancy and later various arrested or psychotic conditions; those with an imaginary relation to reality have very rigid and tightly held views of themselves and their relations with others. The imaginary is associated with the 'mirror stage' in childhood development: the point at which a child is able to recognize an image (in a mirror for instance) as 'me'. Like the simple reflection in the mirror, the imaginary is not the whole person: it is simplistic and rejects troubling complexities. The symbolic entails a more mature engagement with reality and a dialogue open to change and development. The symbolic is associated with effective socialization, and a basic goal of psychotherapy is to bring the subject from an imaginary to a symbolic relation with the real. The symbolic, however, like the imaginary, is a mental, linguistic space. What escapes both these registers is the real, which exists independently of language and is therefore inaccessible to language and the linguistic subject (this bears much similarity to the relation between reality and language of Paul de Man outlined in the section on deconstruction). Also, as in Freud, the unconscious remains inaccessible to consciousness except indirectly through its effects. For Lacan, the unconscious is the discourse of the 'Other', that part of a subject which is part of ourselves we are not aware of and which renders every subject alien from itself. (The idea of the 'Other' is a very resonant idea in Lacan, and is also extremely important for feminism, post-colonialism, and gay and lesbian studies, which seek to identify with that which is other than white, male and heterosexual, a nexus taken as politically and ideologically dominant in the world.) Because we have no direct access to the real or to our own unconscious, the subject is bound to a certain '*méconnaissance*', a mistaking or misknowing. Even in the symbolic register, we are basically misreading the world. Truth, as for Derrida and de Man, is humanly impossible.

For Freud, human sexual anatomy plays a key role in our gendered identity. Lacan transforms the physical penis as Freud understands it into a linguistic entity: the phallus, which is not an actual penis, but a linguistic idea, a controlling signifier which holds in place the possible and acceptable symbolic exchanges between linguistic subjects. As for Freud, males have a different relation to subjectivity than women do, since there is a metaphorical resemblance between the penis and the phallus that causes males to be able to misrecognize themselves as aligned with the phallus as site of power and authority – men feel they have the 'law of the father' on their side, or between their legs. The change from penis to phallus makes a number of differences for the theory of gender in Lacan. Most importantly, differences of gender are no longer biological but linguistic and symbolic. Whether the move from biology to language makes any real difference is a contentious point, however, as can be seen in the two introductions to *Feminine Sexuality*, a collection of essays by Lacan and his '*école freudienne*' (1982). In her introduction, Juliet Mitchell sees the phallus as constituting a kind of fate: there is no subjectivity outside the relation to the phallus and therefore outside masculinity and femininity; for Mitchell there is no subjectivity or even civilization without the phallus and the law of the father. On the other hand, Jacqueline Rose, in her introduction, argues that the distinction between penis and phallus renders male identification with the phallus illusory, and this opens up a space of play and liberty (especially associated with the feminine as free of any such deluded identification) and the possibility of subjectivity and exchange beyond the phallus and the law of the father.

Lacan writes about the same classical and Shakespearean drama as Freud does, but rather than use the drama to psycho-analyse characters or authors, he is more prone to see in works of literature and drama manifestations of the nature of the unconscious and the psyche. In one of his most significant liter-ary studies, of Edgar Allen Poe's 'The Purloined Letter' (Lacan 1972), Lacan traces the way that the unconscious conceals and unconceals its declarations at once, the way it is able to hide in plain sight, as it were, like the Waldos in a *Where's Waldo?* book. When he reads *Hamlet* (Lacan 1977a), Lacan doesn't dwell on primal sexual desires, but on Hamlet's mourning, to show that the loss that he mourns is different from what he has actually lost – that mourning is a mental and imaginary loss independent of real loss. Hamlet's mourning is different from, bigger than, the loss of his father. In Sophocles' *Antigone* (see Kowsar 1992), in which Antigone is buried alive rather than submit to the king's command, Lacan sees a representation of the nature of desire, beyond the law, beyond good and evil, excessive and recalcitrant, which surrenders to no social force. Since psychoanalysis demands that drives be recognized before anything can be done with them, *Antigone* affirms the need to acknowledge the powerful and uncompromising nature of desire – even if society doesn't know how to deal with it.

Drama therapy, role-playing and Spalding Gray

Psychoanalytic theory deals with abstract ideas about the psyche and concentrates on the verbal symptoms whereby the truth about psychological characteristics is revealed. Psychoanalytic therapy, however, is only actualized in the analytic situation, with the patient, or analysand, enacting his or her condition in the presence of the analyst. This enactment involves the emotional investments of transference and countertransference, whereby both patient and doctor play out their habitual feelings by focusing them on each other and rehearse this enactment in therapeutic sessions at regular intervals. Only through these enactments will the patient come to anything more than a superficial understanding of the problems. Psychoanalysis so described is obviously a performative practice and has much in common with theatre and other kinds of performance. Literary psychoanalysis, under the influence of Lacan – who was notorious for shortening the psychoanalytic session – has made relatively little of the performative relations between psychoanalysis and theatre. The recent psychotherapeutic movement of 'dramatherapy', however, has made theatre central to its understanding of the human psyche. Here the concept of 'role', which 'applies to the full range of human experiences through body and sensorium, mind and emotion, intuition and spirit',

> provides coherence to the personality, and ... in many ways supersedes the primacy of the concept of self. And by extension, existence is not only played out as in a drama, but is dramatic in its own right.
>
> (Landy 1993: 7)

We are, in this approach, the roles we play out in order to reject some that are counterproductive and make other healthier ones our own.

In many ways, dramatherapy harks back to the classical and Renaissance idea of theatrum mundi, the theatre of the world, in which the world is thought of as a stage and, in Shakespeare's words, 'all the men and women merely players'. This is a very complex idea which draws often contradictory and unsettling connections between theatre and human identity. Is there a real self behind the role? Is acting therefore a form of deception? Or is role-playing our natural and inescapable means of being in the world and expressing ourselves?

A psychoanalytic study would have to work on a number of the levels already discussed in order to understand a phenomenon such as the American actor Spalding Gray's theatrical monologues. Gray has performed a number of autobiographical monologues in which he sits at a table with notes and a glass of water and recounts incidents from his life, often linked to and by his forays into the film world (as in *Swimming to Cambodia* [1988], which deals with Gray's experiences while at work on Roland Joffe's film *The Killing Fields*). Although partly dealing with Hollywood, Gray's *Monster in a Box* (1992b) is a work in which he discusses the problems – mainly psychological – he had completing his novel *Impossible Vacation* (1992a). *Impossible Vacation* is dedicated to Gray's mother, 'the Creator and Destroyer', and the novel focuses on the thinly veiled fictional protagonist's inability to leave his mother and take a vacation while she is alive and even more so after her suicide. *Monster in a Box* makes explicit the identification of Gray with his protagonist and deals with Gray's inability to write this novel about events before and after his mother's death.

Both *Impossible Vacation* and *Monster in a Box* deal with obviously psychoanalytic material: love for and the attempt to escape from the mother, sexuality, guilt, the inability to escape the traumas of the past, and the working through and overcoming of psychological difficulties. If anything, these matters are eminently transparent: Gray wears his psychoses on his sleeve. The preface to *Monster in a Box* tells how, after a performance of the play, Gray was asked to be the national spokesman for the National Foundation for Mental Health, because he was 'so articulate about [his] mental illness'.

At one point in his story, Gray finds himself undergoing traditional Freudian analysis:

Now we're working very fast and very hard, and I'm telling him the story of my book. Certainly I know what the cure in psychoanalysis is supposed to be, so I'm looking both ways. I don't want it to take me by surprise because I'm not really sure I want the cure. I know the cure is supposed to be the transformation of hysterical misery into common unhappiness. And God knows I have a lot of hysterical misery, but I'm not sure I want to let it go.

(Gray 1992b: 45–6)

If analysis is the talking cure, the therapeutic performance which takes one past or through one's pyschic arrest, what purpose do performance and repetition in theatre serve? *Impossible Vacation* features an epigraph from William Kennedy's *Ironweed*: 'You will not know … what these acts are until you have performed them all…. Then, when these final acts are complete, you will stop trying to die because of me.' The novel presents a series of acts through which the protagonist cures himself of his inability to get past his attachment to his mother. In *Monster in a Box*, the story of writing the novel serves a similar therapeutic function. But what of the performance of *Monster in a Box* itself? Gray creates his theatre pieces by letting them evolve through a series of outlined but unscripted performances. When the process is complete, the text is written down and the performances end. Is this too a therapeutic process? What cure does it entail? Didn't the writing of the novel effect the necessary psychic healing? If so, what does the play do? And what of Gray's desire to hold on to his hysterical misery? Does performance repeat and preserve that misery as much or more than it dissipates it? Perhaps *Monster in a Box* serves no therapeutic role at all, and the performance process is about getting the art right, not the person. If, as Freud says, the artist sublimates his psychological problems in order to make art, is that sublimation therapeutic for the artist or does the artist need to hang on to these problems in order to have something to sublimate? In this regard, there is something strangely distant and dispassionate about Gray's performance, as if the stories he tells don't matter to him any more – almost as if they had happened to another person. Perhaps the movement from life to the novel to the play to final performance is all a process of distancing oneself from the lingering past.

In regard to role-playing, a seemingly simple performance such as *Monster in a Box* leaves us with many unanswered or unanswerable questions. For instance, who is Spalding Gray? The playwright is Spalding Gray, the character is Spalding Gray, the actor is Spalding Gray. Are these three one and the same? Is the actor who speaks the lines at one with the voice of the author? Much current theory would tell us that the author is, in effect, dead and absent before the actor starts to speak: the author's words no longer belong to him or her but to whomever takes them up. When the actor speaks, is he the Spalding Gray he claims to be? If we answer yes, are we saying that there is nothing fictional about the character Spalding Gray? Is playing oneself on stage the same as playing oneself offstage? Isn't it in the nature of dramatic characters to be unreal? Gray (which Gray, though?) claims that he invents nothing: 'I don't know how to make anything up.... I don't know how to tell the lie that tells the truth – I can only tell what happened to me' (Gray 1992b: 16). Psychoanalysis is built on suspicion: we always distort what we say about ourselves. Therefore, both theatre and psychoanalysis tell us that Spalding Gray cannot simply be who he says he is. And yet, can we say that Spalding Gray the character simply is not Spalding Gray the actor or playwright? Isn't our reception of Gray's work premised on a belief that all the Spalding Grays are in some sense the same? What would happen if an actor other than Spalding Gray were to play Spalding Gray? Would *Monster in a Box* then be the same kind of performance? *this demonstrates the individuality of each performance event or experience*

Gray relates taking on the role of the Stage Manager in Thornton Wilder's *Our Town*: 'I could speak from my heart at last, provided I could memorize the lines – and I could use my New England accent' (Gray 1992b: 64). Is playing the Stage Manager *the chageability of theatre.*

completely different from playing oneself? Here Gray can identify strongly with a role other than Spalding Gray, so that the role of the Stage Manager isn't simply other than Spalding Gray. The role an actor takes on cannot be simply other any more than one can simply be oneself. Acting has a topology just as the psyche does: we can divide Spalding Gray into id, ego and superego, into his unconscious and his consciousness, or, in another context, we can divide Spalding Gray into playwright, character and actor. These are not the same topologies; theatre is not a straightforward reflection of the psychoanalytic self. Both theatre and psychoanalysis, however, make clear that human beings are neither simple nor transparent.

Radical psychoanalysis and *Dionysus in 69*

The work of the late French theorists Gilles Deleuze and Félix Guattari covers a wide range of concerns and is classifiable in a number of ways. The two volumes of their *Capitalism and Schizophrenia*, *Anti-Oedipus* and *A Thousand Plateaus*, are concerned with the rethinking and liberation of the human entity. Deleuze and Guattari see humans as presently oppressed and stultified in the relations between oedipal psychic structures, capitalism and the monolithic state: the state makes us into subjects in the passive sense discussed at the beginning of this chapter; capitalism turns us into commodities for sale; oedipalized society, with the help of psychoanalysis trying to make us well adjusted, turns us into dutiful sons and daughters. These forces all work together to limit our freedom. Deleuze and Guattari point toward a future in which de-oedipalized, deterritorialized and deregulated humans are free to become something other, free to travel a thousand plateaus. This other is formulated in different ways: becoming-woman, becoming-animal, becoming-machine – all are attempts to escape the constraints that limit us in fixed identities. These becomings entail first of all a different relation to the body:

Deleuze and Guattari posit a human entity without a face – to the degree that our notion of face locks us in a certain psychological and physical sense of individuality; they also take up Artaud's notion of a 'body without organs', a body not subjected to organization and hierarchy, not processed and trained by society. New human entities also take up different relations to language and thought – animals, for instance, are guided by drives and desires rather than laws and ideas.

Deleuze and Guattari also promote a different possible relation to the real. They call for an understanding based on mapping, 'entirely oriented toward an experimentation with the real', rather than tracing, which reduces multiplicities to known patterns (1987: 12–13). Tracing seems much like Lacan's imaginary, but mapping seems to go beyond what Lacan would call the symbolic to get at reality directly. Deleuze and Guattari believe in the possibility of aligning ourselves and our politics with the real: a world founded on the eternal recurrence of difference on a thousand plateaus leads, if not directly then insistently nonetheless, to a politics of freedom and unfettered becoming.

Deleuze, in 'One Less Manifesto', on the theatre of the Italian playwright, director, and actor Carmelo Bene (discussed in the section on semiotics), outlines some of the institutions and connections whereby theatre is tied to oedipalized society: language in the theatre is the oedipalized language of the master (king, father or patriarch); the author is a figure of authority, overseeing the proceedings as a kind of superego; the actor, gendered and fixed in a societal role, takes up the role of a character similarly conceived of as a fixed psychological individual; within the play, lead characters duplicate societal hierarchy in their mastery over lesser characters (Bene and Deleuze 1979). Deleuze is interested in Bene because Bene is concerned with breaking down these complicities, in creating an anti-oedipal theatre. Bene attempts this through disruptions of standard theatrical elements:

language becomes noise, character becomes chaos, scenography is free of the author's control.

The American Herbert Blau speaks of 'our oedipal drama' (Blau 1983: 441), by which he means that theatre, like ourselves, is caught in the structures of identity, family, desire, misrecognition, repression and so forth delineated by Freud and psychoanalytic theory. While Blau and Deleuze would agree that theatre is oedipal, they would disagree profoundly on the possibility of escaping this condition and on the virtue in doing so. For Blau, to think you can escape oedipal structures of desire and identity is an illusion, and cavalier attempts to do so can be intellectually, personally and politically dangerous.

A perspective in many ways akin to Blau's can be found in the work of the East European theorist Slavoj Žižek. Žižek has written a number of books elucidating the theories of Lacan with reference to examples from popular culture, most prominently from the films of Alfred Hitchcock. There are relatively few references to theatre in Žižek's work, and most of those are to the standard psychoanalytic pantheon (Sophocles' Oedipus plays, *Antigone* and Shakespeare's *Hamlet*) or to Bertolt Brecht. Also, the title of his *Looking Awry* is taken from a scene in Shakespeare's *Richard II*. Žižek's readings are rarely detailed and, strangely for a Lacanian, take more interest in character, theme and ideas than they do in language.

In his interest in totalitarianism and democracy, Žižek – like Deleuze and Guattari – moves psychoanalytic study beyond a focus on the individual to an interest in the largest social and political formations. But Žižek is very sceptical of liberation such as Deleuze and Guattari propose. As a thinker, Žižek has much in common with Jacques Derrida – he writes that deconstruction is 'in a radical sense *commonsensical*' (Žižek 1992: 25n18). By this he means that deconstruction recognizes the limits imposed on human beings by the nature of the real itself, limits which define the human condition as such. This condition entails an irreconcilable contradiction between our need for order and meaning in the world and our traumatic encounter with 'the Real in its utter, meaningless idiocy' (Žižek 1989: 230). There is an inescapable pathology about our relation of misrecognition with reality; at the very bottom the human is a 'symptom' which not even deconstruction or psychoanalysis can get us past. In our rage for order over chaos we always fantasize, taking pleasure in constructing ideological systems which, paradoxically, the more harmonious they are, the more they risk totalitarianism, mass murder and holocaust: our rage for order inevitably has a totalitarian side, the 'Stalinism of language' (p. 212). To think, as do Deleuze and Guattari, that the Anti-Oedipus can escape this fate is naive and probably dangerous. The better task is to acknowledge, rather than attempt to escape, the antagonism at the root of human life and 'to learn to recognize it in its terrifying dimension and then, on the basis of this fundamental recognition, to try to articulate a modus vivendi with it' (p. 5). Like Blau, Žižek holds on to a faith in democracy, despite the contradictions and impossibility of democracy, tied to carefulness in thinking within its illusions and paradoxes:

> The democratic attitude is always based upon a certain fetishistic split: I know very well (that the democratic form is just a form spoiled by stains of 'pathological' imbalance), but just the same (I act as if democracy were possible). Far from indicating its fatal flaw, this split is the very source of the strength of democracy: democracy is able to take cognizance of the fact that its limit lies in itself, in its internal 'antagonism'.
>
> (Žižek 1991: 68).

Of all Brecht's theatre, Žižek is most drawn to the learning plays, with their difficult integrity in facing up to the inescapable paradoxes of political action (Žižek 1992: 174–9). The paradoxes will not disappear even if we ignore them; the dangers are only augmented by our ignorance and precipitousness.

Some of these oedipal and anti-oedipal tensions can be seen in the Performance Group's *Dionysus in 69* (1970), a retelling of Euripides' *The Bacchae*, in which Pentheus is torn to pieces by his mother, Agave, induced to frenzy by Dionysus, the god of excess and disorder. The play deals with forces which break oedipal bonds of selfhood, family, sanity, even the unity of the human body. *Dionysus in 69* was produced in 1968 and 1969, part of a countercultural movement interested in the waylaying of repression through individual and group liberation, nudity, openness, and political and sexual experimentation. Did it succeed?

The process of mounting and performing the play served as a kind of therapy for members of the Performance Group – in fact, they all took part in group therapy sessions throughout the run of the play. The roles in Euripides' play are infused with the individual reality of the actors playing the parts: Dionysus becomes, for instance, 'Joan as Dionysus', or 'Finley as Dionysus' (Performance Group 1970; there are no page numbers in the text). At moments the actors feel at one with their roles, even god-like when playing Dionysus: the actor Joan MacIntosh says of a scene early in the play:

> In this scene I am totally Joan MacIntosh. I have not begun to become the god. The play is a series of revealments in which I find out that I am the god. By the time of the curse [a scene at the end of the play] I am totally transformed.

Another actor finds that he is 'surpassing myself, pursuing an action to its very end, so that my life mask cracks and falls away and I am revealed in my vulnerability'. Another writes:

> I come to the temple to worship. I come to the temple to become more whole. I am acting out my disease, the disease that plagues my inner being, that stops up the flow, the flow that gives to all those who see. Dionysus is not a play for me. I do not act in Dionysus. Dionysus is my ritual.

And 'I am not interested in acting. I am involved in the life process of becoming whole.' The 'becoming whole' goes with a breaking down of limitations, many of them performative and theatrical. The performance space itself is full of irregularities and 'like the performance itself, is designed toward gathering intensities, explosive release'. Nudity (clothes are a 'social mask') and sensual caressing, physical interaction between actors and audience lead to 'an exquisitely polymorphous experience' in which 'resistances fall away'.

Pentheus represents the resistance to this Dionysian ecstasy. He is 'the dictator-king whose word is law', the law against the organism, who stands in the way of liberation and wholeness. By the end of the play he has been seduced by Dionysus and torn to pieces by his mother and Dionysus's other female worshippers. These women get to know what they could be if liberated from being 'the property of men'.

The 'revolution in the heart' that the characters and actors undergo is also a political revolution in which 'the concept of political control is called into question' – Pentheus is also the *paradox* man of the state. So the wholeness and freedom the play points to are personal, gendered and political. The problem is, however, that without the figure of the law this freedom knows no bounds. Dionysus puts an expanding structure in place of a rigid one, 'But he doesn't say where his stops. Just the promise of freedom.' Dionysus asks only 'that you indulge your fantasies of violence and sensuality'. As one of his eager acolytes says, 'If I have to murder every person in this goddam room, nobody is going to keep me from being free.' Ultimately Dionysus becomes, in a way that would not surprise Blau or Žižek, 'tyrant and fascist' with 'absolute ownership of the collective will of the people'. He sends out an army, 'thousands of millions of troops', who will go 'through this country and make it pure again', ending alienation by slaughtering everyone who does not believe.

The sexual reality that the performances engendered was not

always as liberating as planned – would-be Lotharios in the audience took the nudity and caressing as an occasion to touch the actresses in ways the actresses were not comfortable with, and the sensuality eventually had to be curtailed. At the end of *The Bacchae* and *Dionysus in 69*, Agave, Pentheus's mother and murderer, comes to her senses and realizes the horror of what she has done, and 'all the victory she really carries home is her own grief'.

Psychoanalysis and feminism

The relationship between psychoanalysis and feminist thinkers has been particularly ambivalent. Elizabeth Wright notes that psychoanalysis:

> has been crucial for feminists and indeed for all those who want to situate themselves outside a rigid definition of sexual difference.... Nevertheless, feminists have not been slow to undertake systemic critiques of Freud's repeated efforts to define femininity.
>
> (Wright 1998: 174)

Basically, a number of feminist thinkers have taken principles from psychoanalytic thought and practice and used them to critique Freud and Lacan inasmuch as traditional psychoanalysis is seen to support the oppression of women. The argument is that what is valuable and useful in psychoanalysis gives the lie to the sexist assumptions that Freud and Lacan unfortunately, mistakenly and repeatedly fall back on.

The contemporary Bulgarian-French theorist Julia Kristeva is an important figure in feminist theory, and her *Revolution in Poetic Language* can be taken as an important and systematic contribution to psychoanalytic thought. According to Kristeva, human beings begin in infancy in the state she calls the 'semiotic'. By this she means something quite different from what Saussure means. The semiotic is a pre-linguistic order associated with the mother's body, with a space of heterogeneous drives and desires, with the feminine. In coming to language, the subject enters the 'symbolic' order, associated not only with language but also with reason, law, the father and the masculine. In entering the symbolic order, the human becomes the 'thetic' subject, and turns away from the body, the mother and the rhythms of desire; but this loss is accompanied by access to the power of language, reason, society and the law. The story does not stop here, however: the semiotic, which never goes away, returns to disrupt the imaginary unity and coherence of the thetic subject. Through irruptions of desire, rhythms, language not bound by linearity, syntax and reason (like the libidinal cries and babbling of a baby), the semiotic negates and renews the thetic subject, which becomes a 'subject in process' or perpetually on trial. Without this return of the semiotic we would be unfeeling and rigid slaves of reason and order. The subject in process is a subject always renewed in the never-ending struggle of semiotic and symbolic, feminine and masculine forces.

As noted earlier, feminist thinkers differ as to the possibility of escaping patriarchal psychic structures. The desire to escape the patriarch within has led to various attempts to undo the oedipal limitations of theatre and psychoanalysis. For instance, the French feminist playwright and theorist Hélène Cixous has written a number of plays with connections to psychoanalytic theory but which also entail a critique of the sexism that haunts traditional psychoanalysis; two of the most prominent are *Portrait of Dora* and *The Name of Oedipus*. *Portrait of Dora* is an adaptation of Freud's fragment of a case history of a young woman Freud calls Dora. Freud's *Dora* is infamous, especially in feminist circles, for its intertwining of insight and blindness. In it Freud carefully unravels the biases and verbal strategies of his patient, while ignoring the biases and strategies that so obviously structure his own discourse: Freud, along with Dora's family and society, attempts to impose a patriarchal agenda of desire and identity on Dora, which she refuses to accept as her own. In the end she breaks off her appointments with Freud, leaving the analysis and Freud's case history incomplete and frustrated.

Cixous's *Dora* began as a radio play, a strictly verbal exercise like Freud's case history or the 'talking cure' of psychoanalysis. Even so, the dramatization of the work in the voices of the characters decentres Freud's controlling narration and allows Cixous to retell Dora's tale free of Freud's dominance. In this new telling, as in most feminist readings of Dora's story, Dora is both a victim of a patriarchal system which imposes an inappropriate model onto Dora's psyche and a budding heroine who refuses to go along with her own indoctrination. With the help of director Simone Benmussa and film-maker Marguerite Duras, Cixous turned her radio play into a multimedia theatre piece, thus stressing by theatrical means the many levels of reality and understanding that go into the making of any life and subjectivity.

After *Portrait of Dora*, Cixous wrote an opera text called *The Name of Oedipus*, adapting the Sophoclean play so central in psychoanalytic theory. The French title of the play, *Le Nom d'Oedipe*, plays upon the French homonym *nom/non* (name and no), just as Lacan does in the '*nom du père*', the name of the father – patriarchal authority through language – which is also the 'no' of the father, the prohibition and denial that make us subjects within the patriarchal order. Like Kristeva, Cixous takes a special interest in the mother and the realm of the mother, where affirmation, excess and freedom from naming and constricted identity are possible. The play is subtitled *Song of the Forbidden Body*, aligning Jocasta, the mother, with a new and forbidden embodied subjectivity, a new way of being, similar to the semiotic in Kristeva and the Anti-Oedipus in Deleuze and Guattari. Each character in the play is doubled, played by both an actor and a singer, thus marking the subject, the named, the unified, as in reality a place of multiple voices and identities. The play begins with an 'incantatory' overlap of voices and avoids throughout a linear narrative development, rejecting the inevitability of tragedy and fixed oedipalized identity for a fluid and open exploration of psychic multiplicity. In these two plays, therefore, Cixous uses Freud's own material to stage a revolt against and escape from the patriarchal values in Freud's work that imprison women in an oppressive psychological role.

QUESTIONS ONE MIGHT ASK OF A PLAY OR PERFORMANCE

The Canadian theatre director Steven Schipper always discusses the characters of a play with a psychoanalyst before he begins to direct it. Would psychoanalytic information help a director or actor with the play or performance you are studying?

Can you discern in the play or performance a latent content, a psychological subtext, behind the manifest content, the surface meaning? What is the relationship between the manifest and latent meanings?

What is the psychological relation between the actor and the role in the play or performance? Is taking on a role a therapeutic activity? Does the actor heal or grow or learn about him or herself in playing a part?

Does the play or performance reinforce psychological stereotypes and restrictions or does it (try to) break free of them? Are these restrictions personal, societal or gendered? Does breaking free produce elation or terror?

---

2 FEMINIST AND GENDER THEORY

Feminist theory

No theoretical approaches have had as much impact in the last thirty years or so as those concerned with gender and sexuality.

Not surprisingly, therefore, Americans Sue-Ellen Case, Jill Dolan and Gayle Austin have each written a book which introduces feminist theories to the study of theatre and drama (Case 1988; Dolan 1988; Austin 1990). In addition, Elaine Aston has introduced feminism and theatre from a distinctly British perspective (Aston 1995). In these books, feminist theory has been applied to theatre studies more systematically and extensively than has any other area of recent theory. In light of this, the discussion of feminist theory here draws heavily on these works.

Like much materialist theory and unlike, for instance, much phenomenology and post-structuralism, feminist theory is directly and predominantly political. Its purpose is to struggle against the oppression of women as women. This oppression, which is seen to be historically extremely common and widespread, is the result of patriarchy, the supremacy of masculine power and authority most firmly entrenched in the figure of the father (thus the strong relations between feminism and psychoanalytic work). Feminism, therefore, works toward the unravelling and overthrow of patriarchy.

Following the work of the American academic Judith Fetterley, feminism posits the feminist as a 'resisting reader' in the face of patriarchal cultural domination. There is a recognition that traditionally, when women have been allowed to partake of the dominant culture, they have been indoctrinated in masculine values and ways of seeing (identifying with male heroes while viewing female characters at a distance, for example), what Fetterley calls the 'immasculation' of the woman reader (Austin 1990: 27). Feminism attempts to create a woman reader who sees as a woman and thereby brings a different and other perspective to bear on culture.

One project of feminist theory, then, is to look critically at traditional patriarchal culture. Feminist theory searches out the patriarchal values and ideologies that inform, sometimes in silence, sometimes in an overtly cocksure fashion, the prominent work of the masculine canon – the body of works that patriarchal culture has made dominant. This entails a critique of the patriarchal canon and the hegemony of male artists. Sue-Ellen Case, for instance, presents a critical reading of Aeschylus's *Oresteia*, one of the earliest masterpieces of the western dramatic tradition, in the opening chapter of her *Feminism and Theatre* (1988). The *Oresteia* relates the history of Agamemnon and his family: Agamemnon sacrifices his daughter Iphigenia to the gods at the start of the Trojan war; on his return after the war, he is murdered in revenge by his wife Clytemnestra; Clytemnestra is murdered in turn by her son Orestes. The last play of the trilogy, *The Eumenides*, finds Orestes in the law court of Athena in Athens, where it is decided that murdering his mother was justified because of his need to revenge the murder of his father. Case notes that *The Eumenides* is often taken as a play which celebrates the beginning of democracy, the rule of law and the beginnings of western civilization (p. 14). She asserts, however, that 'The feminist reader of *The Oresteia* discovers that she must read against the text' (p. 15), and so 'Many feminist critics and historians have analysed *The Oresteia* as a text central to the formalisation of misogyny' (p. 12), and the decision of the court of Athena, who is 'a male-identified woman in alliance with the male network of power' (p. 15) – immasculated in Fetterley's terms – 'is damning evidence for the public rationalisation of misogyny, for it rests upon establishing the parental line as male' (p. 14). Fathers (men) count; mothers (women) don't.

If most prominent cultural work has been given over to men, it follows that most prominent cultural work is invested in a masculine perspective. Without a large number of prominent women artists or predominantly female audiences, patriarchal culture is seen as the exchange of cultural material – often involving representations of women – within an exclusively male social economy. This recognition often entails a devaluation or rejection of works with high canonical standing – Shakespeare's, for instance – although feminist work also yields complex and subtle revaluations of male texts. The Canadian playwright and novelist Ann-Marie MacDonald's play *Goodnight Desdemona (Good Morning Juliet)* (1990), for instance, is a sophisticated reworking of Shakespeare through the eyes of a main character who slowly abandons her immasculation for a feminist perspective, which both changes Shakespeare's work and maintains a dialogue with it. In this regard, the following analysis by the black American feminist bell hooks of her relation with the Brazilian post-colonialist theorist of pedagogy and activist Paulo Freire is exemplary in its carefulness, consideration and balance:

> There has never been a moment when reading Freire that I have not remained aware of not only the sexism of the language but the way he (like other progressive Third World political leaders, intellectuals, critical thinkers ...) constructs a phallocentric paradigm of liberation – wherein freedom and the expression of patriarchal manhood are always linked as though they are one and the same. For me this is always a source of anguish for it represents a blind spot in the vision of men who have profound insight. And yet, I never wish to see a critique of this blind spot overshadow anyone's (and feminists' in particular) capacity to learn from these insights. This is why it is difficult for me to speak about sexism in Freire's work; it is difficult to find a language that offers a way to frame critique and yet maintain the recognition of all that is valued and respected in the work. It seems to me that the binary opposition that is so much embedded into Western thought and language makes it nearly impossible to project a complex response. Freire's sexism is indicated by the language in his early works notwithstanding that there is so much that remains liberatory. There is no need to apologize for the sexism. Freire's own model of criti-

cal pedagogy invites a critical interrogation of this flaw in his work. But critical interrogation is not the same as dismissal.

(hooks 1993: 148)

Feminist theory is profoundly concerned with the cultural representation of women, sometimes as a strictly masculinist fantasy with no relation to real women, sometimes as the appropriation of women and women's bodies to masculine perspectives. Patriarchal cultural visions often reduce women to stereotypes (virgin, whore, madonna, bitch) and fetishized body parts (breasts, vagina, face). The British film theorist Laura Mulvey discusses, in relation to classic Hollywood film, the system of representation whereby the male 'gaze', of the hero, the camera and the audience, is imposed as the only way of seeing women (Mulvey 1975: 6–18). The male gaze oppresses, silences and distorts female realities, so that, for instance, in classic detective films the women are usually mysterious, unreliable and evil, and in slasher movies they are nubile and often being stabbed to death in showers – although it cannot be true that men are always and necessarily less capable than women of representing women's reality. One task of feminism is to overturn these traditional systems of representation.

The body is one site of oppression for women; subjectivity is another. Drawing, often critically, upon psychoanalytic theory, feminism attempts to understand the ideologies which have limited women's ways of becoming subjects or agents, and to open up new patterns in which women are free to escape the confines of the subjectivity patriarchy sets up for them (related work in theatre is discussed through the example of Hélène Cixous in the first part of this chapter). Representation and subjectivity are made to reveal themselves as gendered fictions and opportunities rather than natural or inevitable realities.

Virginia Woolf, in *A Room of One's Own*, points out the difficulties and patterns of exclusion which have traditionally kept women from taking prominent positions in recognized cultural production – limitations on money, time and space, for instance. Of particular interest to feminist scholars of theatre is Woolf's history of a hypothetical sister of Shakespeare, Judith, with equal talent and equal interest in theatre: given the material barriers which excluded early modern women from exercising their talents in a theatrical career, Judith's story is one of frustration, seduction, abandonment and suicide (Woolf 1977: 46–7). The story of Shakespeare's sister goes with a general awareness of the under-representation of women artists in a male culture which takes itself as universal.

Much more than a critique of masculine culture, feminism is interested in the fostering of women's cultures. In relation to the past, this entails the rediscovery and recuperation of forgotten and overlooked work by women, not only in dominant cultural modes but also in less regarded cultural forms that were traditionally the purview of women excluded from areas of male activity. In theatre studies, feminist history uncovers marginal genres, such as domestic melodrama, which focuses on the tribulations of women in the household (see, for example, the discussion of the nineteenth-century Canadian playwright Sarah-Anne Curzon in Jones 1989), and various quasi-theatrical activities. Part of the task of recouping women's creative past can be seen in a collection such as S.P. Cerasano and Marion Wynne-Davies's *Renaissance Drama by Women* (1996), which collects dramatic works by women from England in the sixteenth and seventeenth centuries, including Elizabeth Cary's *The Tragedy of Mariam* and Mary Wroth's *Love's Victory*, 'the first original tragedy ... and the first original comedy ... to be written by Englishwomen' (p. 4). Cary's play, discussed in the section on post-structuralism, is a sophisticated and compelling work, which offers, 'almost uniquely, a female perspective upon the role of authority within the state and marriage' (p. 45) – although it does so through a complex and contradictory set of voices. Cerasano and Wynne-

Davies note that none of these plays was ever put on in a public theatre; they are all instances of closet drama, written for the page or the private home, the only kind of dramatic production open to women in the period. These playwrights 'chose a literary form which simultaneously liberated and policed their voices; they balanced their works precariously between their private and public roles, and between silence and self-expression' (p. 3).

Feminist theatre history is also interested in those relatively rare women who have managed to succeed in predominantly male artistic spheres. Aphra Behn, for example, becomes both a uniquely and insightfully feminine voice in the masculine world of Restoration theatre and a partly compromised and immasculated player in that world. Anne Russell, in the introduction to her edition of Behn's *The Rover* writes of 'tensions and contradictions' in the play between, for instance, protofeminism and the restoration of patriarchal authority (Behn 1994: 31). Of course, any production of the play is likely to stress one side over the other, as shown in two recent versions of *The Rover*, which deals with the tensions in the courtship of the licentiously unscrupulous Willmore and the virtuous and headstrong Hellena. According to Susan Carlson, John Barton's Royal Shakespeare Company production in 1986 reduced the individuality of the female characters and rendered them in part as sexual objects (Carlson 1995: 522); JoAnne Akalaitis's 1994 production, however, brought out the liberatory and tolerant aspects of the play:

> Both in its rearrangements of text and its enhancement of the visual, Akalaitis' production clearly demonstrates that Behn's play is an exercise in possibility, not a meting of judgment. Behn does not condemn Angellica Bianca's free sexuality, Willmore's rapacious desires, Hellena's naivete, or Blunt's revenge, but she makes all of them possible.

(p. 539)

For feminism, more important than recouping work of the past is the fostering of new work by women, feminist work which would represent women otherwise than patriarchy has heretofore allowed. Here feminist theatre studies take a predominant interest in the work of contemporary women.

The point is often made that, just as there is no universal woman but only women, there is not one feminism but feminisms (Reinelt and Roach 1992: 226). Although this is true of other theoretical movements as well, feminist theories often stress that feminism proceeds in a number of different directions, some of which are at odds with others. Feminism divides into different schools as to what a feminist culture related to women's reality would be like. Radical or cultural feminism assumes a more or less essential or universal feminine mode of being, arising from the female body and its rhythms, the feminine relation to the maternal, and a specifically feminine spiritual, emotional and intellectual make-up. This feminine difference is to be valued, often at the expense of most things masculine. In this light, Hélène Cixous posits an '*écriture feminine*', or feminine writing, a mode of expression faithful to the rhythms and intuitiveness natural to women – although perhaps open to men (Cixous 1986).

Materialist feminism sees the feminine as not natural but constructed in a network with other forces, such as class and race. Women do not constitute one homogeneous group, but are often at odds with each other: the interests of a poor, black woman and those of a rich, white woman are not likely to coincide completely. Materialist feminism refuses to posit a feminine essence of which all women must partake and sees in this idea something coercive and restrictive.

The situation is complicated further by the feminist theory of women of colour, which sees white women as a hegemonic group who have designated themselves to speak for all women. Much feminism, but especially the work of women of colour, is concerned with the position from which anyone speaks and questions those who speak on behalf of others. Here is Sue-Ellen Case introducing her discussion of women of colour:

> Because this description of the position and project of women of colour has been written by a white author, the discourse is necessarily distanced from the actual experiences which shape this position. The distance is not an objective distance, but one which reflects a perspective of racial and class privilege. The white author cannot write from the experience of racial oppression, or from the perspective of the ethnic community, and must thus omit a sense of the internal composition of such a community or of its interface with the dominant white culture. Moreover, within the study of feminism and theatre, this distance creates crucial problems in research and criticism.
>
> (Case 1988: 95)

Women of colour have a different relation than white women do to the white (male) canon, to men of colour and to the hegemonic white discourse. Even more than white women, women of colour have had their perspectives and voices erased from the dominant culture, and therefore have a different struggle in asserting their perspectives and voices (see hooks 1992; Wallace 1992). Black feminism has also argued that theory itself is part of an exclusionary, white discourse that does not relate to the experiences of black women (Christian 1988).

Lesbian feminism adds another element to these negotiations and brings new perspectives to gender identity, heterosexuality, the male gaze, the representation of women and the exchange of women in a patriarchal economy. At its most optimistic, lesbian theory claims that lesbian relations escape patriarchal oppression, representation and the male gaze. (Of course, not all lesbians will be positioned similarly: a poor, Asian lesbian will have different investments than a rich, white lesbian.)

The lesbian film theorist Teresa de Lauretis discusses the problems faced by lesbian work and thought, which seek to assert lesbian sexual difference within the hegemonic context of masculine 'hommosexuality', normative male heterosexuality, whose predominating characteristic is its indifference to (as both an inability to see and a disregard for) whatever lies outside its norms. She writes:

> lesbian writers and artists have sought variously to escape gender, to deny it, to transcend it, or perform it in excess, and to inscribe the erotic in cryptic, allegorical, realistic, camp, or other modes of representation, pursuing diverse strategies.
>
> (de Lauretis 1983: 21)

Stressing the way that heterosexism entraps and assimilates lesbian representation (for reasons of moral condemnation or titillation or both), Jill Dolan has recently stressed not only the need to break representational conventions of the male gaze, but the importance of the explicit presentation of lesbian sexuality as a 'truly radical' (Dolan 1992: 270) and 'sufficiently blatant' (p. 273n17) way of transgressing and subverting the status quo:

> Because gay male or lesbian sexuality is completely out of place – unimaged, unimagined, invisible – in traditional aesthetic contexts, the most transgressive act at this historical moment would be representing it to excess, in dominant and marginalized reception communities. The explicitness of pornography seems the most constructive choice for practicing cultural disruptions.
>
> (p. 272)

In this essay, Dolan is explicitly and forcefully confronting what she calls 'hegemonic antiporn feminism' (p. 270), which sees pornography as both painful to many women and a real threat to all – two claims Dolan treats with dismissive unkindness. She is similarly dismissive of representations of normalized lesbian 'lifestyles' (bourgeois) and relationships (monogamous) and soft-focused lesbian 'eroticism'.

Here we see a difference in general between hard-line and more moderate feminisms, lesbian and otherwise. Also in the hard-line camp is Lizbeth Goodman, who writes, 'Indeed, most schools of feminism are opposed in theory, and most feminist theatre, in practice, to the concept of 'mainstreaming'. In any case, canonization and mainstream production of feminist theatre are both uncommon' (Goodman 1998: 196). Such a view would not see much good in a play such as Eve Ensler's *The Vagina Monologues*, which has received widespread mainstream production with numerous female celebrities taking on the parts. Certainly this is a work which has brought feminist theatre of some integrity into the lives of a great many women and men.

Caryl Churchill and Ntozake Shange

Goodman posits an exception to her assertion that feminist theatre is not mainstream in the plays of the English playwright Caryl Churchill, which have made their way onto the canon of contemporary drama. One of Churchill's most renowned plays is *Cloud Nine* (1985). *Cloud Nine*, which developed out of a theatrical workshop on sexual politics, is a broadly based attack on a number of interrelated hegemonic forces of oppression: sexism, heterosexism, racism, colonialism, classism. The first act takes place in Victorian Africa and is centred around Clive, the father of the family and colonial overlord, who imposes his ideals on those (women, blacks, homosexuals) around him. 'I live for Clive' (p. 251), declares Betty, Clive's wife, and later, 'Clive is my society' (p. 258). Betty is both oppressed and incapable of imagining herself otherwise. Edward, Clive's homosexual son, Joshua, his black servant, and Harry, his homosexual friend, struggle to varying degrees with similar ideological constraints. At the end of act one, Joshua, spurned by Clive, in an act of disillusion and disappointment, shoots his master.

Cloud Nine does much of its feminist work in a specifically theatrical way, in the interplay between characters and actors. The most striking aspect in the mise-en-scène of act one is the relation between actors and characters. Betty, for instance, is played by a man; Joshua is played by a white, Edward by a woman, and Victoria, Clive's daughter, by a dummy. As Betty says, 'I am a man's creation as you see, / And what men want is what I want to be' (p. 251). Each of these characters has imposed on them a social identity which oppresses them and limits the possibility of re-making themselves in a more liberated and self-chosen way. As the actor's gendered or racial reality is distorted in his or her stage role, each character has been saddled with a role which imposes a false sense of self.

Act two takes the same characters, minus Clive, to contemporary London. Now characters are played by actors of their own sex: Betty by a woman, Edward by a man and so forth. The one exception is Cathy (the 4-year-old daughter of Lin, a friend of the now grown Victoria), who is played by a man – in the original production by the actor who played Clive in act one. In large part this rearrangement of roles entails an escape from oppression into more natural identities. As Churchill tells us, 'Betty is now played by a woman, as she gradually becomes real to herself' (p. 246). And yet the play does not present us with a naive or simplistic sense of essentialized gendered identity. Edward, for instance, though now played by a man, clings to the feminine identity he sees as his own. When Gerry, Edward's lover, says to him, 'Eddy, do stop playing the injured wife, it's not funny', Edward responds, 'I'm not playing. It's true' (p. 307). When he begins to explore a sexual relationship with Victoria, Edward says, 'I think I'm a lesbian' (p. 307). Lin, a lesbian, struggles with the limitations that the past imposes on re-making her identity: 'I've changed who I sleep with, I can't change everything' (p. 303).

Even Betty finds it a struggle getting used to her newfound identity. She has a hard time, for instance, becoming comfortable with the act of masturbating she has so come to enjoy:

> It felt very sweet, it was a feeling from very long ago, it was very soft, just barely touching, and I felt myself gathering together more and more and I felt angry with Clive and angry with my mother and I went on and on defying them, and there was this vast feeling growing in me and all around me and they couldn't stop me and no one could stop me and I was there and coming and coming. Afterwards I thought I'd betrayed Clive. My mother would kill me. But I felt triumphant because I was a separate person from them. And I cried because I didn't want to be. But I don't cry about it any more. Sometimes I do it three times in one night and it really is great fun.
>
> (p. 316)

For Churchill, in the second act all the characters 'change a little for the better' (p. 246), but this doesn't mean that they all find their essential selves, only that they are somewhat freed up to struggle and explore – as Betty says, 'if there isn't a right way to do things you have to invent one' (p. 319). In this light, the invocation of archetypal womanliness, though compelling, is fraught with an inevitable failure – as Victoria intones: 'Goddess of many names, oldest of the old, who walked in chaos and created life, … give us back what we were, give us the history we haven't had, make us the women we can't be' (p. 308).

And what about Cathy being played by a grown man, especially the man who was Clive? One way of looking at this is to see the superego which dominated in act one replaced by the id of the rambunctious child and of contemporary sexual 'liberation'. Remember also that in act one the young girl was played by a dummy: to be a young girl in the Victorian past was to be assigned a role so confining as to be lacking in basic humanity.

In act two, on the other hand, the young girl is allowed a verve and presence the equal of an adult male's. Finally, by disjoining character and actor, Churchill intimates that for the pre-oedipalized child there is no inevitable and appropriate identity; she is, at least potentially, free to direct her energies in any way she can imagine.

At the end of the play, the Ghost of Clive returns to haunt Betty, who confronts her earlier self from act one – not that she capitulates to the forces of the past, but these forces do remain with her, as part of her identity and her possibilities. In this moment Churchill both addresses the continuing reality of patriarchy and its phallocentric economy and refuses to be overwhelmed by them. Churchill, it has been noted, 'remains committed to the search for new representational forms, new strategies for encoding the body, new ways to organize the sex/gender relations we live in', while taking cognizance of the cultural conditions under which the new must come into being (Silverstein 1994: 20).

The American playwright Ntozake Shange's *for colored girls who have considered suicide / when the rainbow is enuf* is a renowned work of black feminist theatre. As such, it features a number of concerns common to black feminist theatre and feminist theatre in general. The play, or 'choreopoem', arose in a context of collective creation and collaboration, and in the interchanges between those involved in poetry, dance, music and theatre. (Dance, for Shange, was especially important as a point of access to her African interests.) The work was also influenced by the study of women's history:

> Unearthing the mislaid, forgotten, &/or misunderstood women writers, painters, mothers, cowgirls, & union leaders of our pasts proved to be both a supportive experience & challenge not to let them down, not to do less than – at all costs not to be less woman than – our mothers.
>
> (Shange 1992: xii)

The play itself interweaves music, word and dance in order to show 'a young black girl's growing up, her triumphs & errors, our struggle to become all that is forbidden by our environment, all that is forfeited by our gender, all that we have forgotten' (p. xvii). In part this becoming entails the finding of a language and 'the sound / of her own voice / her infinite beauty' (p. 4). The play features a combination of poetry and black vernacular which invokes an '*écriture feminine*' for women of colour.

The black women in the play have a particular set of relationships with black men (or with white women). On one side there is a connection with black male leaders of the past:

> TOUSSAINT L'OUVERTURE
> became my secret lover at the age of 8
> i entertained him in my bedroom
> widda flashlight under my covers
> way inta the night / we discussed strategies
> how to remove white girls from my hopscotch games
> & etc.
>
> (p. 27)

In this regard, black people stand together against white oppression, including the oppression of white girls and women. On the other side there is the trauma of sexual abuse and rape by which black men have oppressed black women, a trauma which binds black women with white women against men both black and white. The play begins with the characters, seven women, in 'postures of distress' (p. 3), but by the end there is a triumph of voice and self. 'i found god in myself / & i loved her / i loved her fiercely' (p. 63). Here the play taps into a spiritualism important to black culture and to feminist interest in the goddesses of ancient matriarchies, an interest more common in radical than materialist feminism.

In contrast to the confrontational and uncompromising lesbian theatre promoted by Jill Dolan, Shange's twentieth-anniversary production of *for colored girls* in New York in 1995 stressed those aspects of the play which are softer, less alarming, more comforting and nurturing. This effect was achieved in large measure by adding more music and 'organic' movement to the production, so that the general effect was one of solace and community (Lewis 1995: 6). As open and accepting as this production was, however, a 1991 production of the play in Denver went much further. Directed by a gay white male, the production attempted to get at the 'universal aspects' of the play in order to deal with 'all kinds of oppression'. In this regard, the production featured images from the work of the gay American photographer Robert Mapplethorpe (Wiley 1991: 381–2). Such a production runs the risk of effacing, or at least undermining, the particularities of black women's experience that gave rise to the play.

Queer theory

Lesbian feminist theory unites, to some extent, with gay male theory to form the new discipline of queer theory. Queer theory moves from what the American critic Eve Kosofsky Sedgwick calls a 'minoritizing' interest in homosexuality and homosexuals narrowly defined to a 'universalizing' interest in the construction of sexuality in general and its relations with power (Sedgwick 1990: 1). Queers are not just homosexuals, but bisexuals, trans-sexuals, cross-dressers, hermaphrodites and everybody else who doesn't feel particularly straight for some reason. There is an echo here of the American poet and theorist Adrienne Rich's earlier notions of compulsory heterosexuality and the lesbian continuum: compulsory heterosexuality is neither natural nor universal but constructed and enforced in conjunction with other relations of power to the detriment of alternative sexual practices and identities; the lesbian continuum implies that there aren't simply lesbians on one hand and heterosexual women on the other but a broad range of practices and identities in between (Rich 1980). Similarly, scholar Jeffrey Weeks writes of 'sexual flux' (Weeks 1995: 2) and 'a growing sense of our contingency, where nothing but uncertainty and death is certain' (p. 5). Helpful here are distinctions made between the homosocial, the homoerotic and the homosexual. Homosocial refers to same-sex bonding in general, such as men on sports teams and on Sunday afternoons at the pub. Homoerotic refers to sexually tinged but not fully sexualized relations in a same-sex group – think of sexual joking (straight and otherwise) among men in a locker room. Homosexual refers to fully sexual relations between people of the same sex. Of course, the homosocial, the homoerotic and the homosexual have all kinds of tendencies to overlap.

Queer theory, therefore, ultimately points towards a sexuality open to varied and shifting practices and identities. In this it echoes Michel Foucault's call for 'a general economy of pleasure not based on sexual norms' (Foucault 1980b: 191) and Julia Kristeva's for a recognition of the complexity of each person's symbolic as well as biological existence (Kristeva 1981: 35). Some sense of the openness implied in the term can be seen in the following passage:

> The term Queer is manifold; it seeks to encompass that which has been excluded, ridiculed, oppressed. Life caught in the margins. Sex yes, and sexuality, but also gender, race, class, and that which refuses easy taxonomy and suffers the fate of difference. A philosophy never fixed nor realized, but a politics of shared struggle, and a striving for community.
>
> (McNulty 1993: 12)

Seen in this light, Churchill's Cloud Nine appears as a consummately queer play.

Queer theory, therefore, studies the hegemonic institutions, practices and ideologies of heterosexuality and what Sedgwick calls the 'epistemology of the closet' (the practices whereby an oppressed homosexuality is indirectly expressed), on the one hand, and, on the other, the appearance of queerness in all its forms within a heterosexual hegemony, including underlying patterns of sexual variance which give the lie to any idea that our culture is as straight as it likes to think it is. This study gives rise to the ubiquitous gerund 'queering' (as in, for example, 'queering the old boy's club'), describing an activity wherein alternative queer practices and attitudes are found at the heart of a culture, institution or period traditionally taken as heterosexual. Left this open, queer theory and queer studies seem open to any fellow traveller who, for reasons of solidarity or opportunity, wishes to work under the rubric. This causes some unease among gays and lesbians who have long fought against a homophobic culture. Moreover, the 'postmodern' openness of queer studies has been contrasted with more historically grounded and politically focused work in traditional gay and lesbian studies (see Morton 1995).

Following Foucault's *The History of Sexuality* (1980a), queer theory explores the construction of sexuality in history – both heterosexuality and homosexuality come into particular being only in certain historical situations. Like the feminist interest in recouping women's cultural past, queer theory is interested in revealing homosexual activity in past cultures. The work of the American academic Jonathan Goldberg, for instance, explores modes of alternative sexuality in the Renaissance. The early modern period, of course, becomes more queer than it has heretofore seemed (Goldberg 1994). Marjorie Garber's *Vested Interests: Cross-Dressing and Cultural Anxiety* explores the sexual and cultural significance of transvestism (a topic much favoured in recent critiques of gender) both historically and in the present (Garber 1992). In transvestism, gender is related to role-playing and to such materially specific practices as putting on clothes. If clothes make the man, they also sometimes make the man a woman or the woman a man.

The relation between transvestism, role-playing and gender has been fruitfully explored in the study of boy actors playing women's parts in Renaissance theatre. Was it truly a 'woman's part' when played by a boy, or does the phenomenon of boy actors strongly point out how 'women' on stage were a product of masculine imagination and fabrication? Do men kissing boys pretending to be women point to the underlying homosocial and homoerotic realities of early modern theatre? Do, rather, boys playing women highlight the artificiality and complexity of gender identity? Think of Rosalind in *As You Like It*: a boy plays a woman pretending to be a boy, and then a boy plays a woman pretending to be a boy pretending to be a woman. What actor could keep all this straight? How would such a layering of masquerade appear to an audience? Would this layering cast gender identity into a comic vertigo, or was this such an accepted convention that no one saw anything out of the ordinary? At any rate, how different is the Shakespeare we usually get today, when 'women's parts' are routinely played by women?

Some of the possible effects that can be generated by wedding Renaissance practices of theatrical cross-dressing with current sexual politics can be seen in the radical British troupe Cheek by Jowl's production of *As You Like It*. In this version, the old man Adam and young and sexually lively Audrey were doubled, and Rosalind was played by a 6-foot-tall black man. Writing about this production as presented in Brooklyn in 1994, Katie Laris sees it 'debunking the value of such societally-determined attributes as gender, race, and even age'. She adds, 'The ease with which these actors transform themselves and the degree to which the audience accepts these characters, compellingly illustrates how ultimately artificial such categories are' (Laris 1995: 301).

Like feminism, queer theory is interested in recovering the

forgotten art of the past – hence the importance of an anthology such as Laurence Senelick's *Lovesick: Modernist Plays of Same-Sex Love 1894–1925* (1999). In *Out on Stage*, the British academic Alan Sinfield traces a critical history of *Lesbian and Gay Theatre in the Twentieth Century* (1999). Sinfield devotes a chapter of this book to the American playwright Tennessee Williams, focusing prominently on his play *A Streetcar Named Desire* (pp. 186–207). Sinfield explores a number of issues in Williams's work. There are the relations of Williams as a gay man and his gay audience to his female characters: is it one of identification (so that Williams's women are just stand-ins for gay men), sympathy (because of a shared history of oppression) or something more complex, scored by the political and personal differences between women and gay men? There is Williams's ambivalent relation to anti-gay ideology, especially in psychoanalytic theories of deviance, on the one hand, and to more liberated social and political understandings of anti-gay prejudice on the other. Williams comes across as conflicted – inevitably so, given his background and era. Sinfield explores the complex presentation of homosocial relations between 'buddies' in Williams's plays: are they straight, are they gay or are they something harder to pin down? Finally, there is the criticism and denial of gay elements in Williams's work in its rejection and acceptance by mainstream, heterosexist critics – *A Streetcar Named Desire* has been called, for instance, 'the great American play' (p. 203) and given readings which, as often as not, celebrated the heterosexual brutality of the character Stanley Kowalski, while Williams's *Cat on a Hot Tin Roof* had its queer elements systematically and progressively removed as it went from manuscript to stage to film (pp. 197–200). *Suddenly Last Summer*, in which a predatory gay man is cannibalized by young boys, 'Williams' most homophobic play' (p. 192), was a critical and moral success with mainstream critics, including the Catholic Legion of Decency, which approved of the punishment of homosexual activity (p. 193).

In beginning to develop a poetics of gay male theatre, the Canadian academic Robert Wallace calls for a 'homosexual gaze' which 'decentres the aesthetic of the heterosexual male gaze', positing gay experiences as central in a spirit of self-affirmation and assertion. At the same time, gay theatre must not turn away from marginalization as a gay experience, nor from patriarchal oppression and the self-oppression it often imposes. For Wallace, gay theatre, like feminist theatre, is drawn to disruptions of the traditionally realist masculinist gaze by resorting to self- referentiality and the exposure of theatrical illusion. Non-realist theatre also has the advantage of invoking the constructedness and not the naturalness of social norms, including those of gender and identity (Wallace 1994).

Angels in America

The American playwright Tony Kushner's two-part *Angels in America* (*Millennium Approaches* and *Perestroika*) is one of the foremost works of recent gay male theatre. As such, it displays both a traditional 'minoritizing interest' in the lives of gay men and a 'universalizing' interest in new modes of sexuality. The minoritizing side can be seen in the standard references to icons of gay culture – *The Wizard of Oz*, Cole Porter, Blanche Dubois in *A Streetcar Named Desire* (even the use at key moments of extravagant spectacle plays into a stereotypically gay sensibility) – as well as in the focus on particularly gay experiences: one character is a former drag queen, two others suffer from AIDS (which in Kushner's plays remains a gay disease). *Angels in America* is also, however, as its subtitle states, 'A Gay Fantasia on National Themes'; as such, it sets its gay characters and interests at the heart of general concerns of religion, politics, culture and society in America. For Kushner, to be gay is not to be outside American life, but to live it through and through; and the great concerns of American life are gay as much as they are straight. *Perestroika* ends looking forward to a time, which has perhaps come, when gay men 'will be citizens' (Kushner 1994: 148). With its scenes in a fantastical Soviet Union and in a heaven that looks like San Francisco after the earthquake, *Perestroika* takes gay concerns into the international and cosmic spheres as well.

Kushner has consciously enacted a theoretical and political position in his theatre. He is a very theoretically literate playwright, taking a profound interest in such theorists as Walter Benjamin (discussed later), with his interest in apocalypse and utopia. He also follows in the footsteps of Caryl Churchill, whom he considers the 'greatest living, English-language playwright' (Savran 1995b: 138), and takes a similar interest in the complexities and contingencies of identity. Moreover, Kusher aligns his project with the politics of groups such as the American activists Queer Nation:

> Like Queer Nation, *Angels in America* aims to subvert the distinction between the personal and the political, to refuse to be closeted, to undermine the category of the 'normal', and to question the fixedness and stability of every sexual identity.
>
> (Savran 1995b: 132)

As in much recent queer theory, *Angels in America* plays with set notions of sexual preference. The most troubling character in the two plays is Roy M. Cohn, a right-wing power broker dying of AIDS, who asserts, 'Homosexuals are men who know nobody and who nobody knows. Who have zero clout. Does this sound like me ...?' 'Roy Cohn is not a homosexual', he declares. 'Roy Cohn is a heterosexual man who fucks around with guys' (Kushner 1993: 45–6). As reactionary as Cohn's attitudes are, they speak to the complexities of personal, social and sexual identity. Furthermore, the angel who visits and copulates with Prior Walter, also an AIDS patient, has eight vaginas and is 'Hermaphroditically Equipped as well with a Bouquet of Phalli' (Kushner 1994: 48).

And yet the angel preaches a reactionary sermon of going back and staying put, of a return to the past, which the plays reject. 'The Great Work Begins', says Prior at the end of *Perestroika*, taking on a commitment to '*More Life*', to the re-making of America as a place free of sexual and racial oppression. *Perestroika*, writes Kushner, is essentially a comedy, but one with high stakes and a terrific amount of struggle (Kushner 1994: 8). If there is a problem with Kushner's work, it is that there is a lack of precision and clarity as to how all the themes brought forward hang together, and if the struggle and stakes are high, specifics of strategy and goal remain unclear. This lack of clarity can be taken in at least two ways. First, it may be a necessary part of the utopian instinct directed toward an unknown future: 'a teleology, not a guarantee' (Savran 1995b: 144). On the other hand, it can be taken as a symptom of the circumstances of confusion and complicity in which *Angels in America* arises; given this particular 'field of cultural production', David Savran argues, the play could hardly avoid certain ambivalences' (Savran 1995a: 208). Similarly, Alan Sinfield has trouble with the way *Angels in America* uses, and has been celebrated for, presenting a sense of America's 'spiritual destiny' (1999: 206) and for the way it 'slides into the cloudiness of irony, symbolism and pro[f]undity at moments where clear elucidation would be valuable' (p. 207) – although this critique does not stop Sinfield from using an image from the play as the cover illustration for his own book.

Here we see, as in feminism, the conflict between a pliant and a hard-line queer cultural politics. The Canadian academic Douglas Arrell writes in a review of David Roman's *Acts of Intervention: Performance, Gay Culture and AIDS* (1998), 'We soon anticipate the negative judgements Roman will pass on "mainstream" plays, realistic plays, and plays that center on an AIDS death – which, he says, result in "the reinscription of gay men, especially those with AIDS, as victims"' (Arrell 1999: 461). Commenting on Roman's championing of more radical works, Arrell asks,

'Have some of the rarefied solo performances which satisfy all of Roman's theoretical concerns really successfully "intervened" in the AIDS crisis, or have they merely pleased an "in crowd" of gay intellectuals?' (p. 461).

Masculinity and Oedipus

Of course, it is also possible to make masculinity in general, rather than queer masculinity, the object of study, and masculinity can be dealt with in many of the same ways that gender is dealt with in feminism and queer theory: one can attempt to understand traditions of masculinity, either to celebrate or criticize them; one can explore masculinity in the past and in the present; one can seek to liberate men who have been or continue to be oppressed in their masculinity. Volume two of Foucault's *The History of Sexuality*, *The Use of Pleasure* (1985), studies (male) sexuality in classical Greece, where sexuality appears as part of a personal discipline that the free male can subscribe to: sexuality is part of the art of forming and controlling the self, an idea that returns in the Renaissance as 'self-fashioning' and which runs counter to the oppressive gender restrictions on women in Ancient Greece and to the later notion of women's and homosexuals' sexuality as something pathological that must be controlled from without, by hospitals and psychiatrists. Two recent books have studied masculinity in ancient Greek drama. In *Acting Like Men* (1998), Karen Bassi says of Oedipus, for example, that he, like other Greek heroes, is 'born from the desire to resurrect an idealized and ever receding past and the masculine subject who occupies and sanctions that past' (p. 245), and audiences during and after classical Greece – and readers such as Freud – have identified with Oedipus and other Greek heroes in a way that perpetuates nostalgia for idealized masculinity and mastery. Indeed, Thomas Van Nortwick, in his *Oedipus: The Meaning of a Masculine Life* (1998), embraces such an identification with Oedipus:

The pattern of emotional and spiritual development I will be tracing through Sophocles' metaphors is one that the Greeks tended to see as biologically based and characteristic of the male sex....

...I am a man – a man who cannot sort out what is biological and what is cultural in my own response to the world. I am inclined for these reasons to talk about 'men' here as the principal modern recipients of the ancient heroic myth I describe, but with no great confidence that what I say might not apply in some way to women as well.

(pp. x–xi)

Here we see opposite approaches to the western tradition of masculine identity – one critical and from the outside, one celebratory and from the inside.

QUESTIONS ONE MIGHT ASK OF A PLAY OR PERFORMANCE

What assumptions about gender identity and gender relations are at work in this play or performance? Which gender's point of view is being presented?

Are men and women cast in traditional roles or does the casting call into question gender conventions? Does the casting run with or against the gender assumptions of the drama text?

How do your own gender and gender assumptions affect your understanding of and sympathy for this play or performance? Are you a patriarchal reader, an immasculated reader, a resisting reader or some other kind of reader?

Is this play or performance part of the traditional canon or not? Do the gender of the playwright or the work's assumptions about gender have anything to do with this?

3 READER-RESPONSE AND RECEPTION THEORY

Reader-response and reception theory, taken together, are concerned with how people other than the author or creator contribute to the meaning and import of a work of art. For these theories, an unread book or an unwatched play, like a tree falling in the forest with no one to hear it, are nothing more than lifeless objects. Indeed, certain artistic effects assume an audience to be affected: surprise endings demand an audience curious yet kept in the dark – that's why it is infuriating to be told the ending of a mystery (although the telling has an effect only on the observer and not on the work of art itself); IMAX films are pointless if there is no audience whose stomachs are being churned by flying over one extremely high precipice or another. Although an interest in the effect of art on the observer goes as far back as classical Greece – with Aristotle's *Poetics*, which speaks of the way tragedy excites pity and fear in the audience (Aristotle 1965: 49–51) – recent reader-response and reception theories have arisen since the late 1960s, mainly in Germany and the United States. In literary matters they are concerned with the practice of making meaning on the part of a reader or readers. As we can see, however, reception in theatre or film is not specifically about readers but about spectators. If we think even more widely about reception, myriad receivers affect the significance of cultural works: readers, viewers, literary agents, film companies, gallery owners, critics, publishers, government cultural agencies and so on. Since theatre is not read in private like a book, and since it demands resources and people to be performed, it has a particularly rich relation to reception.

Widely conceived, as a general theory of the appropriation of works of art by all the forces involved in their transmission and reception, reader-response and reception theory have connections with all the theoretical approaches we have encountered so far. Saussure does not seem particularly concerned with how the signifier invokes the signified in the person who encounters it – his seems a closed system running on its own, like a movie theatre that keeps operating automatically after a nuclear holocaust; Peirce, however, stresses that the act of interpretation is inherent in the sign and that signs generate interpretation and 'unlimited semiosis' among their interpreters (in Makaryk 1993: 186). Phenomenology, we have seen, is interested in listening, seeing, unconcealing – acts of reception – and sees in the work of art a special kind of truth worth getting to know. Phenomenology has had a special influence on German reception theory: Wolfgang Iser, a key figure in this movement, was influenced by the theories of reading of the philosopher Roman Ingarden, who was a student of the phenomenologist Edmund Husserl (Holub 1984: 83). For this group, the reader encounters the work of art in a way analogous to our encounter with the world: the work of art (a play, for instance) unconceals its truth to us in the time of the act of listening and perceiving. Our task is to listen faithfully, aspiring to be the 'implied reader' (Iser 1978; Holub 1984: 84–5), the reader who hears what the work is truly saying.

Post-structuralism has also been interested in the act of reading, most notably in Roland Barthes's distinction between the readerly and writerly text: the readerly text leads the reader along by limiting and imposing its meaning; the writerly text is open to, and encourages, the reader rewriting and recreating the text in the joy of open reading (Barthes 1974: 4). Is it the text, however, which makes for a readerly or writerly reading, or is it the reader who brings an open or closed approach to whatever text? How much agency, how much freedom, does the reader have? Deconstruction, with Derrida's notion of iterability, implies that there is no faithful reader but only an infinite possibility of different readers, none of whom are any more true than any others. Similarly, author and reader are no longer in a hierarchical relation whereby the author imparts meaning to the reader. Rather, the reader gives as much to the author as the author does to the reader. As Derrida says:

> But it would be necessary to analyze very closely the experience of hearing someone else read a text you have allegedly written or signed. All of a sudden someone puts a text right in front of you again in another context, with an intention that is both somewhat yours and not simply yours.... It can reconcile you with what you've done, make you love it or hate it. There are a thousand possibilities. Yet one thing is certain in all this diversity, and that is that it's never the same.
>
> (Derrida 1985: 157–8)

Paul de Man sees literature as an allegory about the impossibility of reading, in the sense of finding an author-imposed set of meanings. As allegories of reading, works of literature become self-reflexive or self-referential meditations on their own interpretability (de Man 1979).

Freud, in his psychoanalytic theory, sees that the task of the analyst is to read past the manifest content (of the patient's dream or the genius's work of art), which tries to hide the awful truth, to the latent content, the awful truth itself. In feminism there is Fetterley's distinction between the immasculated reader, trained to follow the attitudes of patriarchy, and the resisting reader, who brings a feminist critique to patriarchal works and attitudes. Here who the reader is becomes important: a radical feminist reads differently from the pope.

All these theories, therefore, have a great deal invested in understanding the reception of works of culture. We may see in them two general tendencies, which overlap and combine in complex ways. One tendency is prescriptive, attempting to say how culture should be received. Here there is a right and a wrong reading, or at least one we support over another. Iser, Freud and Fetterley all fall into this tendency, although Iser prescribes a faithful reading while Freud prescribes a suspicious and Fetterley a hostile one. The second tendency is descriptive, attempting to understand the way reception works without advocating one particular approach. Derrida's notion of iterability is, in large measure, descriptive, although he seems to embrace the wild and free-flowing dissemination of meaning iterability allows – just as Barthes prefers writerly to readerly texts. The German reception theorist Hans Robert Jauss and the American reader-response theorist Stanley Fish are perhaps better examples of the descriptive tendency.

Hans Robert Jauss is more interested in the changing inter-pretations of a work of art from era to era and in this way he moves reception theory in a historical direction (Jauss 1982). A historicized reception theory traces the rewriting of the sig-nificance of a text in changing circumstances. The significance of *Othello*, for instance, has changed with shifting societal attitudes toward race, as *The Taming of the Shrew* is affected by attitudes about women and *The Merchant of Venice* by attitutes toward anti-semitism. On a sociocultural and political level, Stanley Fish goes further in this direction: he relates, for instance, the ability of his students to read a list of the names of linguistics scholars mistak-enly as a seventeenth-century devotional poem – which shows the power that their classroom experience has over their percep-tions. According to Fish, there are no meanings inherent in works of art except those which 'interpretive communities' in any particular era foster or allow, while disallowing and discour-aging others (Fish 1980). Institutions play a big role in this: stu-dents can, for instance, put forward their own idiosyncratic interpretation of a play in a drama class, but they will be dis-couraged when their grade plummets and friends begin to shun their company. Even if they refuse to abandon their reading, it is unlikely anyone else will carry it on. The pressures of power determine which meanings are posited and accepted.

From a Marxist perspective (discussed more fully in the section on materialism in the next chapter), Tony Bennett writes, 'Marxist criticism has assumed that every text has its politics inscribed in it, but that politics has to be made', and 'In this sense, literature is not something to be studied; it is an area to be occupied' (Bennett 1977: 167–8, 137). The British Marxist Terry Eagleton posits the multi-faceted task of the 'revolutionary cultural worker' as not only participation in the production of new works but also the appropriation of existing works through radical criticism and reinterpretation (Eagleton 1981: 113). What is being argued here is that works of culture, even when carved in stone, are open to being seen in new ways, and, like the resisting reader of feminism, the revolutionary reader is less interested in being faithful and doing justice to the work of art than in making political use of it, appropriating it in whatever ways are useful. This may entail denouncing a traditional masterpiece for its reactionary tendencies, finding something progressive in a work heretofore taken as conservative, or even rewriting a work to make it more palatable to one's political viewpoint. Why not, after all?

Reception theory has been developed by a number of theatre theorists. Marvin Carlson has written about the importance of the audience for semiotic theory of the theatre. The complexity and openness of signification on the stage create in the audience a 'psychic polyphony' which allows individual audience members to focus their attention in any number of ways, allowing the theatrical spectator 'an unique and individual "synchronic" reading as the play moves forward diachronically' (Carlson 1990: 99). This is to say that each spectator takes in particular facets of the performance moment by moment and also has a particular sense of how the performance unfolds in time. Thus, no two spectators see exactly the same play. Similarly, theatre's 'local semiosis' (p. 113) means that the specific arrangement of signs in any performance is unrepeatable. From night to night a performance changes in subtle or striking ways. Furthermore, the re-mounting of any drama text in another time and circumstance will change its semiotic content and reception even more extensively.

The Canadian scholar Susan Bennett analyses the role of the audience in theatre from a number of recent theoretical perspectives, including semiotics, post-structuralism, and reader-response. She concludes that the audience in traditional theatre enters into a 'social contract' in which audience members agree to be passive in their behaviour but open, eager and active in their acceptance and decoding of the signs presented to them. Prescriptively, she calls for the 'emancipation of the spectator' evident in non-traditional and often marginalized theatre practices, which allow for a more active role for the audience (Bennett 1990).

The American Gerald Rabkin, in 'Is There a Text on This Stage?' – a title which echoes Stanley Fish's *Is There a Text in This Class?* – uses reader-response theory, as well as ideas from Barthes, Derrida and Foucault, to undermine the traditional importance of the author/playwright and the written text he or she creates, and to stress the importance of open and radical interpretation often at odds with the author's intentions. Rabkin discusses the Wooster Group's *L.S.D.*, which appropriated and rewrote Arthur Miller's *The Crucible*, and the American Repertory Theatre's production of Samuel Beckett's *Endgame*, which resituated the play in an abandoned subway station. Both productions provoked lawsuits from the outraged authors, a response, it seems, little informed by sympathy for contemporary critical theory. Rabkin writes, 'The playwright's intentionality is, then, not irrelevant, but this intentionality is perceived within a complex matrix of interpretation' (Rabkin 1985: 158) and 'we have in theatre two sets of readers – the theatre artists who traditionally "read", interpret, the written text, and the audience who read the new theatrical text created by the mediated reading' (p. 157).

Theatrical adaptation

Much of this theory of reception undermines the notion that a reader or interpreter can or should be faithful to the truth of the work or to the author's intentions. Post-structuralism argues that such fidelity is impossible; feminism and Marxism argue that we owe less allegiance to the work of art than we do to our political struggles. This means that the reader may feel free or compelled to rewrite a work of culture to fit present circumstances. To 'adapt' means to 'make fit' in just this way. Thus, another practice in which past works are appropriated and rewritten is theatrical adaptation, which we have seen at work in Grotowski's *Akropolis*, Blau's *Elsinore* and *Crooked Eclipses*, the Performance Group's *Dionysus in 69*, and MacDonald's *Goodnight Desdemona*.

Theatrical adaptation is particularly rich in the methods available for re-making the meaning of past works. The drama text, of course, can be altered in any number of ways. In *Goodnight Desdemona*, MacDonald jumbles Shakespearean lines with her own parodies of Shakespearean-sounding verse. Blau's *Elsinore* mixes snippets of *Hamlet* with lines developed by the actors in rehearsal; his *Crooked Eclipses* works only with the lines of Shakespeare's sonnets, but cuts and pastes drastically. Blau subtitles *Elsinore* an 'analytic scenario' and *Crooked Eclipses* a 'theatrical essay'. Here we see explicitly how adaptations wed two kinds of readings: the critical and the creative. They are both criticism of the old and new dramatic art in their own right.

Moreover, there is staging to be adapted. A radical staging changes the meaning of a work even when the words remain relatively the same. An all-woman cast of *King Lear* is in some ways an adaptation. At this level of specifically theatrical adaptation, there enters into the reception and re-making of meaning in the theatre a complexity missing in strictly literary cultural practices. In theatre there is more than just words to read and re-make and more than just readers who respond. *Dionysus in 69* shows how, as Rabkin argues, various sets of readers are involved in theatrical production – especially in the kind of radical production advocated by Susan Bennett. In *Dionysus in 69*, each night the actors are free to re-make the play, and they do so at least partly in response to the reactions of the audience, who become collaborators in the ongoing adaptation of Euripides' *The Bacchae*. Moreover, as Marvin Carlson asserts, changing context has a role in re-making meaning. *Dionysus* is one thing, but *in 69* is another: this production takes much of its meaning from the turbulent counterculture of the late 1960s; its significance is very much of its time.

David Mamet's *Oleanna*

Narrowly conceived, drama texts are open to theories of reader response in the same way that works of literature are. David Mamet's controversial *Oleanna* is a case in point. The play deals with the troubled relations between a male professor and his female student, relations which lead to sexual harassment charges that ruin the professor's career and provoke him at the play's end to assault the student in his office. Many have read the play as an attack on so-called political correctness, but with different levels of approval. Daniel Mufson gives an overview of the controversy surrounding the play, which he sees as one-sided and sexist, even as he relates how others have taken a contrary view (Mufson 1993). Indeed, the play remains controversial and open to different interpretations, not only in itself but also because of the charged social context in which issues of sexual harassment continue to be debated.

For instance, when *Oleanna* was produced in Toronto in 1994, one male student wrote in the University of Toronto student newspaper:

> Mamet's play is a brilliantly written and scathing attack on the insidiousness of political correctness and militant feminism....
>
> Militant feminists, or 'feminazis', as one individual coined the phrase, and vitriolic mandarins of political correctness would have the masses believe that everyday life is untenable without a suffocating web of complex rules, regulations, and safety nets at every turn. They would have you believe humanity's dearest longings, that of loving and physical closeness, are fraught with ambiguity, perversity, and ulterior motives.
>
> (MacPherson 1994: 5)

In a less strident article, and one staying closer to the play, Bronwyn Drainie, in the *Globe and Mail*, found the play's success deeply disturbing, because the female student is presented as a 'monster', and productions in various cities have provoked audience members to shout encouragement when she is being beaten at the end of the play:

> I'm not saying *Oleanna* shouldn't be there or that you shouldn't go and see it in your community. But when you do, think very carefully about what you are watching: decide for yourself whether Mamet is presenting a fair fight or a cleverly crafted match with the conclusion long foregone.
>
> (Drainie 1994: E5)

Both these readers see the play as slanted against the politically correct student, though they respond differently to this bias. In a third local review, this time of the film of *Oleanna*, which was released at the time of the Toronto stage production, a second University of Toronto student saw the film as a disturbing representation of two equally unmeritorious characters:

> Her reactionary response to what has occurred makes Carol as unsympathetic as John. She reduces his veiled abuse to actual rape and charges him with assault. But even then, John does

not see what is occurring. He is still stuck in his academic and paternal role.

(Huffman 1994: 15)

To what degree are the differences between these perspectives the product of differences between the theatrical production and the film, and to what degree are they the product of differences among readers?

Another interesting aspect of these debates is the interplay between theatre and the academy, an interplay that Stanton B. Garner takes up in a discussion of teaching *Oleanna* in a university drama course. Garner is struck by the controversy surrounding the play: 'indeed, the fury of the debate *Oleanna* occasioned in the press and the academic community is in many ways as remarkable a phenomenon as the play itself', and, stressing the importance of reception, he writes, 'If the ability to spark such debate (and such passion) is one of the signs of a work's power, then *Oleanna* must be acknowledged as one of the landmark cultural texts of the early to mid-1990s' (Garner 2000: 40). Teaching the play, Garner finds '*Oleanna* in the classroom becomes a powerfully reflexive text, framing the student–teacher relationship and the larger institutional structures within which this relationship is articulated' (p. 41). Curiously, for instance, although his students overwhelmingly side with the male professor against the female student, in class, since Garner sides with the student, they rebel against Garner's authority with an intensity not unlike the student's in the play. Garner writes, 'Mamet's play blew the cover off our institutional reactions in a way that made our week and a half one of the most interesting classroom experiences I have ever had' (p. 50).

It is possible to read the play as enacting allegorically within itself the problematic of reading. Act one presents us with a first meeting, which seems more or less innocuous, which is reinterpreted in later acts as a scene of harassment. In act two, the two characters interpret the events of act one from opposed points of view; in this process the audience, too, is made to read its own responses in act one: did we miss something? was everything as innocent as it seemed? is the student all wrong? does she have a point? Even if the play is unfairly slanted against her, in the structure of reconsideration much of what she says forces us at least to revisit what we have seen. And is everything she suggests wrong, or are some of her accusations right? And if so, which ones, exactly? In such a state of questioning, even if we conclude that the professor was not very guilty to begin with, should we think that at the end, despite any yahoos in the audience who cheer him on, when he stands over her prostrate and beaten on the floor?

And how would our reading be affected by slight changes in staging? What if, in the first act, there was something a bit more suspicious and fawning about the professor, something a bit more sexualized about his treatment of the student? How sexual would he have to be before we could agree that his actions were problematic, unacceptable, harassment? In this regard, the first act of the play as it exists on the page is hardly more than a cipher; we only have actions we can begin to judge after we have seen a particular performance. Or, more radically, 'How would the encounter change', Garner asks, 'if the gender roles were reversed?' (p. 49). And yet, no matter how *Oleanna* is played, hypothetical alternatives suggest themselves. *Oleanna* is a strong work for reader-response analysis not only because it polarizes an audience, not only because it provokes audience members to question their own responses, but because it opens on to the theatrical possibilities of production choices as well as audience responses as constitutive of meaning and reception.

Peter Brook's *A Midsummer Night's Dream*

One of the major thrusts of reader-response theory is to downplay the centrality of the author in artistic production. Theatre, however, has already long decentralized the playwright in favour of producer, director and actors. The generation of meaning in the theatre is more complex, and involves more kinds of participants, than literary practice does. Some of this complexity is suggested, for instance, in accounts of Peter Brook's renowned and well-documented production of *A Midsummer Night's Dream*, which opened in Stratford-upon-Avon in 1969 and eventually toured Europe and North America. Looking at accounts of this production opens up notions of drama text, author and theatre text to the multiplicity of agency and collaboration in the making of theatrical significance.

How is the drama text to be understood? Is it merely the words on the page? Words and intentions put there by the author? Brook believes that *A Midsummer Night's Dream*, like *King Lear* or *Coriolanus*, is a masterpiece, an 'absolutely perfect play' (Brook 1987: 87), which can only be reduced by textual amendment. He felt no need to change a word (Berry 1977: 128). David Selbourne, who watched the rehearsals for the Stratford production, noted this 'fidelity to the text-as-written' (Selbourne 1982: 19), in which the text was 'inviolable' and there was 'no question ... of additions or subtractions, cuts or alterations to the writ of Shakespeare' (p. 65).

What becomes apparent, however, is that merely repeating the proper words does not guarantee a fidelity to the 'original meaning'. Selbourne becomes bemused that Brook attributes to the words of the text 'near-unfathomable depths' (p. 65); he complains that Brook makes more of Shakespeare's text than is there (p. 79), that Brook tries 'to induce responses which the text does not yield' (p. 93), that Brook continually misreads the text (pp. 137, 181, 219, 229) – ultimately, that Brook shows a reverence for the written coupled with a rejection of the writer (p. 67).

For Selbourne, fidelity to the words of the text is not enough; there must be fidelity to the sense of those words, and that sense is to be determined by authorial intention. He speaks of 'the playwright's truth in the last instance' (p. 13), of 'Shakespeare who conceived the whole in his imagination' (p. 17), of truth 'contained only in the mind of Shakespeare' (p. 21); he identifies with 'the author' (p. 41) and wonders what Shakespeare would think 'if he rose from his tomb down the lane' (p. 65). For Brook, however, Shakespeare is taken to be quite a different phenomenon, or set of phenomena. On the one hand, Shakespeare is what has traditionally come to be associated with the name, a code word in each country for a set of values and expectations (Berry 1977: 124). In Brook's England, Shakespeare is the linchpin of the nineteenth-century, Victorian tradition which comes down to him as 'the deadly theatre' (Brook 1968: 10) with its admonition to 'Play what is written' (p. 12), devoid of liveliness and creativity. But this nineteenth-century fidelity to the text is a bore (Brook 1987: 71) and gives rise in Brook only to the desire to 'fuck Shakespeare' (Berry 1977: 123). This Victorian bore, however, is not the real Shakespeare. The real Shakespeare isn't a bore. Nor is he a Victorian. He is an Elizabethan, and Elizabethan England was almost totally different from Victorian England (Brook 1987: 45). Elizabethan England was harsh, 'the violence, the passion, and the excitement of the stinking crowds, the feuds, the intrigues' (p. 71), like Eastern Europe in our own day (p. 45), and so the real Shakespeare, as Jan Kott says, is our contemporary (p. 9). Rather, to be more precise, we are a strange cross of the Victorian and the Elizabethan (p. 45), and while the Shakespeare of *Timon of Athens* is our contemporary, the Shakespeare of *Othello* is not (p. 9).

Ultimately, Brook is not really interested in Shakespeare the author any more than in Shakespeare's words: 'what passed through this man called Shakespeare ... is quite different from any other author's work'; 'it's something which actually resembles reality'; 'it is the thing itself' (Berry 1977: 115). Shakespeare is a 'creator', and his words are a set of codes for 'vibrations and impulses' (p. 130). Shakespeare is the 'miracle of Shakespeare' (Brook 1987: 16), and it is not his method which interests us, it is 'the Shakespearean ambition' (p. 55). Brook, then, is not trying to be faithful to Shakespeare or Shakespeare's words, but to something he takes to be more originary: 'The text is not the play. Only a small part. Words change or say different things in another time and place. The director has to go beneath them and find the author's true intent' (Loney 1974: 13). The author's intent, behind the words, is to recreate processes and rhythms of thought, pre-verbal impulses (Selbourne 1982: 39), 'the life behind the text' (p. 217), in the case of *A Midsummer Night's Dream*, to recreate magic (Loney 1974: 25). Shakespeare's '*mots rayonnants*' (Berry 1977: 121), his shining, resonant words, play a part in this re-creation, but 'all the printed word can tell us is what was written on paper, not how it was once brought to life' (Brook 1968: 12). Sometimes the words are only approximations (Selbourne 1982: 101); sometimes they interfere with feeling (p. 99).

Selbourne quotes the Romantic William Hazlitt who said that all that is finest in *A Midsummer Night's Dream* is lost in the representation (p. 37); Brook, on the other hand, says that 'the only way to find the true path to the speaking of a word is through a process that parallels the original creative one' (Brook 1968: 13). Drama text gives way to theatre text. This will yield to us the 'secret play' that can only be discovered in rehearsals (Loney 1974: 54). Yet Brook is just as dismissive of faithful historical reconstruction as he is of the deadly theatre: reconstruction is guesswork (Brook 1968: 13) and only of antiquarian interest (p. 16). The only way to recreate Shakespeare's magic is by contemporary theatrical means. Somewhat xenophobically, Selbourne notes these 'alien' tools (Selbourne 1982: 29) whenever they arise: 'imported' Japanese theatre (p. 83); Chinese circus (p. 85); Japanese wrestlers (p. 109); Pacific island ritual (p. 139); Grand Guignol and Kurasawa (p. 175); 'Grotowskian effect'

(p. 297); 'Oz not Arden' (p. 323). We can note others: African ritual (Berry 1977: 125) and music (Loney 1974: 72); jazz or rock performance (p. 72); Vedic chant (p. 70); Persian folk plays (p. 17); Indian theatre (p. 56).

What we see, then, is a complex play of fidelity and infidelity: a fidelity to the words of the text is matched by an infidelity to Shakespeare's intended meaning; a fidelity to Shakespeare's ambition is matched by an infidelity to his theatrical method. An ultimate fidelity to life and magic is not a fidelity to Shakespeare, but in sympathy with Shakespeare's own fidelity to these concerns. Shakespeare as author, as playwright, was really a reader and presenter of life.

If our interest is now in the theatre text, we still must face the particulars and differences that arise in different performances even of the same production. Let us set aside the complex social and cultural materiality of the theatrical event, not attempting to define and reconstruct all those elements that would go into a full account of a theatrical production: the text, the multiple borrowings from world theatre, the actors in all their specificity, their delivery and movement, costumes, make-up, the set design, the lighting, the auditorium, ticket prices, the exact composition of the audience and the specificity of each individual member, the socio-political organization of the theatre company, the entire theatrical world. Let us keep the question on a more general level. Loney's acting edition, for instance, is 'an American adaptation, based point-by-point on the prompt-book of the World Tour version'. It is 'perhaps the most definitive because it represents the refinements and simplifications which the production achieved in the Paris rehearsals for the tour and the later modifications introduced as the show travelled to such cities as Budapest, Helsinki, and Los Angeles' (Loney 1974: 3a). Are we to believe that only those who saw the World Tour version towards the end of its run were privy to the 'definitive' production? Selbourne's book, on the other hand, ends with the last dress rehearsal before the opening night of the first Stratford production. His is an account of rehearsals. The production he talks about is not definitive, but constantly changing.

To ignore the rehearsal process would be to ignore an essential aspect of the production. The specificity of Brook's rehearsal process is what sets his work apart from the deadly theatre:

> In a living theatre, we would each day approach the rehearsal putting yesterday's discoveries to the test, ready to believe that the true play has once again escaped us. But the Deadly Theatre approaches the classics from the viewpoint that somewhere, someone has found out and defined how the play should be done.
>
> (Brook 1968: 14)

In rehearsal things don't stay the same; things are erased (Selbourne 1982: 279); those involved change from day to day and moment to moment (p. 273). Rehearsals are performances in their own right (p. 77), with their own strange logic; one day the actors 'wreck the entire studio' (Loney 1974: 28):

> Anyone watching the play that morning would have found it unrecognizable and yet those of us who had participated in the chaos sensed that we had been in contact with elements of the play that no amount of discussion or carefully plotted 'production' could have revealed.
>
> (p. 58)

If rehearsals are performances, performances must retain the quality of rehearsals: 'Creation and exploration need not and, in fact, must not stop on the last day of rehearsal' (p. 57); 'theatre is always a self-destructive act and is always written on the wind' (Brook 1968: 15). The 'endlessly moving, endlessly changing' nature of Shakespeare's material is best served by a production in which there is 'no definitive moment of public realization'

(Selbourne 1982: xxvi). Every performance, like every rehearsal, produces 'another truth' (p. 293): sometimes certain lines take on a meaning only for the nonce (p. 327); sometimes an accident happens which will never happen again – a black dog wanders across the stage (p. 311), a tray of candles causes a fire (Loney 1974: 35). There are multiple possibilities in the so-called definitive prompt-book itself: 'Puck spins plate, drops it to Obe[ron], who spins it on his own rod – if he catches it. If he drops it, a Fairy passes a spinning plate to him' (p. 46a). A rehearsal, a performance at the Midland Arts Centre, the 'full-scale experience' of opening night, the simplified versions of the world tour, none are definitive, 'but quite simply "other"' (Selbourne 1982: xxvii).

Kenneth McClellan, in his snide and reactionary book *Whatever Happened to Shakespeare?*, argues that it's not 'Brook's *Midsummer Night's Dream*', 'it's Shakespeare's *Midsummer Night's Dream*' (McClellan 1978: 9–10). Selbourne begins his book with the same opposition: 'Will this be Brook's *Dream*, or Shakespeare's?' (1982: 7). But this narrow opposition between author and director gives way in Selbourne as a reader to a fuller understanding of theatrical agency: Brook runs up against the limitations of his actors, who possibly can only play conventional Shakespeare (p. 215); after a certain point the play is in their hands, not Brook's (p. 267); eventually the technicians take charge (p. 319), and the setting, not the text, imposes a structure of feeling on the actors (p. 321) – 'If the preverbal comes before the verbal, does place come before both of them?' (p. 167). Brook as director, like Derrida as author, is faced with his work coming back to him in almost unrecognizable form:

> Seeing a first public performance of a play one has directed is a strange experience. Only a day before, one sat at a run-through and was completely convinced that a certain actor was playing well, that a certain scene was interesting, a movement graceful,

a passage full of clear and necessary meaning. Now sur-
rounded by an audience part of oneself is responding like this
audience, so it is oneself who is saying 'I'm bored', 'he's said
that already', 'if she moves once more in that affected way I'll go
mad' and even 'I don't understand what they're trying to say.'

(Brook 1968: 127–8)

In performance the audience ultimately becomes the true master
of the situation (Selbourne 1982: 299), and every audience is
different: children are disillusioning (pp. 207–13); the Stratford
audience conventionalizes (p. 285); the Los Angeles audience
doesn't get it, while the students of San Francisco do (Loney
1974: 76). Finally, Loney's acting edition, with its long list of
contributors, ends with three blank pages for 'director's notes':
new authors, actors, technicians and audiences await the next
Peter Brook.

QUESTIONS ONE MIGHT ASK OF A PLAY OR PERFORMANCE

Are there things you could say about the play or performance
which are patently true or patently false? On what grounds could
you say this?

Have you ever seen the same play produced at different times
in your life? Did the meaning change? Was that because of differences in production, because of differences in you, or because
they took place in different times and circumstances?

What aspects of the significance of a production you see here
and now might be different in another time and place?

What aspects of you as a person affect the way you read and
interpret the play or performance?

How are your responses limited and regulated by those around you? What happens if your friends all disagree with you or your instructor tells you you're wrong?

How much power does an actor, director, or scene designer have to affect the meaning of who a character is and what he or she says?

3

WORLD AND THEATRE

Materialist, Postmodern and Post-colonial Theory

A performance text is a transmission tuned to a highly specific wave-length and a specific set of atmospheric conditions.

(Gurr 1987: 3)

You sit and watch the stage
Your back is turned –
To what?
The firing squad
Shoots in the back of the neck
Whole nations have been caught
Looking the wrong way
I want to remind you
Of what you forgot to see
On the way here
      (Bond 1983: xliv–xiv)

In the first two chapters of this book, I have for the most part set aside the question of the relation of theatre to the broad social and political world in order to focus on the theatrical event in itself and then on the human subjects and agents at work in the theatrical event. But of course theatre happens in a larger context. Indeed, with its need for a public place, for physical resources, workers and an audience, theatre is more complexly and intimately intertwined with the outside world than many literary and other artistic activities. Moreover, changes in the world are bound to produce changes in theatrical production. Any well-rounded theory of the theatre, therefore, must take account of how theatre relates to the forces of the outside world.

As in the previous chapters, here I have chosen to focus on three theoretical approaches. All of the theories discussed in the first two chapters make some contribution to understanding the place of theatre in the world. Feminism, as I have noted, is a profoundly political and social mode of understanding: women become gendered and oppressed by a patriarchal system at work everywhere in the world around us. But even deconstruction, in the hands of Derrida, has been brought to bear on such issues as apartheid and nuclear apocalypse. Nonetheless, I have chosen to focus here on materialist theory, postmodernism and post-colonialism.

Although materialist theory has arisen historically in the context of western capitalism, and although it has traditionally affirmed a Marxist emphasis on the dominance of economic factors over other social and political forces, materialism widely conceived is a general historical theory arguably applicable to any time and place. This is not true of postmodernism and post-colonialism, which attempt to account for a narrower range of historical situations. For both postmodernism and post-colonialism, however, the period accounted for includes that of our present world, and therefore they are both particularly relevant for an introduction to the relations between world and theatre. Also, there are a number of overlapping concerns between the three theoretical fields: the Marxist theorist Fredric Jameson, for instance, has written extensively on postmodernism, and Karl Marx, to whom all materialist theory owes a great debt of influence, ends the first volume of *Capital* with a chapter on the place of colonization in the development of capitalism.

1 MATERIALIST THEORY

It has been claimed on occasion that Paul de Man is a materialist thinker, inasmuch as his theory of language as inescapable metaphor posits language outside notions of intention and makes of it a binding force in human existence, history and exchange. Language is the material reality in which we do all our thinking and acting. Such a claim, however, radically misconstrues the basic principles of materialist thought. When Marx writes in the first volume of *Capital* that the history of capitalist expropriation 'is written in the annals of mankind in letters of blood and fire' (Marx 1977: 875), he is not just speaking metaphorically – although he is doing so – nor would a materialist think that these words circulate in a linguistic sphere without connection to the real. 'Letters of blood and fire' implies that language takes place in a wider range of human material concerns which give to words their meaning and import. A basic task of materialist theory is to understand the elaborate relations between language, literature and art, on the one hand, and society, history and the material world, on the other.

All materialist theory has a few basic premises. It does not have much sympathy for a belief in the natural, freestanding individual. Like semiotics and deconstruction, it rejects the belief that we are independent agents who are free to impress our ideas on the world – rather, the world impresses itself on our ideas. Our thoughts and ideas are made by the world around us. If we want to understand ourselves and our world, we have to understand the material forces at work in our world. Marxism says that we can best understand those forces in terms of modes of production, the structure of economic relations in any society. This structure is characterized by two factors: the relation of workers to the work situation and the relation of the workers to what they make. Under capitalism, workers have relatively weak claims to the work situation and to the products of their labour. Imagine the stereotypical scene often depicted in film and on television: after many years with a company, a man is fired and told to clean out his desk. We see him leaving with a shabby cardboard box containing a few pencils and personal photos. He has no right to his job, his desk, his tasks, his place in the workforce. He also leaves behind all the profit that his long labour has produced for the company. This is in partial contrast to feudalism, the mode of production that preceded capitalism. Under feudalism the worker handed the profits of his labour over to the feudal lord, but he had some expectation that he would not be let go or turfed out, that he had a right to his serfdom – in fact, it was a crime for 'masterless men' not to have some connection to a feudal household. This is not to say that feudalism was a kinder, gentler system than capitalism; rather, both exploit and alienate workers in their own ways.

In traditional Marxist materialism, culture is thought of as a superstructure dependent upon a socioeconomic base. The base/superstructure model sometimes tends toward an oversimplification in which culture is more or less completely determined by economics and art is most often a direct reflection of economic conditions. The character of the base changes historically through variations in the mode of production, and much Marxist literary criticism is concerned with understanding the relations between economics and literature in a specific time and place: the Canadian scholar N.N. Feltes, for example, has studied the modes of production of novels in Victorian England and the effect that modes of production have on the structure and content of those novels (Feltes 1986).

Much Marxist literary criticism, and much Marxist theory, escapes the reductionism threatened by the base/superstructure model. The French Marxist Louis Althusser, for instance, argues that the relations between economics and culture are 'overdetermined', that is, subject to the influence of any number of historical forces not narrowly economic. Althusser sees cultural activity as one of many 'ideological state apparatuses', systems (schools, institutions, families, the media, corporate culture) whereby people are made to submit to capitalist activity not through force and coercion (that is the sphere of the army and the police) but through 'interpellation', whereby people are brought to identify with the roles capitalism needs them to play (Althusser 1971: 123–73). Ideology leads us to think that capitalist exploitation, for instance, is natural, inescapable or good. We come to believe that human beings are inherently competitive and back-stabbing, that looking out for number one is the only way to get by in the world, or that, despite any evidence to the contrary, capitalism is in the long run good for everybody. 'Ideology' – like difference and the other, an extremely resonant concept in recent theory – is the imposition and enactment of these beliefs. Althusser borrows from Lacan the notion of the subject, but for Althusser the subject comes into being in ideology, economics and politics, rather than in language and sexual identification. For Althusser, however, art is not strictly ideological, but provides a kind of distance and insight that ideology obscures. Marxism is a science, according to Althusser, and provides a clear understanding of the reality of capitalism. Art does not provide scientific understanding, but it does expose the tensions and complexities that ideology tries to keep us from seeing. The French theorist Pierre Macherey has attempted to systematize the understanding of how the internal tensions in a work of art expose the reality that underlies ideology (Macherey 1978). Basically, since ideology is a misrepresentation, when artists write within that ideology, in following through with what they want to present, there will be moments, large or small, when the ideology is exposed as untrue or contradictory.

The British theorist Raymond Williams complicates the relations between socioeconomics and literature in a different way. In place of monolithic capitalist forces of production, he introduces the tripartite idea of the 'dominant', the 'residual' and the 'emergent' (Williams 1977: 121–7). The dominant are those hegemonic forces (of capitalism, in our world) which are most strong at any moment of history; the residual are those once strong forces associated with the past which are now weakened yet still capable of influence (the way family and clan loyalties, for instance, work against the dog-eat-dog individualism of the market place); the emergent are forces in ascendance which have not yet come into full strength. In any era, the dominant forces exert the most influence; residual and emergent forces, however, can also have effects. A work of culture can combine elements of all three forces, thereby rendering complex and even relatively autonomous its relations with the socioeconomic order.

In The Political Unconscious Fredric Jameson redraws the base/superstructure model in such a way as to equalize cultural and economic forces as determinants in the mode of production (Jameson 1981: 32–8). Economics affects culture and culture affects economics. Think of the way that cultural and political advances in women's rights have reshaped the workforce over the last fifty years. The German theorist Theodor Adorno sees in modern art not a reflection of capitalist oppression but more or less unfettered works of reason and enlightenment which, especially in their formal liberations, point beyond the blinkers of capitalism (Adorno 1984). In their complexities, avant-garde music or novels such as James Joyce's Ulysses escape being pawns of capitalism in the way that mainstream television and magazines, for instance, are. From this view, nobody is made a more subservient worker by listening to the twelve-tone music of Arnold Schoenberg. Adorno does think, on the other hand, that most popular music, even that with leftist content, helps to keep people in line. Imagine the office worker on lunch break listening to the latest big rock band on a Walkman before dutifully returning to the office for the afternoon. In some way, the music has refreshed the worker to go back to the job.

Despite these complications, much Marxist theory ultimately falls back on the determinant power of the economic. Althusser's sense of overdetermination is tied to his sense of the economic as determinant 'in the last instance', although the last instance 'never comes' (Althusser 1969: 113); Jameson's redrawing of the balance between cultural and economic forces leaves the economic still 'privileged'. Jameson also holds on to the notion of 'totality', which implies a coherence and unity to any social order, no matter how complex and qualified. Some materialist thinkers have tried to posit a materialism without a centre, as in the work of the French theorist Chantal Mouffe and the Latin-American Ernesto Laclau, who add gender and race to class as determinant considerations (Laclau 1988; Mouffe 1988). Similarly, cultural materialism, a Marxist-influenced attempt to politicize the study of culture, as practised in such works as Jonathan Dollimore and Alan Sinfield's *Political Shakespeare*, opens materialism on to a more heterogeneous, particularized and non-systematized understanding of the interplay of cultural, economic and social forces (Dollimore and Sinfield 1985). Terry Eagleton's stridently Marxist work has moved to a more flexible materialism, as in his relatively recent *Ideology: An Introduction*, which is less systematizing than exploratory (Eagleton 1991). In the United States, new historicism, associated most strongly with Stephen Greenblatt, is a materialist movement inasmuch as it seeks to find broad cultural connections between historical situations and particular works of art that arise in those situations, but its theoretical and practical connections with Marxism and Marxist politics are much weaker than in most materialist theory (Greenblatt 1988).

Two other materialist theorists worthy of special attention are Walter Benjamin and Michel Foucault, each discussed elsewhere. Benjamin posits the 'Now of recognizability', the historically limited perspective from which anyone must perceive the world, especially the past (Benjamin 1989: 50). Partly due to a perspective defined by his Marxist understanding, Benjamin sees art, which has traditionally been hallowed by an 'aura' of beauty and spirit which privileges it and separates it from the world at large, in a new light:

> Whoever has emerged victorious participates to this day in the triumphal procession in which the present rulers step over those who are lying prostrate. According to traditional practice, the spoils are carried along in the procession. They are called cultural treasures, and a historical materialist views them with cautious detachment. For without exception the cultural treasures he surveys have an origin which he cannot contemplate without horror. They owe their existence not only to the efforts of the great minds and talents who have created them, but also to the anonymous toil of their contemporaries. There is no document of civilization which is not at the same time a document of barbarism.
>
> (Benjamin 1969: 256)

Thus, for Benjamin, we must bring very ambivalent feelings to our understanding of art, since it is often the product of, and in sympathy with, a history of exploitation and oppression. Benjamin's work is infused with a messianic faith in a utopian moment when 'one single catastrophe which keeps piling wreckage upon wreckage' gives way to a leap into the 'free heavens' of the future.

Michel Foucault offers historical materialist alternatives to both Marx and Freud. Much of Foucault's work traces the effects of the discursive practices of various scientific disciplines at certain times in history on the production and limitation of knowledge. The rise of scientific thought brings with it possibilities and limitations for how we understand the world. Like Derrida and de Man, Foucault undermines the belief in science and reason as truth – truth is what is made or allowed to seem true. Foucault moves in his work from the study of discursive formations (scientific or medical discourse, for instance) to the study of apparatuses – systems and institutions (prisons, hospitals) through which power is enacted. For Foucault, these apparatuses, more than economics and modes of production, are what constitute human social patterns. These apparatuses are also responsible for enacting human subjectivity. Here Foucault posits a history of the subject different from those of both Freud and Althusser. In *The History of Sexuality*, Foucault takes issue with Freud's sense of human sexuality as repressed: for Foucault, society rather fosters and channels sexuality, which only exists as instituted by social apparatuses (Foucault 1980a). In place of Freud's psychic models, Foucault offers a theory of the human as a conglomerate of sub-individuals, each enacted by different aspects and apparatuses of power (Foucault 1980b: 208): I, for instance, am a conglomerate of son, heterosexual, father, academic, citizen, consumer, etc. Behind this socially activated set of sub-individuals lies nothing, perhaps, and 'man' as thought of in the West is historically no more than a face drawn in the sand to be washed away by the sea of future institutions (Foucault 1973: 387).

As a practice of studying the relations between a society and its theatre, materialist theory is potentially useful for the understanding of any historical situation and could address the effect of a slave economy and the cloistering of women in the household on the theatre of ancient Athens, as well as the effect of high commodification on recent musical theatre, such as Andrew

Lloyd Webber's *Phantom of the Opera* or the Disney corporation's *Beauty and the Beast*, whereby theatre becomes more economically and technically endowed and more profitable, and yet more precarious and directly susceptible to market forces than ever before – a theatre that sells out in a number of senses.

Materialism and Shakespeare

Shakespeare worked in a period of transition from feudalism to capitalism. He and his co-workers were officially feudal servants in the household of the king – the 'King's Men'. But he was also a shareholder in the theatre company, entitled to part of the profits, and the company hired other workers, not owners of the company, who were paid only modest wages and who, lacking job security, were relatively easy to let go. One of the most accomplished studies of the relationship between a particular theatre and its historical situation is Walter Cohen's *Drama of a Nation: Public Theater in Renaissance England and Spain* (1985). Cohen finds the pre-conditions for Renaissance public theatre in the emerging capitalism of early modern Europe, which made possible everything from the economics and structures of the theatre companies to the existence and function of professional dramatists. Cohen also traces the influence of class relations and attitudes on particular genres: romantic comedy, for instance (*As You Like It* or *The Merchant of Venice*), arises in the tensions between the aristocracy and the up-and-coming bourgeoisie (Cohen 1985: 189–90). Finally, Cohen traces the economic and social forces that led to the demise of the public theatre and the birth of more elitist and exclusive theatres throughout the seventeenth century.

Another approach to understanding Shakespeare's theatre and its relation to Renaissance culture arises from the work of the Russian theorist Mikhail Bakhtin. In a study of the French Renaissance writer Pierre Rabelais, Bakhtin develops the sense of Rabelais' connection, in his writing, to forms of popular peasant culture such as feasts and carnivals (Bakhtin 1968). These forms of popular culture are characterized by talking back to the established ruling-class ideology, through irreverence, humour, parody and bawdiness – qualities which have come to be called the carnivalesque. The voicing of popular attitudes in Rabelais' work makes them 'polyphonic' (multi-voiced) and 'dialogic' (creating a dialogue between different positions – popular and aristocratic, for instance – without allowing one position or voice to dominate). Now, strangely enough, Bakhtin did not think that theatre and drama were particularly polyphonic or dialogic; he saw these qualities much more in novels, especially those of Fyodor Dostoevsky (Bakhtin 1984: 34). Others, however, have found popular, carnivalesque, polyphonic and dialogic elements in theatre, especially that of Shakespeare. The German critic Robert Weimann, for instance, has studied the way that Shakespeare's theatre voices both the official position of the ruling class and the objections of the people. This happens not only through the structure of the stage itself – upstage is mainly a place for authoritative pronouncements; the lip of the stage is a place for characters to become informal and intimate with the lower-class audience – but in the putting on stage of both kings and clowns (Weimann 1978). David Wiles has written a book on the role of clowns in Shakespeare's theatre. He notes, for instance, that most public performances ended with a bawdy jig in which the clowns got the last word, even if the play that day had been austere, conservative and elitist (Wiles 1987). It would have been difficult, and probably not something anyone set out to do, for public theatre to take an unadulteratedly subversive and anti-authoritarian position in Shakespeare's time, but there are ways of seeing that his theatre did set one ideological position in dialogue with another.

Looking at Shakespeare in a contemporary setting, Robert Wallace and Richard Paul Knowles have done materialist studies of Canada's Stratford Festival. In a study of alternative and marginal theatre in Canada, Wallace discusses in passing the conditions of production at Stratford. He notes the effect of government arts grants to the festival: such grants to Stratford profoundly limit the money available to smaller, more experimental and indigenous theatres, even while shrinking grants to Stratford itself mean the festival must rely more and more on box-office success for its survival. Needing to draw large crowds, Stratford has been forced to rely on Broadway and West-End style musicals; appeal as much to American tourists from neighbouring states as to the people of Ontario and Canada; and stick to a formula of proven success and low-risk accessibility, often at the expense of its original mandate to produce serious Shakespearean theatre (Wallace 1990: 97–105).

In work more narrowly focused on the festival, Knowles lays out Stratford's shifting history, from 'the founding itself, ... a delayed colonial celebration of a 19th-century brand of imperialist British nationhood (one that allows Canada's national theatre to be dedicated to the plays of the canonical British writer)' to 'the current "multinationalist" moment, which extends from the early 80s to the present, in the context of free trade, "globalization", and intercultural tourism' (Knowles 1994a: 2). In a review of the 1993 season, Knowles outlines his materialist suppositions:

> No production of Shakespeare can be reviewed outside of its material context.... At Stratford, Ontario, in 1993, where even more than at most theaters the institutional context tends to function with remarkable directness as an Ideological State Apparatus, funded by government and corporate grants, and catering to an audience it presents as monolithic, the production of Shakespeare is necessarily the reproduction of a complex and shifting but nevertheless conservative, affirmative culture.
>
> (Knowles 1994b: 225)

In other words, Knowles argues that the economic situation of the festival, its corporate sponsors, the corporate structure of the festival company itself, its high ticket prices and reliance upon well-off, older, often American, tourists mean that the festival is bound to present productions attuned to the dominant corporate-capitalist ideology. In Benjamin's terms, a Stratford production is a document of barbarism.

Such readings have the advantage of a straightforward logic and groundedness, but they run the risk of downplaying the intangibles and undecidables of literature and culture. For instance, in a number of plays – in the epilogue of *A Midsummer Night's Dream* and in the choruses of *Henry V* and *The Winter's Tale* – Shakespeare addresses his audience as 'gentles'. Such a tradition continues in our own day when an audience is addressed as 'ladies and gentlemen'. Most of us are not ladies and gentlemen, at least not in the sense of belonging to a certain privileged class. In our day, such class associations have been largely lost, and 'ladies and gentlemen' is more or less a term of mild flattery intimating that we are a polite and civilized group. In Shakespeare's day, the class associations of a term like 'gentles' were much stronger, and a large portion of the audience were decidedly not members of the class that could legitimately be called 'gentles'. Certainly it is important to realize this, and to note the discrepancy between this form of address and the composition of the actual audience. But what does it mean? Are the plays symbolically recognizing only part of the audience to the exclusion of others? Do they rather level the audience by raising all to the same social status? Do they merely flatter in a way that no one present would really take seriously? *A Midsummer Night's Dream*, it is believed, was first presented at an aristocratic wedding. Was 'gentles', therefore, an accurate and exclusionary description of its initial audience? What of the other two plays, which have their origin in the public theatre? And what of *A Midsummer Night's Dream* when later presented to a heterogeneous public audience? Perhaps there are no simple and concrete answers to our questions, and whatever effect was intended or achieved is not one we can easily identify. We are left in the realm of perspective and conjecture.

Similar problems confront us if we seek to tie the representations of complex theatrical and dramatic works to historical reality. For instance, much recent English social history tells us that the family in early modern England was an institution of affection and care. *The Winter's Tale* is an early modern play which represents the life of a family. Its first half is a nightmarish depiction of jealousy, paranoia and cruelty; its second half presents a fanciful recovery of lost loved ones. Do either of these aspects of the play relate to the family as historians present it? If not, why not? If so, how? Is it possible to make both parts of the play, seemingly diametrically opposed, relate to the same history? And what do we think when we realize that some social historians present, in contrast, a much bleaker account of the early modern family? Materialist criticism will seem simplistic and mechanical if it underplays the complexities of the relations between culture and society.

In his *Theses on Feuerbach*, Marx declares that the point is not merely to interpret the world but to change it. Materialist analysis of theatre is concerned not only with positioning theatre as a consequence of its place in history but also with seeing how theatre can affect the world. Artaud calls for a theatre which would have as direct an effect on society as the plague, but theatre is rarely so bluntly powerful. Stories of plays changing the course of history are woefully rare: the Earl of Essex staged the deposition of the king in *Richard II* to stir up support when he rose against Elizabeth, but the insurrection failed anyway. Those who study the political force of theatre have to look for more subtle modes of influence.

In *Radical Tragedy* (1984), Jonathan Dollimore discusses the political force of theatre in early modern England. Treating the plays mainly as intellectual drama, he sees the tragedies of Shakespeare and his contemporaries as undermining and interrogating the ideology and institutions of religion and state in a way that ultimately contributes to the outbreak of the Civil War and the overthrow of the monarchy in the 1640s (Dollimore 1984: 4). Thus, the drama of the period not only articulates ideological crisis but also precipitates it (p. 5). *King Lear*, for instance, with its display of dysfunctional and self-serving power-grabbing, demonstrates to the audience how the so-called 'laws of human kindness operate in the service of property, contractual, and power relations' (p. 198) and presents ideas closely related to those in radical pamphlets of the Civil War period.

Dollimore is a cultural materialist, writing in a British tradition of intellectual activism, and for strategic reasons over and above scholarly ones he perhaps overemphasizes the potential for culture to act forcefully and decisively on political and social issues. In the United States, cultural materialism has been less influential than new historicism, spearheaded by Stephen Greenblatt. New historicism has been strongly influenced by the work of Foucault on the ways that institutions of power both foster and channel such forces as sexuality, madness, illness and crime (think of Renaissance theatre as one of Foucault's 'apparatuses'). This has given rise to the twin concepts of subversion and containment: the state needs to foster insurrection in order to exercise its powers of response; representations of radical and subversive activity and thought on the stage, especially when ultimately overcome, contribute to the legitimacy and authority of the powers that be. Moreover, monarchical power in the early modern period worked in part by representational display akin to theatre, inspiring awe, reverence and fear into the public by parading its might before them, further drawing politics and performance into close complicity. Renaissance drama and theatre, from this perspective, contribute inescapably to the regeneration of the state. Foucault, however, does not preach only defeatism in the face of power – he himself was a committed activist in areas such as prison reform; nor is there any essential reason why subversion must always be coupled with containment – such a coupling makes the world, of the Renaissance or the late twentieth century, seem more absolutist and fated than it necessarily is.

Brecht and *Coriolanus*

Earlier, I made mention of Terry Eagleton's discussion of the task of the 'revolutionary cultural worker' as, in part, the appropriation of works of art through radical interpretation. Sometimes this manifests itself in seeing, as Benjamin declares, the barbarism in cultural treasures; other times it comes in seeing the revolutionary import in seemingly conservative or reactionary works. An example of this second approach can be seen in Bertolt Brecht's materialist analysis of the opening scene of *Coriolanus*. Brecht is willing to rewrite Shakespeare, if necessary, but in this case he sets his troupe the narrower task of analysing without adding to or changing Shakespeare's text, and of bringing out aspects of interpretation by staging and production alone (Brecht 1964: 259, 265). In contrast to the 'bourgeois theatre', which focuses all its attention on the hero, and thereby aligns itself with the patricians' cause (p. 255), Brecht is explicitly interested in examining the class struggle in the opening scene from the plebeians' situation: 'we want to find out as much about the plebeians as we can' (p. 256). Brecht reads such an interest in Shakespeare's text itself.

For Brecht, Shakespeare's play is 'splendidly realistic' (p. 254). The opening scene demonstrates 'how hard it is for the oppressed to become united' (p. 252) and teaches, among other things, 'That the position of the oppressed classes can be strengthened by the threat of war and weakened by its outbreak' (p. 264). The play is rich in conflict and contradiction, and, because it offers no easy solutions, it 'gives rise to discomfort' (p. 255); in this way it offers 'first-hand experience of dialectics' (p. 265), of working through oppositions.

The point of producing the scene becomes to 'strengthen' these aspects of Shakespeare's text. For example, by making the weapons of the plebeians makeshift and yet ingenious and effective, and by contrasting them with the professional soldiers and their weaponry under patrician control, we can see that the plebeians are a force to be reckoned with and yet in a precarious position in their class struggle (pp. 257–8). At the end of the scene, when an external threat of war has united – but only partly and temporarily – the classes of Rome, it is important to show the limits of this union in the way the members of the two classes interact (pp. 262–3).

For Brecht there is great revolutionary potential in reason and understanding, and a careful analysis of Shakespeare furthers our understanding: 'The wealth of events in a single short scene. Compare today's plays with their poverty of content!' (p. 255). He notes, 'within these complex events on a particular morning in Rome ... there is much that a sharp eye can pick out. And certainly if you can find clues to these events, then all power to the audience!' (p. 259).

When Brecht came to adapt the play, however, he went some measure beyond interpreting it, to changing it. In his version, the plebeians are a much more dedicated force than in Shakespeare. They never waver in their belief that it was right to banish Coriolanus, and one of them says:

> I have the feeling, shared, I'm told, by many
> Others, that Rome's a better place
> With that man gone, a city worth defending
> Perhaps for the first time since it was founded.
>
> (Brecht 1972: 138)

Coriolanus doesn't give up his attack on Rome because he's tied to his mother's apron strings, but because he realizes that the people of Rome have banded together to resist him. His failure is not so much tragic as something to be celebrated.

Materialism and Utopia

As an alternative to questioning or subverting the status quo, cultural forms can also take on a utopian or romance function, presenting a vision of a different social order preferable to our own. As a public space, theatre functions as what the anthropologist Victor Turner calls the liminoid, a place set apart for the process of social or personal transformation, or what Foucault calls heterotopia, a quasi-public space which functions to reflect, expose, invert, support or compensate for the outside world (Foucault 1986: 24–7). Thematically, there is in many of Shakespeare's plays the 'green world', a place of retreat from the dominant social order. In the romances, the possibility of open and endless transformation – 'storm perpetual' or 'unpath'd waters, undream'd shores' in The Winter's Tale – is suggested, only to be foreclosed by happy return at the end of the play.

Many materialist theorists are wary of the utopian mode in culture. In a recent study of the English Romantics, the deconstructionist-Marxist Forest Pyle argues that the idea of a transformed future is always unproductively limited by imaginative efforts to represent it, and that it is better to leave it as an absence or gap open to unforeseeable conditions to come (Pyle 1995: 173–5). Similarly, Jameson argues that, although the utopian drive is inherent in culture and is not unconnected to the revolutionary drive, it often takes a nostalgic or reactionary form, finding solutions in unfortunate places (Jameson 1981: 281–99). Cohen, however, stands by the importance of the romantic drive in theatre and society:

Indeed, Marxism has always wagered that in the long run human history would have, or at least could have, the structure of romance. Precisely in its utopianism, then, romance may offer a legitimate vision not of the prehistory lived in class society, but of that authentic history that may someday succeed it.

(Cohen 1985: 391)

Similarly, the theorist of pedagogy Paulo Freire, discussed more fully elsewhere in this chapter, writes:

On the other hand – while I certainly cannot ignore hopelessness as a concrete entity, nor turn a blind eye to the historical, economic, and social reasons that explain that hopelessness – I do not understand human existence, and the struggle needed to improve it, apart from hope and dream.

(Freire 1994: 8)

If the utopian drive is important – as is, at the same time, a sense of actuality and possibility – then the task is, in the phrase of Raymond Williams, 'to make hope practical, rather than despair convincing' (Williams 1983: 240).

Some of the problems and tensions around the adequacy of any utopian model can be seen in Northrop Frye's regard for The Tempest. For Frye, romance is the most profound literary form, and The Tempest is one of our most important visions of an ideal community. Because of Frye's faith in western liberal democracy, romance for him is merely a movement forward – albeit a giant leap forward – from the way things are in the modern world. Many materialist thinkers do not have such faith in the western tradition. Post-colonial writers, for instance (as discussed in the final part of this chapter), have seen in The Tempest not a vision of an ideal society but rather a vision of imperialist practice and ideology. In an early introduction, Frye denies the relevance of colonialism for an understanding of The Tempest:

> It is a little puzzling why New World imagery should be so prominent in *The Tempest*, which really has nothing to do with the new world, beyond Ariel's reference to the 'still-vexed Bermoothes' and a general, if vague, resemblance between the relation of Caliban to the other characters and that of the American Indians to the colonizers and drunken sailors who came to exterminate and enslave them.
>
> (Frye 1969: 1371)

Later, Frye is able to see the relation between imperialism and the play, but only by turning away from the extermination and enslavement he has already recognized. Frye connects the play to the idealized imperialist vision of Samuel Daniel in *Musophilus*, 'where the poet speaks of extending English into unknown parts of the world'. Frye adds, 'Note that Daniel is talking about language, not military conquest: the power of art, not arms' (Frye 1986: 184). But Shakespeare's play is filled with much more force and cruelty than this implies. It may be that any utopian expression is bound to trip up somewhere along the line; *The Tempest* itself recognizes this in the utopian vision of Gonzalo, the end of which contradicts the beginning (there would be no kings; he would be king). Utopian visions are to be taken with a grain of salt, but whether they should be avoided altogether is another question.

Cultural Studies

A currently busy area of materialist work is what is called Cultural Studies, which began at Birmingham in Great Britain in the 1950s and has since arisen in various permutations in the United States, Canada, Australia and parts of Africa (Davies 1995). Although it is by definition and practice an open and provisional activity, Cultural Studies has shown certain characteristics which have remained more or less important in its wanderings. First and foremost, for many Cultural Studies is not merely academic but politically engaged (although this is the aspect that has been lost the most, especially in the United States). The politics of Cultural Studies has moved from a narrowly Marxist focus to an expansive inclusion of new issues such as gender and race. Connected with political engagement, Cultural Studies has been predominantly interested in contemporary popular culture and struggle. As a consequence, in its travels Cultural Studies has embraced the local conditions of culture, so that each locale must reinvent the particulars of Cultural Studies, what it is about and what it sets out to accomplish (Grossberg et al. 1992: 1–16).

Cultural Studies tends to focus on popular culture in two senses: mass culture and the marginal, alternative forms of activity of the 'people' in a socialist sense. In Theatre Studies, this might entail, on the one hand, The Phantom of the Opera, and on the other, various alternative theatrical collectives at work in a particular locale. The studies of Knowles or Wallace of Stratford or queer theatre could be taken as instances of localized Cultural Studies, specifically Canadian, as it relates to theatre.

The cover of a recent cultural theory reader features images of the Mona Lisa used in an advertisement for dairy cream (Easthope and McGowan 1993). Cultural Studies is interested in high western culture predominantly in the ways it is appropriated in current contexts. Much recent study of Shakespeare – in which the visual device of reconfiguring Shakespeare's picture is commonplace – could be taken in this regard as Cultural Studies. Gary Taylor, for instance, writes of 'Shakesperotics' as 'everything a society does in the name ... of Shakespeare' (Taylor 1989: 6), while Graham Holderness, in The Shakespeare Myth, writes, 'For every particular present, Shakespeare is, here, now, always, what is currently being made of him' (Holderness 1988: xvi). Think of t-shirts, coffee mugs, ads for computer software, national theatres, tourist-town economies, school systems and radical theatrical adaptations. Canadian Cultural Studies, for instance, will be interested in Shakespeare inasmuch as his work takes root in a specifically Canadian institution such as Stratford, or the writing of Northrop Frye, or the feminist collective Nightwood Theatre and its production of Ann-Marie MacDonald's *Goodnight Desdemona*.

Although there are ways in which Cultural Studies can take an interest in something like Shakespeare or the *Mona Lisa*, works from the past are by no means the central focus of Cultural Studies work. The compendious collection *Cultural Studies* features only one article out of thirty-nine on material not explicitly contemporary (Grossberg *et al.* 1992: 593–612). That this article is on Shakespeare is less telling than that it stands alone, isolated and somewhat forlorn. For Cultural Studies, Shakespeare and the past are just not that important.

Cultural Studies perhaps here plays its hand a little too strongly. Shakespeare may have been dead for almost 400 years, but his work continues to play an active role in the world around us. A recent collection of essays on Shakespeare, *Marxist Shakespeares*, includes not only various analyses of the relations between Shakespeare's plays and theatre and the economic and political realities of the seventeenth century, but also essays on recent developments regarding Shakespeare's place in the current global economy. These include essays on the new Globe Theatre in London and the recent burgeoning of mainstream films based on Shakespeare: Kenneth Branagh's *Henry V* and *Hamlet*, the adaptation of *The Taming of the Shrew*, *Ten Things I Hate About You*, and Baz Luhrmann's *William Shakespeare's Romeo + Juliet* (Howard and Shershow 2001).

QUESTIONS ONE MIGHT ASK OF A PLAY OR PERFORMANCE

What economic and material forces allow you to study or practise theatre? Family background, class, state or private educa-

tion, government grants, part- or full-time work? What ideology
lies behind you believing that studying theatre is a good thing?
To what degree is your interest in theatre contingent on the job
prospects associated with it?

What material factors did it take to mount a play or performance you have seen or been in? How do economics affect a
performance? Think of the realities of securing a theatre, sup-
porting more or fewer actors and technicians, paying for rights,
costumes, sets, advertising, etc.

What elements of society make up the audience at any particular play or performance? Is it class based? Is the ideology of the
play geared to the make-up of the audience? Who would be out
of place at this play or performance?

What is the relation between the play or performance and
capitalist ideology? Does it support or subvert status quo ways
of thinking? Does it do this in content, in form, or both?

2 POSTMODERN THEORY

The theorist Nick Kaye notes the difficulties with 'any categorical
definition of what the 'postmodern' actually is' (Kaye 1994: 1).
Part of the problem has to do with 'post'. The prefix 'post' in a
term can indicate a range of relationships with something that
comes before. At its simplest, it indicates that something comes
after something else, that one thing has ended and another
begun. Post-structuralism, therefore, comes after structuralism,
and, as we have seen, puts an end to many of the assumptions of
structuralism, replacing them with new ideas of its own. But
'post' also indicates that one thing follows another, proceeding
under its influence and effects. Post-structuralism works from
many of the premises of structuralism, taking them further.
There would be no post-structuralism without a structuralism to

build on. These complexities are also at work in the relations between postmodernism and modernism.

But what is modernism, the thing that postmodernism is said to come after? Perhaps a better place to start is to ask what is modernity? Modernity is the condition, the characteristic patterns, of the modern world. The modern world has been developing for 500 years or so, beginning in Europe and gradually spreading to the rest of the globe. The world has become more and more modern over this period, so that in some ways modernity really comes into its own only in the nineteenth century. It is hard to give a simple set of characteristics of the world over a 500-year period, but it is relatively safe to say that modernity has seen the rise of such things as science, technology (in everything from communications to warfare to medicine to transportation), urbanization, population growth, the nation state, individualism, capitalism, civil rights, and experimentation in the arts and sciences. Modernism, then, is the pattern of social and cultural responses to life in the modern world, to modernity. Again, it is difficult to catch everything, but modernism in art has seen, for instance, the birth of the novel, film, photography, classical music, jazz, ballet and modern dance. In theatre, modernism includes Chekhov, Ibsen, Shaw and Brecht. Modernism has often been characterized by experimentation in the arts, by a drive towards the new.

Understanding postmodernism, therefore, should begin with understanding its relation to modernism. This relation, however, is open to different interpretations. The critic Jon Whitmore, speaking of postmodern theatre, writes that it 'carries modernist principles beyond anticipated boundaries or ... rejects modernist principles altogether' (Whitmore 1994: 3). Even if these approaches are not exactly opposites, they are very divergent. It might help to begin with some ideas about the relationship between postmodernity and modernity. Something striking seems to have happened to modernity in the last fifty years or so. Some of its aspects seem to be unravelling – the nation state, for instance, seems to be swamped by international political and economic unions and forces; on the other hand, modern cities just keep getting bigger and technology continues to change the way we live. If anything, what is new in postmodernity is the speed at which changes occur. It's as if modernity has been put on overdrive. We may also notice how certain compelling aspects of modernity are changed by this. Individualism and personal freedom are important in modernity because they were striking notions and ran against patterns of conformity, servitude and slavery that were a long time in being overcome. For the contemporary city-dweller living on his or her own, personal freedom is taken for granted. At the same time, however, how individualist can you be when you are one of 6 billion people on the planet and most of your tastes, dictated by market trends, are shared by millions of others? Also affected is the importance of the new. When the French modernist poet Gerard de Nerval walked a lobster on a leash in nineteenth-century Paris, he was doing something strikingly individual and unique; when one of our contemporaries adopts the latest fashion trend, even if it is done a few months before everybody else jumps on the bandwagon, is it really very individual or very new? Often these fashion trends are consciously 'retro', not new at all but picking up an out-of-fashion trend from the past – hence the resurgence of children's scooters and martinis and martini glasses in the last few years. Even true breakthroughs in technology are so commonplace that they no longer have the feeling of being new that invention had in the past.

Postmodernism, then, can be seen as the social and cultural patterns of response to being in the postmodern world, to postmodernity. What those patterns may be are characterized differently by various theorists of the postmodern.

Postmodern theory and theories of the postmodern differ depending on what they understand the focus of postmodernism to be. For the French theorist François Lyotard and the Italian Gianni Vattimo, postmodernism is a way of thinking. In *The Postmodern Condition*, Lyotard argues that postmodernism entails the failure of all master narratives, such as the myth of progress and the idea of one true religion, which might allow for a total and unified understanding of the world. In place of master narratives, Lyotard posits micronarratives and language games, performability over truth, pluricity over unity, exchange over legitimation (Lyotard 1984): people act out and exchange many different ways of understanding rather than relying on one overarching truth. We mix and match values and outlooks as circumstances demand. For Vattimo, as we saw in the section on phenomenology, postmodern thinking entails 'weak thought', provisional and ongoing, without a foundation in universal or trans-historical truth (Vattimo 1988). To live in the postmodern condition, phenomenologically speaking, is to live without a grand and deep sense of abiding truth.

For the Canadian theorist Linda Hutcheon, the postmodern is much more an artistic style, recognizable by its self-reflexivity – its self-awareness – and irony, especially in its relations to the practices and objects of the surrounding culture and the cultural past. Postmodernists like to play with the cultural images of the past – remember the Mona Lisa in the ad for dairy cream. Postmodern work often takes the form of parody, which has a highly divided and ambivalent relation to its object of imitation. Does it celebrate or deride the work being parodied? Although Hutcheon recognizes that the postmodern, as she defines it, has been commercialized and appropriated by hegemonic forces, such as capitalism and imperialism, she insists on the power, no matter how ambivalent, of postmodern art to contest the status quo (Hutcheon 1988).

For the French theorist Jean Baudrillard and the American Marxist Fredric Jameson, in very different ways, postmodernism is first and foremost a social and cultural predicament.

Baudrillard is interested in a history of simulacra, or simulations, from the Renaissance, when the rise of public theatre brought acting and simulation to a new prominence, to the present, which ends in the present stage of third-order simulacra in which simulation is so widespread as to create a 'hyper-reality' which has subsumed the place of nature and the real (think of Disneyland and 'reality' television shows such as *Survivor*) (Baudrillard 1983). With the new cultural order comes a new economic and political order: 'the political economy of the sign' (Baudrillard 1981). We don't so much make things any more, but rather exchange images. In light of this new prolifera-tion of image and information, thinkers from Marx to Foucault, still concerned with production rather than reproduction, are rendered obsolete (Baudrillard 1975, 1987). Jameson's under-standing of postmodernism is evident in the title of his book *Postmodernism, or, The Cultural Logic of Late Capitalism* (Jameson 1991). For Jameson, postmodernism is the cultural predicament brought on by late capitalism's extension of commodification into virtually all aspects of social and cultural life. There's noth-ing that isn't bought and sold anymore: babies, body parts, the Royal Canadian Mounted Police. Cultural production under late capitalism's volatile and transient market configurations often takes the form of 'pastiche', a borrowing from anywhere with-out a commitment to anything, satire without any bite. Moreover, the proliferation of technologies, commodities and information renders the world 'sublime', that is, complicated beyond a human scale of understanding. Think of the Internet or a particularly big shopping mall: the human mind can never have a sense of the whole thing all at once. Only Marxism, argues Jameson, can effect a 'cognitive mapping', a totalizing understanding, which would begin to make the world knowable and eventually – although not immanently – transformable (freeing us from the dictatorship of capitalism).

Since Heidegger and, in a more detailed way, the Canadian theorist of the media Marshall McLuhan, thinkers have been concerned with the effects of technology – implants, interfaces, connections, prostheses – on the human body, and the postmodern condition has only served to heighten such interests. McLuhan calls the media 'extensions of man', implying that new media extend our bodies, especially our sensory system: we hear, see and touch in new ways because of radio, television, computers (McLuhan 1964). Rock music, for instance, has made many of us partly deaf. The American theorist Donna Haraway sees the present age as enacting 'the invention and reinvention of nature – perhaps the most central arena of hope, oppression and contestation for inhabitants of the planet earth in our times' (Haraway 1991: 1), and this reinvention entails reinventing ourselves. In 'mapping the biopolitical body' (p. 3) (whom we are made to be by social and scientific forces), Haraway sees hope in 'cyborg feminism'. Cyborgs are hybrid creatures, composed of organism and machine, and 'The cyborgs populating feminist science fiction make very problematic the statuses of man or woman, human, artefact, member of a race, individual entity, or body' (p. 178). Rejecting universal and totalizing theories, Haraway sees in the cyborg the possibility of transgressing and reconstructing boundaries and thereby taking responsibility for biopolitical configurations of body and self: 'The cyborg is resolutely committed to practicality, irony, intimacy, and perversity. It is oppositional, utopian, and completely without innocence' (p. 151).

Postmodern theory tends to combine a certain emotional distance – often an ironic or 'cool' relation to contemporary culture – with a generalized pessimism about the possibility of social change and revolution: the cultural, political and economic system that dominates the world is a truly formidable and overwhelming opponent. Even with those theorists who see promise and possibility through postmodernism (Haraway, for instance), there is a concomitant sense of danger and oppression. Often postmodern theory resembles traditional Marxism in the determinist relations it draws between culture and the socio-technological order: there is no outside to the postmodern condition; all one can do is work within its possibilities and limitations. Granted, talk of revolution is often replaced with talk of transgression and subversion, but it is not completely clear what these are or what good they can do.

What are the features of a postmodern work of art? If post-modernism is the condition of contemporary culture, then all culture produced in our time is by definition postmodern. To try and single out (any more than provisionally) certain works for stylistic reasons as postmodern while ignoring others is empirically unsound and limiting. Postmodernism is as postmodernism does. After all, irony, allusiveness and tricks of self-referentiality are nothing new in western culture (see *The Knight of the Burning Pestle*, *Tristram Shandy* and *Ulysses*, for example). Does that mean that these works are postmodern? That hardly seems to make any historical sense. But if modernist works often feature characteristics we think of as postmodern, what makes postmodernism so distinctive? If we begin with a narrowly stylistic definition of the postmodern, this question remains unanswerable. Rather, what we can do is observe the particular forms and relations that post-modernism takes in any particular cultural phenomenon. Although this may well result in certain patterns appearing to be 'typically' postmodern, we will probably find postmodern works that don't follow these patterns much at all.

Postmodernism and theatre

Theatre *per se* is a somewhat marginal cultural activity in the postmodern world. As Baudrillard points out, theatre has gone from a dominant art form in early modern Europe to a relatively minor one in a postmodern world where everything is theatricalized (think of those exhibitionists who broadcast their daily lives on the web), but where the theatrical is more commonly presented through television, computers, film and other technological and easily transmitted media. We have seen, in recent years, the rebirth of extravagantly spectacular musical theatre in the work of Andrew Lloyd Webber, a rebirth in a new commodified format in keeping with the markets of global capitalism; but such theatre indicates more the ability of capital to appropriate whatever makes money than the resurgence of theatre as a defining feature of our culture. In some thinkers and practitioners – Hélène Cixous, for instance – theatre is seen as a residual form useful and attractive because it goes against the grain of our technological and simulated culture, promising, in a way reminiscent of phenomenological thought, an encounter with real time, lived experience and death (Shiach 1991: 106–9).

Some of these issues are addressed in Johannes Birringer's *Theatre, Theory, Postmodernism*. Birringer laments the marginalization of theatre in postmodern culture, and, while theatre's resistance to being on 'the cutting edge' is charming, it is also incapacitating (Birringer 1991: x–xi). Birringer does not see postmodernist late capitalism as an attractive situation – it is a time of dehumanizing effects on the 'dispossessed body' and of 'pervasive social and economic displacements' (pp. xii–xiii), what one might have once called exploitation and alienation. There is no point, however, in refusing to engage with this situation. Birringer calls for theatre to have a 'critical connection to postmodern culture' (p. xiii). Postmodernism is a process still under way and not an irresistible *fait accompli*. For Birringer, theatre's resistance to postmodern impoverishment lies not in its anachronistic 'liveness' (an idea we saw undermined by Philip Auslander in the section on phenomenology), but in its obsessive exploration of representation and its limits, in its ability to contradict and rupture the indifference of contemporary culture:

the practices and countermodels I have described allow us to think that the theatre cannot be absorbed by the spectacle of a technological culture as long as it can still experience and reperform the contradictions produced by this culture.

(p. 228)

A similar, even more sanguine, position is taken by Auslander, who sees, in performances such as the Wooster Group's L.S.D. and the stand-up comedy of Andy Kaufman (discussed later in this section) and Sandra Bernhard, instances of postmodern political resistance to the status quo of postmodern commodification. Much like Linda Hutcheon, Auslander argues that, although 'all cultural production is politically compromised' (Auslander 1992: 4), postmodern performance restores critical distance, which strategically allows us to reconsider the world we live in, thereby performing a resistant political function (p. 7). The political critique in postmodern performance, however, is not straightforward in the way traditionally political art has been. First of all, Auslander says, the import of a work can only be seen in a subtle and complex understanding of its context (p. 4). Moreover, postmodern performances do not contain explicit commentary or take political positions, but raise uncertainties by representing our own compromises without taking a clear position.

Auslander's readings of both context and performance text are supple and sophisticated. There is, however, something extremely attenuated about the political resistance he claims to observe. To further understanding can be effective politics. The postmodern strategies Auslander observes, however, are often so subtle and uncertain it's not clear how much an audience is capable of appreciating them. As Auslander admits, the difference between being inside the postmodern situation and representing it is 'a small one' (p. 81). As an effective strategy for political resistance, it may be smaller than he thinks.

Tom Stoppard, Anna Deavere Smith and Heiner Müller

A certain kind of postmodernism – elegant if trifling – can be seen in a number of the plays of Tom Stoppard, for instance *The Real Thing* (1983). The title itself of this work indicates a postmodern concern with authenticity and simulation, which in the play is presented structurally as an opposition between real life and the stage – not exactly a stunning new analogy, but one here deployed with sophistication. The play's characters are all involved in theatre and scenes from plays in which they are acting – *'Tis Pity She's a Whore*, for instance – are interlaced abruptly with scenes of 'real life'. The play also features a pastiche and overlay of high and low cultural references: John Ford (the seventeenth-century playwright), Italian opera, the Righteous Brothers, the Crystals; this juxtaposition raises the question of the 'real thing' in art, a question left open in a typically postmodern tip of the hat to mass culture:

> I like Herman's Hermits, and the Hollies, and the Everly Brothers, and Brenda Lee, and the Supremes.... I don't mean everything they did. I don't like *artists*. I like singles ... the Righteous Brothers' recording of 'You've Lost that Lovin' Feelin'' on the London label [is] possibly the most haunting, the most deeply moving noise ever produced by the human spirit.
>
> (Stoppard 1983: 25)

An ironic scepticism is at play throughout, including in the political debate between the conservative and proper on the one hand and an impolite and awkward leftist commitment on the other. And yet there remains, along with the play of pluralism and artifice, an abiding faith in art, words, love and reality which runs counter to the reputed postmodern investment in overriding irony. Does this mean that *The Real Thing* is not truly postmodern? Rather, we might find in it the tensions of the postmodern condition, in which tradition and the longing for certainty are bound up with a deep cultural and formal scepticism.

Anna Deavere Smith's *Twilight: Los Angeles, 1992* also exhibits many of the characteristics that have been taken to be postmodern. The play is a one-person show about the Rodney King riots in Los Angeles (which took place when white police officers who had beaten an inner-city black man were acquitted by a suburban, mainly white jury). Smith taped interviews with various people who experienced the riots and in performance she mimics those she interviewed, using edited versions of the interview tapes as text. Smith's procedure raises interesting questions of simulation and reality: on the one hand, she uses the exact unrehearsed words of her subjects and spends much time perfecting their exact gestures – in this way she participates in a heightened but traditional realism. On the other hand, she learns her parts from videotape, and so technological representation lies behind her exacting verisimilitude. Moreover, as careful as she may be, her re-enactments cannot escape being simulation, and distortion is inevitable – some she has interviewed have complained that she exaggerates their accents and gestures. Also, as in the theatre of Brecht, Smith does not present reality in all its wayward complexity; rather, she presents character with the help of a few carefully chosen props and costumes: caps, ties, a phone, a billy club. Alice Rayner, whose work is discussed in Chapter 1, sees Smith's performance strategy, however postmodern in the detail of its situation, as 'well within the tradition' of theatre phenomenology, in that there is always a gap between theatre and reality, and even documentary-like representation is simulation:

> however much it uses the real in its material, [Smith's work] precludes a designation of the real and of verifiable truth. It cannot close off its representation in reference because the very

> acts of selecting, combining and theatricalizing dissolve the
> terms of the real and put them into the terms of the imaginary.
> (Rayner 1995: 12)

Here postmodern and phenomenological analysis come together
in a manner reminiscent of that of Gianni Vattimo.

Twilight: Los Angeles, 1992 is structured by fragmentation and juxtaposition: many different voices are given short monologues; no
one voice is allowed the space to dominate. In this way, Smith's
play escapes the master narratives discussed by Lyotard. In many
ways, dramatic form, with its lack of narrative overview, is more
conducive to decentred authority than many literary forms, but
this effect can be heightened or diminished depending on how
it is put into play – Shakespeare gives rein to more points of
view than Shaw, for instance. Smith is interested in embracing
formal and material diversity, in making a theatre which
attempts to reflect the complexity of society (Smith 1992:
xxi–xxii). Just as there is no one unifying voice capable of speaking for society, Smith does not present a naive solution to complex social problems. Rather, she is interested in presenting 'the
processes of the problems'; solutions, to come later, 'will call for
the participation of large and eclectic groups of people' (p. xxiv).

Twilight: Los Angeles, 1992 is rich in characters who, in the condition of sublime incomprehensibility outlined by Jameson, feel
overwhelmed by forces beyond their understanding and control.
Such a condition begins with the figure behind the play, Rodney
King, a man at the centre of forces (institutional racism, the
media, American politics) which reduce him to confusion and
powerlessness. Most pointedly within the play itself are Walter
Park and his family. Park, a Korean convenience store-owner, was
shot in the head during the rioting and was given a frontal
lobotomy. He continues to be, at the time of the interview, heavily sedated. 'Then why, / why he has to get shot?' asks his wife,
June Park, 'You know, / I don't know why' (p. 147).

Twilight has a number of meanings in the play. One, put forward by the post-colonial theorist Homi Bhabha (discussed in the next section), whom Smith interviewed from London by phone, is that twilight is 'the moment of ambivalence / and ambiguity. / The inclarity, / the enigma, / the ambivalences' (p. 232). Here is another variation on the postmodern theme of confusion and incomprehensibility and the absence of master narratives. Twilight is also the name of a young black gang leader and trucemaker who is given the last speech in the play. Here Smith embraces some of the themes of post-colonialism: 'The relationships among peoples of color and within racial groups are getting more and more complicated' (p. xxi), Smith writes, in a way resembling what Gayatri Spivak (discussed in the next section) argues. Twilight the character embraces a perspective not unlike Edward Said's call for a hybrid identity (discussed in the next section) and understanding: 'in order for me to be a, to be a true human being, / ... I can't forever dwell in the idea, / of just identifying with people like me and understanding me and mine' (p. 255). In our multicultural, postmodern predicament, Smith, like Twilight, calls for 'multifaceted identities' (p. 25).

If there is any postmodern characteristic missing from Smith's play, it is the irony and depoliticization discussed by Hutcheon and Jameson: here is a non-ironic and committed postmodern theatre. In this way, it has been noted, Smith exhibits a politically purposeful postmodernism aligned with Habermas's belief in the possibility of complex, engaged and rational consensus and change (Lyons and Lyons 1994: 62–3).

If the postmodern constructs a world in which human lives are, like everything else, exchangeable commodities in a shifting and inescapable market that commodifies the heretofore uncommodified and discards whatever is outmoded, then Heiner Müller and his work seem a particularly compelling example of theatre in the postmodern condition. Müller began his career in the 1950s in what used to be called East Germany or the GDR.

In the late 1970s and 1980s, he was in the rare position of working back and forth between East Germany and the West, and it was in this capacity that he became a prominent figure in international theatre. During this period, Müller often commented on the differences between society and theatre in East and West. Life in the East was ultimately better: socialism gave people a sense of security and community, and the utopian drive toward a just society, although severely compromised by totalitarianism, was still alive. Because of technological and societal limitations, theatre in the East was not swamped by other media and remained a form of expression of central importance. Nonetheless, Müller was in a position to live out the 'common fantasy' of the East: 'to go to the West from time to time and to come back' (Müller 1982: 44). Consequently, Müller's attitude to the postmodernism associated with the West was complex and contradictory. His 'Reflections on Post-Modernism' is a poetic and dense critique of the depoliticization of culture in the West (Müller 1979). In a more iconoclastic mode, Müller writes, 'The only Postmodernist I know of was August Stramm, a modernist who worked in a post office' (Müller 1984: 137); and yet, when asked where he would prefer to mount his plays, he answers, 'I would like to stage MACBETH on the top of the World Trade Center for an audience in helicopters' (p. 140) – which sounds (in terms of technology, capital, the recontextualization of the past and the complicity of the artist with the established order) like a postmodern performance if ever there was one.

Many of these attitudes and tensions are played out in Müller's *Hamletmachine*, a radical adaptation of Shakespeare. Stylistically, *Hamletmachine* is typically postmodern in its fragmentation, complex irony, overlaying of cultural quotations (it ends by citing Susan Atkins of the Manson gang), and mixing of traditional and current cultural images, as in 'the madonna with breast cancer' (Müller 1984: 55). Moreover, Müller's Hamlet finds himself in a position of privilege much like Müller's own:

In the solitude of airports
I breathe again I am
A privileged person My nausea
Is a privilege
Protected by torture Barbed wire Prisons.

(p. 57)

Like Müller, Hamlet exists between a world dominated by Stalin and one dominated by Coca Cola. As a white male, he is a spent force, but new figures of liberation arise in his place: Marx, Lenin and Mao as three naked women (Müller is interested in the rebellion of the oppressed body against what western and patriarchal power has done to it); change, when it comes, will be brought about by revolutionary, Third World and feminist forces.

Hamletmachine is, however, a very bleak work, and many commentators, including Herbert Blau, have noted the despair and hopelessness in Müller's theatre – he himself has declared, 'I am neither a dope- nor a hope- dealer' (Müller 1984: 140). Critics have been particularly troubled by Müller's collaborations with Robert Wilson – Birringer writes of Wilson's production of Hamletmachine 'sucking the political thought out of the images and spilling a cool, architectonic-technological brilliance over the stage' (Birringer 1991: 62). Nonetheless, Müller's bleakness in this period was tied to the possibility of a long, difficult process of social revolution.

Things have been quite different since 1989. The fall of the East bloc to capitalism has, first of all, erased the position from which Müller formulated his unique position: there is no longer a betwixt and between but only monolithic commodification. Much of Müller's work has become irrelevant, or at least anachronistic and out of fashion. On a larger scale, East German theatre has suffered profoundly under unification. Carl Weber notes that in the GDR 'no other medium enjoyed equal tolerance

to conduct a discussion of the state's fossilized political structure', and, on a strictly economic level, theatres in the GDR
received large government subsidies and functioned independent of a market economy (Weber 1991: 48). Since reunification, theatres in the East have been forced to raise ticket prices
drastically, thus running the risk of losing the audience that
made theatre in the GDR so vital; the influx of western affluence
and media further threatens the centrality of the theatre.

After reunification, Margaret Croyden finds in Müller an
unmatched pessimism and a sense of tragedy and despair
(Croyden 1990: 98). Müller has even less hope than in the past:

> What I liked about the GDR was that money was not the first
> value and now money is the first value and this is the end of
> history for a while.... Apparently people need money and pos-
> sessions, and my only hope is that one day there will be a giant
> nausea and a national vomiting. And then you can talk to
> Germans about the 'third way' [not communism, not capital-
> ism, but something else – nobody knows what] and not before.
> And that will take a long time.
>
> (Croyden 1990: 106)

In this spirit of 'posthistoire', or the end of history (for now),
Müller presented in 1990 a seven-and-a-half-hour Hamlet,
including in it Hamletmachine, which was a 'requiem for the GDR'
(Croyden 1990: 98). Andreas Höfele positions this production in
a theatre of 'exhaustion' in which the possibilities of the future
are exhausted and the 'potentially liveliest art has been invaded
by images of stagnation, deadness, and decay' (Höfele 1992:
81). The play begins with Hamlet's dying words: 'How the play
ends is a foregone conclusion; it has, in fact, ended already'
(p. 84); 'and in the end Fortinbras, wearing a business suit and a
gold mask, a star warrior of capitalism, takes over' (p. 85).

Postmodernism and performance: Andy Kaufman and Abe Lincoln

Looking through the index of Stuart Sim's *Critical Dictionary of Postmodern Thought* (1998), one is struck by how few entries there are for anyone involved in theatre. There is no entry for Heiner Müller and one page citation for Robert Wilson, for instance. The theatre practitioner with the most references is, in a way that is both strange and familiar, Shakespeare. Certainly one could say with some justification that Sim's dictionary neglects postmodern theatre; on the other hand, however, this neglect points to the relative marginality of theatre in postmodern thought. Philip Auslander, we have seen, argues that recording technology has undermined the notion of live theatre, putting it under the sway of television, and Jean Baudrillard argues that the simulation once only to be found in theatre is now characteristic of all postmodern cultural forms. We are much more likely to receive such simulation from television or over the Internet than we are from a stage. What we end up with is a world in which important work in theatre is done by postmodernists at the same time that theatre itself has become a very marginalized medium under the influences of the postmodern world. If theatre is less than prominent in our culture, however, performance, broadly conceived, is, according to Nick Kaye, 'a primary postmodern mode' (p. 22).

The American stand-up comic Andy Kaufman, discussed by Auslander, is a striking figure in postmodern performance. Like many, if not most, stand-up performances, Kaufman's work is heavily under the influence of television, both in its content and in its presentation. His subject matter is often taken from television and the mass media: the cartoon hero Mighty Mouse, Elvis Presley, professional wrestling, stand-up comedy itself. Much of his performance work took place on television, for instance in his appearances 'as himself' on David Letterman's late night television show, staging confrontations that were then treated as real in newspaper reports. Two of Kaufman's longest running performances were as the offensive nightclub performer Tony Clifton and as a professional wrestler, finally as a male chauvinist wrestler who thought women belonged in the kitchen and the bedroom, taunting women and challenging them to take him on. In each case Kaufman presented his performance as reality – going to great lengths to make it appear that Tony Clifton was a real person, for instance. In each case the performance was based on truly obnoxious behaviour: Clifton would insult his audience in remorseless bad taste and pour glasses of water on people's heads; Andy the wrestler goaded his audience with attacks on the hygienic practices and intelligence of southern Americans and the equality of women. One assumes it was all an act and that Andy Kaufman didn't hold in private the views he presented in public. And yet, in a strangely postmodern play on appearance and reality, it doesn't make much difference: the performance is so obnoxious in itself that whether or not Kaufman is pretending doesn't matter. The relentless onslaught of hostility and insult takes on a life of its own. Think of the way friends sometimes compulsively tease each other. Eventually the teasing, whether based in truth or not, becomes irritating in its own right. Or think of the way an offhand, unconsidered and inappropriate remark can ruin a public figure's reputation, no matter how uncharacteristic, and no matter how sincerely it is disavowed afterwards. By saying over and over in his smug, superior way, 'I'm from Hollywood', Kaufman gets under our skin whether or not he personally buys into this smugness. Kaufman took some pains to maintain his illusions, staging confrontations and behind-the-scenes revelations that reinforced them – illustrating the mean-spiritedness behind a saccharine showbiz, for instance – but these precautions only thicken the confusion rather than clarifying the reality. The real is not ultimately at issue here any more. Performance and confrontation have created their own hyperreality, their own Andy Kaufman.

Is Kaufman ironic then? Irony means to say one thing and mean another. It's not clear, however, what if anything the other thing that Kaufman means would be; there is only the saying. Is it satire? If so, who is its target? Is it pastiche? It seems somehow more fully entered into than that. What is most striking is Kaufman's enthusiasm, his embracing of the game – he leaps in the way the mudwrestler leaps into the mud. To ask why seems pointless. The mountaineer George Mallory, asked why he wanted to climb Mount Everest, answered, 'Because it's there.' There may have been other unacknowledged reasons (personal glory, British cultural imperialism); but Kaufman's actions are on their surface (and what else is there?) similarly lacking in ulterior motive. Where in this performance is any subversive politics?

Another performance that seems particularly postmodern happens several times each day at Disney's Magic Kingdoms in Florida and California. There is a room containing robotic versions of all of the presidents of the United States. These robots, or cyborgs, fidget in their chairs until one of them, Abe Lincoln, rises and recites the 'Gettysburg Address'. Here we have Madame Tussaud's on batteries. We see a number of postmodern elements: the prominence of cyborgs and technologies of representation; simulation of reality (both of history and of live performance itself); repetition. Moreover, here we are in a pop culture performance, at some of the most visited tourist attractions in North America. But there is nothing very ironic about the performance, nor anything politically subversive. Abe Lincoln seems, in this performance, to serve some rather grand narratives, such as American patriotism. We can also see Jameson's cultural logic of late capitalism at work: here history and patriotism have become commodities, yours for the price of a ticket. The past has been bought and sold, so that, as Walter Benjamin writes, 'even the dead are not safe' from the forces of capital.

QUESTIONS ONE MIGHT ASK OF A PLAY OR PERFORMANCE

Does the play or performance make use of technology? If so, does this have an effect on the representation of reality or on the way your senses receive the performance?

The Canadian theatre critic Kate Taylor writes of how state-of-the-art movie theatres, DVDs, home theatres and surround sound have changed the way people expect sound to be heard and have contributed to a 'lost art of hearing' which affects the theatre audience, so that more and more live theatre performances resort to microphones for sound projection (Taylor 2000). Do you find theatre, after going to the movies or listening to your stereo, hard to hear? Is there a sense that theatre is somehow backward and out of date because of this?

Does the play or performance recycle other cultural material – through allusions, reproductions, recordings, parody, pastiche? How does it make something new of earlier cultural references?

Does the play or performance rely on a master narrative to make sense of things or does it present a fragmented and disunified understanding?

Does the play or performance show an acceptance of the way things are, a capitulation, or does it offer ways to think and act outside or against the status quo?

3 POST-COLONIAL THEORY

Like postmodernism, post-colonialism is an attempt to describe our contemporary situation and its culture, this time by focusing on the effects of the western imperialism that has dominated the world since the sixteenth century and that has been unravelling since the end of the Second World War, as independence has come to most of the former colonies of Europe. Certainly, however, the domination of a few nations over the others has not ceased – the military and economic influence of the United States being the most important example. The term post-colonialism implies both a situation coming after colonialism and a situation in the heritage or aftermath of colonialism: both an ongoing liberation and an ongoing oppression. Like feminism, post-colonialism aims to give voice to an oppressed group by under-standing and critiquing the structures of oppression and artic-ulating and encouraging liberation and revolution. In this case the group is those who have lived under the imperialist domina-tion of western colonial powers. In very different ways, this includes, for instance, Ireland, Canada, Australia, South Africa, Palestine, Algeria, Brazil, India and Vietnam. Post-colonial theory, therefore, has arisen over the last fifty years in response to the developing relations of power and influence among the nations and peoples of the world. Unlike much postmodern theory, post-colonial theory often combines individual emotional com-mitment and outrage with a defiant optimism. It is much more strident and activist than an acquiescent postmodernism.

Post-colonial theory has taken many turns, mapping the com-plexity of the post-colonial condition. The work of the Palestinian-American theorist Edward Said, for instance, begins with a critique of 'orientalism', the reductive ideology and culture of western imperialism and the 'imaginative geography' which entrenches clear and asymmetrical divisions between 'orient' and 'occident' to the advantage of the West. Orientalism divides the world into the white, moral, rational West, deserving and des-tined ruler of the world, and the non-white, conniving and irra-tional East, which needs the West to watch over it (such attitudes are satirized in the first act of Cloud Nine, discussed earlier). Such thinking is everywhere present in the history of western imperi-alism and continues to colour thinking even today (Said 1978).

As in the thought of Walter Benjamin and much feminism, for Said patterns of oppressive orientalism are to be found not only in the most egregiously jingoistic and racist examples, but in the 'masterpieces' of the western tradition:

> Most professional humanists ... are unable to make the connection between the prolonged and sordid cruelty of practices such as slavery, colonialist and racial oppression, and imperial subjection on the one hand, and the poetry, fiction, philosophy of the society that engages in these practices on the other.
>
> (Said 1993: xiii–xiv)

One facet of post-colonial work, therefore, is to challenge the canon of western art, a challenge which takes myriad forms, from outright rejection to re-appropriation and reformulation.

Said's later work moves to the acknowledgement and acceptance of existing and developing hybridity – the entanglement of cultural identities in a migratory and diasporic world. Think of the child of Vietnamese immigrants living in Toronto, for instance, or someone of mixed African and Asian descent living in the Soho of London or New York. In the name of hybridity, Said calls for a subjectivity that transcends the restraints of imperial, national or provincial limits (Said 1993). In his discussion of hybridity, Said, like many others, sees that patterns of migration have rewritten post-colonial geography as well as identity: today the post-colonial is a part of London, Paris, Berlin, New York and Toronto, as it is of Hong Kong, Jerusalem, Soweto and Recife.

In *The Wretched of the Earth*, the North African theorist Frantz Fanon writes, 'In decolonisation, there is therefore the need of a complete calling in question of the colonial situation' (Fanon 1965: 30). In post-colonial theory, this has come to mean a subtle examination of the many and often conflicting strands that make up the post-colonial situation and identity. The Indian theorist Gayatri Chakravorty Spivak, based in the United States, brings a powerful commitment to Marxism, deconstruction (she is the translator of Derrida's *Of Grammatology*) and feminism to her analysis of the situation of the colonial 'subaltern' (the person in an inferior position who has others speak on his or her behalf), especially the situation of non-western women. Moreover, she is interested not only in the critique of the Eurocentrism of western culture ('I teach a small number of the holders of the can(n)on, male or female, feminist or masculist, how to read their own texts, as best I can' [Spivak 1987: 92]) but in understanding the complex forces that define the 'interests' of any subject position. In this light she posits not a monolithic idea of woman or brown person, but the subaltern as a divided rather than transparent subject. From Marxism and especially deconstruction, Spivak takes up a call for a 'productive bafflement' (Spivak 1988: 286), in which concepts, definitions and positions are always deployed provisionally and strategically and are always open to questioning and rethinking. The influence of deconstruction on her post-colonial thought can be seen in the title of her recent book *Critique of Postcolonial Reason* (1999): she seeks to question the entrenched certainties of post-colonial thought and politics. She remains, however, militantly dedicated to radical politics and has been critical of Derrida's rather depoliticized reading of Marx in his *Specters of Marx* (Spivak 1995).

The Indian theorist Homi Bhabha, who divides his time between England and the United States, is concerned specifically with the discourse of colonialism, how its language, its metaphoric and metonymic patterns, structure the other as fetish and stereotype in order to reduce, dominate, discriminate against and exploit non-European peoples (Bhabha 1986). The positive associations surrounding the word white and the negative associations surrounding blackness are simple and widespread examples of how language plays a part in racism and imperialism. For Bhabha, imperialist ideology follows the logic of language and affect as much as it does the dictates of Enlightenment reason: racism is not merely a matter of rational self-interest on the part of the West; rather, it is very difficult, given the way our language works, to think outside racist patterns. For those who attempt to resist imperialist ideology, therefore, it is necessary to work in 'betweenness', in strategies tied to fragmentation and displacement, which can be a form of revolt against the seemingly monolithic, seemingly rational, authority of imperialism (Bhabha 1992). Similarly, the Vietnamese-American theorist and filmmaker Trinh T. Minh-Ha invokes the fragment that 'stands on its own and cannot be recuperated by the notion of totalizing whole' (Minh-Ha 1992: 156). For her the post-colonial subject is constructively hybrid and unfinished and not tied to an imperialist ideal of unity and completeness. Minh-Ha is interested as a woman, an Asian-American and an artist, not only in how 'woman, native, other' have been represented in imperialist ideology, but also, more creatively, in experimenting with the ways she can represent herself. Consequently, for example, her theoretical work, much influenced by western thinking, is interspersed with poetry and Zen philosophy (Minh-Ha 1989). The East is not essentially anti-rational any more than the West is inherently rational, and any particular subject position in a world as variable as our own will call for the bringing together of disparate elements in new and unexpected ways.

Many special issues of academic journals have been dedicated to post-colonial topics; a number of readers have recently been published (see, for example, Ashcroft *et al.* 1995 and Williams and Chrisman 1994). Bill Ashcroft, Gareth Griffiths and Helen Tiffin's *The Empire Writes Back* (1989) has provided an introduction to post-colonial theory and literatures. Post-colonialism also gives rise to comparative studies of national cultures; for instance, a number of volumes have compared Canadian and Australian literature and drama, especially in terms of aboriginal work (see, for instance, Goldie 1989). For post-colonial theatre, geographical disparateness is coupled with a wide range of performative practices, often para-theatrical or ritualistic, which fall outside the parameters of the western theatrical tradition. The section of Reinelt and Roach's *Critical Theory and Performance* (1992) dedicated to such material (which the editors have chosen to call, somewhat misleadingly, 'Cultural Studies') indicates some of the breadth that ensues: a South Indian *King Lear*; the rituals of Shamans in Thailand and Chicago; the trickster in Ntozake Shange; the Chinese American in *Yankee Dawg You Die*; political demonstrations in Tiananmen Square and Berlin, and at Kent State University; Mardi Gras in New Orleans.

Aimé Césaire's *A Tempest*

In the engagement with the canon of western theatre, Ashcroft, Griffiths and Tiffin stress the importance of Shakespeare's *The Tempest* for post-colonial thought:

> *The Tempest* has been perhaps the most important text used to establish a paradigm for post-colonial readings of canonical works. So established are these readings that in contemporary productions 'some emphasis on colonialism is now expected.' In fact, more important than the simple rereading of the text itself by critics or in productions has been the widespread employment of the characters and structure of *The Tempest* as a general metaphor for imperial–marginal relations or, more widely, to characterize some specific aspect of post-colonial reality.... [W]riters throughout the post-colonial world, particularly writers of the Anglophone and Francophone white and Black diasporas, have written answers to *The Tempest* from the perspectives of Caliban, Miranda, and Ariel.
>
> (Ashcroft *et al.* 1989: 190–1)

Especially in backlashes against political correctness, post-colonial readings of *The Tempest* have been high-profile targets of attack – the American conservative Dinesh D'Souza, for instance, has called it unfair and an indignity to reduce Shakespeare to a mere function of colonial forces (D'Souza 1991: 70–1). These attacks try to ignore the actual historical sources of Shakespeare's play in accounts of new world discovery and turn away from those textual moments when the colonialist implications of the relation between Caliban and others in the play are made overt and urgent. Furthermore, these attacks fail to appreciate the post-colonial reading project as it manifests itself especially in theatrical adaptation: reading is always in part political and adaptation is always a remaking with different emphases and with a new purpose. Dignifying Shakespeare is not the main concern.

The Caribbean playwright Aimé Césaire's *A Tempest* is the foremost post-colonial adaptation of Shakespeare's play. In general outline, Césaire's plot follows Shakespeare's relatively closely, until the end when Prospero remains behind in a bitter conflict with Caliban for control of the island. Throughout, however, Césaire uses various means to change the emphasis, from Shakespeare's on romance and reconciliation to his own on imperialism, domination and struggle.

Parts of Shakespeare are retained more or less intact: foremost is Césaire's retention of Caliban's song of freedom and defiance '*As in Shakespeare*' (Césaire 1985: 49). At other times, Césaire takes a moment from Shakespeare but expands or reformulates it: Caliban's 'You taught me your language' becomes an attack on the strategic political limitations of Prospero's pedagogical project:

> You didn't teach me a thing! Except to jabber in your own language so that I could understand your orders – chop the wood, wash the dishes, fish for food, plant vegetables, all because you're too lazy to do it yourself. And as for your learning, did you ever impart any of that to me? No, you took care not to. All your science and know-how you keep for yourself alone, shut up in big books like those.

(p. 14)

Trinculo's discussion of putting an Indian on display in England is expanded and directed much more explicitly at Caliban (pp. 43–6). In Shakespeare, Prospero tries more or less successfully to impose a chaste atmosphere on the wedding masque he stages, although thoughts of Caliban ultimately interrupt the festivities; in Césaire, Eshu, a 'black devil-god', interrupts the masque with an 'obscene' song (pp. 52–4). Prospero is more completely a tyrant than he is in Shakespeare's play, and the European characters are more overtly colonizers.

In these instances, Césaire is taking his cue from something explicit or hinted at in Shakespeare. At other times, however, he adds something much less evident in the original. Most important are two new scenes, in the first of which Caliban debates with Ariel on the best way to work toward freedom (pp. 23–7), and in the second of which Caliban debates with Prospero on the nature of the imperialist project (pp. 69–73). Central to Césaire's revision, Caliban has intelligence and resolve to go with his rebellion and resistance.

Césaire's *A Tempest* is labelled an 'Adaptation for a Black Theatre'. As such, it presents the events of Shakespeare's play not only from another perspective but for another audience, one for which Caliban is the hero and Prospero the monster. The play is also, however, a 'psychodrama' (p. 1) in which black actors take up all the roles, playing out not only the external and political but also the internal and psychological structures of oppression which go with imperialist domination. Here Césaire's play begins to address the complexities of post-colonial subjectivity.

Intercultural theatre: Wole Soyinka and Rustam Bharucha

Wole Soyinka, the Nigerian playwright, has written about the role of theatre in African resistance to western colonial values. 'The history of West African theatre in the colonial period', he writes, is 'largely a history of cultural resistance and survival'

(Soyinka 1996: 241). He sees the 'survival strategies' of theatre mixing traditional, folk and ritual forms with more westernized practices. He has been most interested in the traditions of his own Yoruba people, mixing their traditions of music and storytelling with his interest in such western figures as Aristophanes, Euripides and Shakespeare. He has worked in this way not only by incorporating western elements in his own plays but also by incorporating African elements in adaptations of western classics, such as in his *The Bacchae of Euripides* (Gilbert and Tompkins 1996: 39–41).

Soyinka's 1959 play *The Lion and the Jewel*, a relatively early work of post-colonial drama, functions by combining western dramatic forms (verse drama, comedy of ideas à la George Bernard Shaw and bedroom farce) with African traditions of folk tale, dancing and storytelling – the play ends with an enactment of traditional Yoruba betrothal ceremonies. *The Lion and the Jewel* tells the story of two men vying for the affections of a beautiful young girl. Lakunle is a young, impoverished, westernized schoolteacher, who categorically rejects the 'bush minds' of traditionalists and African traditions such as the 'bride-price' (which the male suitor gives to his betrothed), which he characterizes as:

> A savage custom, barbaric, out-dated,
> Rejected, denounced, accursed,
> Excommunicated, archaic, degrading,
> Humiliating, unspeakable, redundant,
> Retrogressive, remarkable, unpalatable.
>
> (Soyinka 1974: 8)

He wants a 'modern', western marriage:

> Together we shall sit at table
> – Not on the floor – and eat,
> Not with fingers, but with knives

And forks, and breakable plates
Like civilized beings.

(p. 8)

Lakunle seeks a modern Africa: 'Where is our school of ballroom dancing? / Who here can throw a cocktail party?' (p. 34). What becomes clear, however, is that in rejecting the bride-price and espousing western ways, Lakunle is serving his own patriarchal interests over Sidi, the 'village belle'. He says, 'Women have a smaller brain than men / That's why they are called the weaker sex' (p. 6).

Also interested in Sidi's affections is Baroka, the 'bale' or village head, an aging traditionalist who thwarts all attempts at modernization and westernization. In a way that combines the folk trickster figure with Ben Jonson's Volpone, Baroka is always feigning illness and impotence, although he remains in truth supremely robust. In the end, through superior wiles, he seduces Sidi, who comes completely under the sway of Baroka's traditional and sexual power. As she says to Lakunle:

Why, did you think that after him
I could endure the touch of another man?
I who have felt the strength
The perpetual youthful zest
Of the panther of the trees?

(p. 57)

The Lion and the Jewel seems an allegorical wish fulfilment in which traditional African culture bests the forces of westernization, although it is not clear how this theme relates to the mixing of African and western elements in the form of the play. Nor is it clear that Sidi's escape from the western patriarchal attitudes of Lakunle is furthered by her being taken under the traditional masculine sway of Baroka.

Mixing different cultural dramatic traditions – intercultural theatre and performance – is a practice fraught with aesthetic and political pitfalls. At its most noble, interculturalism attempts, in the words of Patrice Pavis, to 'call [...] into question Western universalism, in order to give greater respect to cultural differences and their relativity' (Pavis 1996: 12). The effects are not always so successful as this. One of the strongest critics of intercultural performance is the Indian writer Rustam Bharucha. Bharucha's primary targets are western practitioners of interculturalism, rather than those working from non-western positions as Soyinka does. Peter Brook is such a western intercultural director – as we have seen, his production of *A Midsummer Night's Dream* incorporated elements from many non-western traditions. Bharucha sees a number of problems here. First, the power relations between the West and the rest of the world are such that the exchange will never be fair and balanced:

> For my own part, I believe that as much as one would like to accept the seeming openness of Euro-American interculturalists to other cultures, the larger economic and political domination of the West has clearly constrained, if not negated the possibilities of a genuine exchange. In the best of all possible worlds, interculturalism could be viewed as a 'two-way street', based on mutual reciprocity of needs. But in actuality, where it is the West that extends its domination to cultural matters, this 'two-way street' could be more accurately described as a 'dead-end.'
>
> (Bharucha 1993: 2)

Bharucha's second concern is that interculturalism always displaces traditions from where they really mean something. The worst thing is 'when a traditional performance is stripped of its links to the lives of the people for whom it is performed. Nothing could be more disrespectful to theatre than to reduce its act of celebration to a repository of techniques and theories' (pp. 4–5). Given these concerns, Bharucha condemns Brook's intercultural production of the Indian epic poem *Mahabharata* for blatantly trivializing Indian culture and reducing Hindu philosophy to platitudes (p. 4). Bharucha criticizes even the co-opting of tribal and rural performances by urban theatres of the same culture; he writes of his own cultural situation, 'Today, "Indian culture" is being reduced to a commodity by our own government and a new breed of bureaucrats, who have shaped, marketed and transported this "culture" to different parts of the world' (p. 7). In reality, therefore, unlike in Soyinka's *The Lion and the Jewel*, the Barokas of the world, with their village traditions, are overwhelmed by an onslaught of the western, urban and modern forces of the world at large.

David Henry Hwang and Tomson Highway

The rootedness and purity Bharucha espouses may be good for certain isolated, rural forms of traditional performance, but how can people who live in the cities and cultures that function as points of interchange between various traditions (most of North and South America, for instance) make theatre that is relevant to their hybrid conditions?

The Chinese-American David Henry Hwang's highly successful *M. Butterfly* (1989) exhibits many of the concerns of postcolonial theory. In the tradition of Benjamin, Said and Césaire, Hwang reveals the oppressive structures at the heart of a masterpiece of western culture – this time Giacomo Puccini's nineteenth-century opera *Madame Butterfly*, in which Hwang sees 'a wealth of sexist and racist cliches' (Hwang 1989: 95). For Hwang, *Madame Butterfly* is a paradigm of western male attitudes toward Asia and Asian women, attitudes both profoundly mistaken and profoundly oppressive. In short, Puccini's opera is a prime example of the orientalist ideology discussed by Said and to be found in many of the masterpieces of western culture.

In Hwang's play, the French diplomat Gallimard has taken a Chinese lover (Song Liling, whom Gallimard takes to be a submissive female but who is really a transvestite Chinese spy). Gallimard uses the music and words of Puccini's opera to help him – as in the discourse theory of Homi Bhabha – fetishize and confine his lover and their relationship. In this way Hwang explores the mindset that guides western attitudes toward the East (the play is presented as the recollections of Gallimard): in the western imaginary, the East is feminine, passive and always victimized. Both Puccini and Gallimard attempt to foist this western imaginary on eastern reality, but ultimately this vision says more about, is truer of, the West than it is the East. Hwang sees his play as 'a deconstructivist *Madame Butterfly*' (p. 95) in which he reveals the truth behind the western cliché by turning Puccini's story upside down: in the end it is Gallimard who is the true M. Butterfly, the victim dying for unrequited love. 'I am pure imagination', he declares. 'And in imagination I will remain' (p. 91).

Although he posits his play as deconstructivist, M.*Butterfly* moves inexorably toward a revelation of, literally, the naked truth (this was discussed more fully in the section on post-structuralism). Like Césaire's Caliban, Hwang's Song Liling is a cocky and confident character who seems to have escaped all the self-destructive illusions that Gallimard brought to their relationship – indeed he has clear-headedly exploited them for twenty-five years. Hwang's play too, despite its self-reflective and theatrical toying with representation, is extremely self-assured and single-minded. M.*Butterfly* is not interested in the more difficult areas of complicity in the post-colonial subject; in this way Hwang's deconstruction remains strategically one-sided. Nor is there in the play – despite Hwang's own position as a Chinese-American – any interest in hybridity as a subject position. In M. *Butterfly*, East is East and West is West and never the twain shall meet.

A more complicated engagement with post-colonial subjectivity from within can be found in *Dry Lips Oughta Move to Kapuskasing* (1989) by Tomson Highway, a Cree-Canadian born in northern Manitoba and now based in Toronto. *Dry Lips* is the second of seven proposed plays set on the fictional Wasaychigan Hill Indian Reserve. The first is *The Rez Sisters* (1988), which deals with seven reserve women who travel to Toronto for the world's biggest bingo game. The only male character in *The Rez Sisters* is the traditional trickster figure Nanabush. *Dry Lips*, on the other hand, features seven male characters, and Nanabush, basically a non-gendered or doubly gendered figure, is this time female. Set side by side, the two plays reveal a symmetry in their representation of gender in native society, although it is telling that Highway has chosen in these first two plays to represent men and women on the reserve as two solitudes. Especially in *Dry Lips*, the separation echoes the tensions and power struggles between native men and women – the attempt by the reserve women to start a hockey team is taken as an affront to male control and esteem. Highway's theatre is profoundly concerned with the differences between native women and native men; at the same time, especially in the figure of Nanabush, Highway presents a place beyond simple gendered identity and oppression. Nanabush presents a native alternative to restrictive binary identities, which for Highway are in large measure the imposition of western patriarchy on native culture. In a similar tension, *Dry Lips* combines a culturally acceptable, often restrictive, male homosocial structure with hints of a repressed homoeroticism that upset the binary order from another direction.

Highway, who is gay, professes strong feminist sympathies and sees his plays in part as representations of the damage imposed by western patriarchy on native women and native communities. Nevertheless, when the play received its second production, which ran at a large, mainstream Toronto theatre, it was attacked by a number of feminist critics. Two central, horrific events in the play are the birth of a child with foetal alcohol syndrome and the rape of a young woman with a crucifix. The representation of these events in the context of an almost entirely male cast was felt by some to be inescapably misogynist. Alan Filewod has surveyed these responses and discussed the factors that went into creating such an impression: the hollowness of the large commercial theatre space; the loss of the context of the play and its relation to *The Rez Sisters* (Filewod 1994). What most interests Filewod is the way responses of native women critics, uncomfortable with the production, were downplayed in the controversy. At any rate, these events reveal the complexities of post-colonialism and gender politics not only on the textual level but also on the level of reception.

Dry Lips is also complex in its relation to western culture. Ashcroft, Griffiths and Tiffin outline how the politics of language plays a major role in colonial and post-colonial projects (1989: 7–8). Western discourse, as discussed by Homi Bhabha, imposes western ideology; a return to indigenous languages is often seen as a means of cultural liberation. Much of Highway's play is written in the richly textured English of the reserve; often, however, the characters speak in Cree and Ojibway, languages which, for Highway, are invested with special emotional and semantic qualities (for instance, in terms of their freedom from gender [Highway 1989: 12]). The play ends with Zachary Jeremiah Keechigeesick haltingly learning phrases in Ojibway from his wife, Hera. On a different cultural front, the play presents a conflict among the characters between Christianity and native spirituality – most localized in the differences between the tellingly named Spooky Lacroix and Simon Starblanket. Although the play's sympathies are decidedly with Nanabush and Starblanket, Highway presents the complexity of religious identity on the reserve. Finally, although Highway is outspoken in his criticisms of western patriarchy and religion, he is much more accepting of western art. Unlike *A Tempest* or *M. Butterfly*, *Dry Lips* does not take to task any masterpiece of the western canon, and Highway himself, like Edward Said, is a classical pianist, and learned much about playwriting from the English-Canadian James Reaney and the French-Canadian Michel Tremblay.

The doubleness of Highway's representation of native life can be seen in the play's tragicomic mood. On the one hand, *Dry Lips* is an extremely painful play. Its epigraph, from Lyle Longclaws, is '… before the healing can take place, the poison must first be exposed … ' (the snake is western patriarchy, and the bitten are native males). On the other hand, it is a very funny play and, in its final moments, a joyous celebration of native beauty and life:

> The baby finally gets 'dislodged' from the blanket and emerges, naked. And the last thing we see is this beautiful naked Indian man lifting this naked baby Indian girl up in the air, his wife sitting beside them watching and laughing. Slow fadeout. Split seconds before complete black-out, Hera peals out with this magical, silvery Nanabush laugh, which is echoed and echoed by one last magical arpeggio on the harmonica, from off-stage. Finally, in the darkness, the last sound we hear is the baby's laughing voice, magnified on tape to fill the entire theater. And this, too, fades into complete silence.
>
> (pp. 129–30)

Augusto Boal

One area in which post-colonial thought has been particularly rich and suggestive is the theory and practice of pedagogy. Foremost in this field is the work of the Brazilian Paulo Freire, especially his seminal book, *Pedagogy of the Oppressed* (1970). Freire aligns political oppression with oppressive pedagogy. Traditional, oppressive pedagogy is learning by rote, in which teachers who know deposit their information and ideology into the passive minds of students taken as knowing nothing on their own. Such a practice posits students – especially the oppressed – as incapable of thinking for themselves or taking up action. It also instils a sense of the unquestioned inevitability of the oppressive status quo. Against this model, Freire calls for a dialectical pedagogy in which all are thought capable of active contribution – so-called teachers can learn from so-called students. Here the oppressed bring their own experience and understanding to the pedagogical process, solving problems for themselves, and thereby training themselves to take an active role in changing the world. Freire and Henry Giroux have also developed the idea of 'border pedagogy'. Like Said's hybridity, border pedagogy takes account of patterns of migration whereby people develop a comparative sense of the relations between different environments and ways of knowing. For instance, members of minority groups in large cities live by moving back and forth between at least two different cultures. Again like hybridity, border pedagogy calls for us to distance ourselves from our own subject positions in order to see things as others might (Janmohamed 1994).

These pedagogical ideas have been applied to theatre in the work of the Brazilian political exile and theorist Augusto Boal. The first sections of Boal's *Theatre of the Oppressed* (1985) are dedicated to an elaboration of Brecht's criticisms of 'Aristotelian' theatre with the help of ideas from Freire. Aristotelian theatre, which is the hegemonic form of western theatre (Boal traces it from classical Athens down to contemporary soap operas), is a form of political indoctrination, intimidation and coercion, whereby an ideological acceptance of the status quo and fear of change is instilled in a passive and oppressed audience. Remember how, for instance, Susan Bennett sees spectators in traditional theatre as passive recipients with no active role in what goes on on stage. For Boal, as for Brecht, the oppressive ideology and passivity of theatre are highly complicitous: the manipulative ideology of the status quo means the audience is not allowed to think for itself, and the audience's passive position as spectators means it is not allowed to act for itself.

Brecht saw this structure at work, but his epic theatre was only able to allow the audience to think and judge for itself, with its continual admonitions to the audience to find its own solutions and effects to distance them from incapacitating emotional pitfalls. Boal's project takes the next step and seeks to find ways of allowing the audience not only to think but also to act for itself, thereby turning theatre from an ideological state apparatus into 'a rehearsal of revolution' (Boal 1985: 141).

Boal has proposed myriad theatre exercises in which revolutionary theatre can be enacted. A number are described in later sections of *Theatre of the Oppressed*. In an example of what he calls 'invisible theatre', actors take up places in a hotel restaurant. One of them loudly orders an elaborate meal which, it turns out, he cannot pay for. This causes a scene and the other actors start a public debate about poverty, wages, the cost of food, the right to eat and so forth. Eventually others in the restaurant, not part of the troupe, enter into the debate and the discussion goes on through the night. Here those who participate are allowed to think and speak for themselves. As Boal comments:

> In the invisible theater the theatrical rituals are abolished; only the theatre exists, without its old, worn-out patterns. The theatrical energy is completely liberated, and the impact produced by this free theater is much more powerful and longer lasting.
>
> (p. 147)

A second example is called 'Breaking of Repression' (p. 149): a member of the audience relates an incident when he or she was (for reasons of race, class, sex or age) repressed, accepted the repression, and acted in a manner contrary to his or her own desires. This person arranges for the actors to act out this incident. Then the scene is replayed, this time with the protagonist resisting the repression. In this way, and in discussion afterward, measure is taken of the possibilities and limitations of resistance, and the actors and audience thereby undertake a step towards revolution. For Boal, it is also important to move from the particular to the general, 'from the *phenomenon* toward the law' (p. 150). In this way, Boal's poetics discourages identification with an individually fixed plight and encourages something like the hybrid and improvised thinking of the border intellectual.

Another theatrical project is called '*Knowing the Body*' and entails making the oppressed aware of the 'muscular alienation' imposed on the body by different kinds of work:

> A simple example will serve to clarify this point: compare the muscular structure of a typist with that of the nightwatchman of a factory. The first performs his or her work seated in a chair: from the waist down the body becomes, during working hours, a kind of pedestal, while the arms and fingers are active. The watchman, on the other hand, must walk continually during his eight-hour shift and consequently will develop muscular structures that facilitate walking. The bodies of both become alienated in accordance with their respective types of work.
>
> (p. 127)

The body's shape and gestures, along with dress and language, are part of the sociopolitical 'mask' of behaviour imposed on everybody in particular ways – remember the discussion of the policeman and the motorist in the section on semiotics. The task becomes to analyse and come to understand what has been done to the body in order to open up the possibility of making it and using it differently.

For Boal, traditional theatre widely conceived is 'the most perfect artistic form of coercion' (p. 39). Conversely, while the Theatre of the Oppressed is not in itself a revolution, it does help prepare the way for one. In these opposed forms, Boal stresses the importance and centrality that theatre still has in our time. Such a heady emphasis might cause us to rethink the importance and meaning of theatre, not only in a post-colonial context but in other contexts as well. Think, for instance, of a context most likely very present for anyone reading this book: the theatre classroom. Theatre may be marginal in many activities of contemporary life, but one doesn't have to expand the idea of performance very much at all to see the classroom as a theatre and teaching and learning as a performative situation. Education may be one area in which the theatrical remains a central aspect of our culture.

What kind of performative pedagogy should we bring to the theatre classroom? Is it most important that we study the classics of the western canon or should we rather focus on the local works and performances that we undertake wherever we are: which means more to us, reading a masterpiece or mounting a small production of our own? And what forms of theatre should interest us? Should we be out in restaurants ordering meals we can't pay for, or at least undertaking something less brashly unconventional? For Boal – as for Brecht, Artaud, Blau and many others – theatre is thoughtful, and whatever form it takes, should it not make us think, especially when we undertake it in a pedagogical and intellectual context? Finally, should our study be passive or active? Should we read the classics and sit while an expert lectures to us about them, or should we get up on our feet, produce, enact and discuss? The study of theatre, as much as any discipline, brings with it the drive to make and perform rather than simply to ingest.

Many of us are highly privileged and it would depoliticize Boal's project to reduce the Theatre of the Oppressed by universalizing and abstracting it: if everyone is oppressed, the category loses its meaning, or at least its political import. Nonetheless, the post-colonial pedagogical and theatrical project holds exciting possibilities for situations beyond its borders narrowly drawn.

After Brazil ceased to be a dictatorship, Boal returned to his native country and in 1992 he was elected to the national legislature. He then began developing a new mode of theatre, 'Legislative Theatre', which 'includes all the previous forms of the Theatre of the Oppressed plus others which have a specifically parliamentary application' (Boal 1998: 5). Legislative Theatre works to foster participatory, interactive democracy. Whereas the Theatre of the Oppressed transformed the spectator into an actor, Legislative Theatre transforms the citizen into a legislator (p. 19). Boal writes:

> We do not accept that the elector should be a mere spectator to the actions of the parliamentarian, even when these actions are right: we want the electors to give their opinions, to discuss the issues, to put counter-arguments, we want them to share the responsibility for what the parliamentarian does.
>
> (p. 20)

One form Legislative Theatre takes, for instance, is 'The Chamber in the Square', a mock-parliament in which there is a public discussion and debate of a very precise legislative question, so that 'participants must not only vote but must also explain their positions' (p. 93). These public debates then influenced Boal's vote in the national legislature; in this way theatre becomes 'one of the ways in which political activity can be conducted' (p. 20).

Coco Fusco and Guillermo Gómez-Peña

Not everyone, even among those on the left, gives unqualified support to Boal's theatre projects. The Latin American performance artist Coco Fusco, for instance, finds that Boal's work has created a restrictive straitjacket for Latin American artists. She writes:

> As brilliant and necessary as the contributions of Paulo Freire and Augusto Boal have been to the understanding of radical pedagogy and social change, the desire to restrict the validity of

Latin American cultural production to its capacity to politicize the underprivileged is a symptom of the frustration of leftist intellectuals and a way of ghettoizing Latin American cultural production. It has also been turned in the U.S. into an insistence that all 'authentically' Latino artists perform this function – even though the reality is that many Latin American artists' primary audience consists of their peers, other intellectuals, and audiences that do not respond receptively to what they perceive as outdated and dogmatic paradigms. Too many Latin Americans have suffered at the hands of authoritarian systems that reduce all forms of expression – public, private, religious or aesthetic – to a certain political value or meaning for there not to be an enormous amount of skepticism about such approaches to culture.

(Fusco 2000: 4).

Fusco's performance work is very different in style from Boal's theatre projects: it features the ironic playfulness and cultural density of much postmodern art. One of her pieces, with her regular collaborator Guillermo Gómez-Peña, is *Two Undiscovered Amerindians Visit* …, in which she and Gómez-Peña were placed in a cage and exhibited in various cities as two people from a fictional undiscovered island off the coast of Mexico. The performance was staged around Europe and the Americas, often in ethnological museums with an attachment to the history of putting native people on display for Europeans. The two Amerindians were shown performing 'traditional tasks', including sewing voodoo dolls, dancing to rap music, lifting weights, watching television and working on a laptop computer (Fusco 1994: 145). Although the performers originally expected their 'use of satiric spectacle' to be readily apparent, many people believed the entire set-up to be true (one man remembered having read about the island in *National Geographic* [p. 160]), and they reacted in a number of ways, from fear to paternalistic (or dehumanizing) concern – one viewer called The Humane Society to complain about their treatment (p. 157). The complex and unexpected response of viewers changed the effect of the performance, complicating its interplay of truth and fiction. Some of the 'traditional tasks', for instance, although unlikely to be the activities of people who have had no contact with the West, are more in keeping with the lives of many contemporary Latin Americans, who, as 'other', continue to be on display. The performance also called attention to the oppressive politics and fictionality of past practices of ethnographic and 'objective' study of native peoples – museum directors were bewildered to find that viewers took the performance in the same way they took their own 'scientific' displays. The performers expected that their performance would show that viewers had not moved past cultural stereotypes in their thinking and hoped to confront viewers with their own stereotypical reactions. They did not expect the performance to be taken as reality; nor did they expect to be accused of 'misinforming the public' (p. 143). What was actually the case, perhaps, was that with an already misinformed public, lines between fiction and reality became very difficult to disentangle.

A similar playfulness with reality and cultural stereotypes can be seen in Gómez-Peña's performance piece *The New World Border*, the title itself an allusion to George Bush Sr's declaration of a new world order. The piece, very self-aware of its play of fiction and reality, labels itself repeatedly in contradictory ways: 'This is an authentic Indian ritual' (Gómez-Peña 1994: 125); 'This is what it is' (p. 125); 'This ain't performance art but pure Chicano science-fiction' (p. 127); 'Is this re-a-li-ty or performance? Can anyone answer?!' (p. 127); 'I want everyone to repeat after me: "This is art (*pause*); this is not reality (*pause*). Reality is no longer real"' (p. 131). Reality has become, in one of the work's many plays on words, 'Reali-TV' (p. 123).

The New World Border grew in reaction to Bush's new world order based in the hegemony of the United States and its affinity in

1992 with the celebrations around the 500th anniversary of Columbus's 'discovery' of the new world; the performance was presented in a number of cities as a radio broadcast by members of 'Gringostroika', 'a continental grassroots movement that advocates the complete economic and cultural reform of U.S. anarcho-capitalism' (p. 122). It presented an imaginary future in which the dominance of Anglo-Americans over Latinos has been reversed. One version of the performance, for instance, began with unilingual whites being picked out and segregated from the rest of the audience (p. 125). In this imaginary future, the United States has been dissolved, 'All major metropolises have been fully *borderized*' (referring to the process 'also known by sociologists as "calcutization" or "third-worldization"' [p. 121]); and 'there are no longer visible cultural differences between Toronto, Manhattan, Chicago, *Lost Angeles*, or *Mexico Cida*. They all look like downtown Tijuana on a Saturday night' (p. 128). In this future, racial purity is rare and frowned upon, and the world is full of the kind of hybrid identities espoused by Said: common ethnic groups include '*Germanchurians*', '*Afro-Croatians*' and '*Jap-talians*' (p. 132). This future is both the opposite of what exists, in terms of the reversal of US domination, and an exaggeration of trends that actually exist – toward hybridity and miscegenation, for instance. In a similar way, Gringostroika puts forward political principles which mix the ironic and the politically compelling:

1. No nation, community, or individual can claim racial, sexual, or aesthetic purity.
2. Starting in January of '95, all borders on the American continent will be open. No passport will be required.
3. All nations will operate with only one currency: the mighty peso.
4. Members of monoracial minorities of European descent must be granted equal rights, voting power, and a free multicultural education.

(p. 131)

How different is this, really, from Boal's work? Like Boal, Fusco and Gómez-Peña politically engage their audience in fictions that call from them strong responses which become the subject of reflection and, hopefully, drivers of social change. Boal, however, works in a straightforward way to bring his audience to a clear understanding of issues; Fusco and Gómez-Peña are more willing to immerse their audience in confusion and contradiction. Boal's audience is ideally an audience that can be led directly to truth; the audience of Fusco and Gómez-Peña is sometimes a lost cause mired in prejudice, sometimes an audience that understands. But understanding is ironic, complex, contradictory and entails a sense that reality and fiction are anything but simple.

QUESTIONS ONE MIGHT ASK OF A PLAY OR PERFORMANCE

What is the relation of the place where this play or performance is taking place to the history of western colonialism? Does that relation colour the play or performance in any way?

Does the play or performance feature multi-racial casting? Does this serve to reinforce or undermine cultural stereotypes?

Does the play or performance use traditional, 'Aristotelian' techniques or does it attempt to give the spectator a more active (or liberated) role?

Is interculturalism at work in this play or performance? If so, does it serve western domination and appropriation, undermine western cultural hegemony, or make for a fair and constructive exchange? Does your answer to this question depend on your own identity and place in the post-colonial situation?

CONCLUSION

What Next?

Every wink of an eye some new grace will be born.
  (Shakespeare 1974: *The Winter's Tale* 5.2.110–11)

What is the use of talking, and there is no
end of talking,
There is no end of things in the heart.
                    (Pound 1971: 136)

If you have read this far, where does it leave you? Do you now know theory? Some may feel they now know more than enough: some may have begun with a dislike for theory which has only been magnified; some may have had their initial curiosity more than satisfied. For such readers it is time to move on to something else. But for those whose interest in theory has been pricked by this introduction, what is there to do next?

It seems to me that three tasks lie open before you. One is to continue reading. You will find that this conclusion is followed by a section of recommendations for further reading. Having read this book, you have only begun the endless task of pursuing theory in your reading. You need to read more. Having said that, however, I think a few precautions are in order.

One aspect of postmodern life is the radical proliferation of information. There is always more and more to read; there is no end of things to read. Academic study in the postmodern age partakes of the postmodern sublime: there is always too much for anyone to get his or her mind around. There is no escape from perplexity.

In such a situation, even those who wish to pursue theoretical knowledge may become overwhelmed, discouraged and intolerant. Is it necessary, one may ask oneself, to read one more essay, albeit the latest thing, on some slight yet over-trodden theoretical issue? Is the most current work always the most important work? Why? Often it seems theory is not done for the sake of fuller understanding, but because careers are riding on its continuing overproduction. The result is often a kind of intellectual white noise which makes no one the wiser.

There is no end of thinking. As long as we live, we think. And there will always be unresolved issues. We will never, as hard as we try, have the answers to everything. Theory, in the sense of ongoing reflection and contemplation, is an important part of life. While theory sometimes seems overly difficult and abstruse, at other times it forces us to realize that many of life's pressing issues are complex and difficult and not susceptible to ready answers.

If we can borrow from the theatrical terminology of Peter Brook, what the reader needs to develop is the power to discern between living theory and deadly theory (Brook 1968). Living theory can be difficult, complex and taxing; but the difficulty is necessary in order to give adequate consideration to something important. Theory, too, can be a thing in the heart. Deadly theory, on the other hand, will be verbally, notionally, gratuitously opaque, and it will be unrelated to anything we can think of as important in our lives. Sometimes, however, it will not be easy to tell living theory and deadly theory apart, and the point is not a facile dismissal of anything we don't understand.

Finally, the postmodern age is often said to be about speed. But the most sophisticated theoretical understanding is as often about the slow contemplation of a single work or idea as it is about the rapid processing of endless volumes of information. Ignorance is not a defensible theoretical position, but each reader must decide when silence and isolation are best allowed to settle temporarily over the mind.

The second task that lies before you is to continue to think through the stickiest, most nagging question this book has raised, which is the relationship between theory and theatre, between theory and theatrical practice. If you haven't already given up on theory as basically useless, if you think that theory and contemplation are a necessary aspect of any thoughtful and interesting performance, then this remains a pressing question for you.

Childhood, as I experienced it, is a time in which one encounters, everywhere from cheap paperbacks to bubblegum wrappers, endless weak jokes based on rudimentary word play. I think, for instance, of something like 'Why do monkeys eat bananas? Because they want to have appeal', or 'Why did Edison invent the electric bulb? Because he sought enlightenment.' Both of these jokes function in the same way: they take an abstract idea – appeal, enlightenment – and through a trick of language equate it with something tangible – a (banana) peel, (electric) light. In their own basic way, these jokes show us much of what language-based theory has taught us: the way language controls or plays with our thinking and at the same time the absurdity of equating language and reality. They also present characters –

monkeys, Edison – with a rather strange kind of motivation, one in which it is easy to move from the abstract to the concrete or the concrete to the abstract. Most of us know, however, that gaining appeal or enlightenment is never as easy as eating bananas or turning on a light.

So are we as foolish as monkeys if we assume that moving from theory to theatre or theatre to theory is an easy or straightforward process? We have seen that someone as theoretically astute as Bonnie Marranca has questioned the relevance of much theoretical work to the practices of the performing arts. Theory and theatre can be irrelevant to each other. But there is nothing inherent about them which means that this must be so. Nor is there anything about them which guarantees a productive relationship. The question of their usefulness for each other will have to be answered over and over again always in new and particular circumstances.

The final piece of unfinished business is to tackle some of the nagging issues that have arisen in the theoretical discussions in this book, questions for which there are no easy or final answers. One of those questions is the one postmodernism and other theories pose about the future of theatre. In the fall of 1995 an international conference called 'Why Theatre?' was held at the University of Toronto. A major subject of discussion was the future of theatre in the twenty-first century. Given technological developments in virtual reality and communications, it is not clear what, if any, purpose will be served by live theatre in the not-too-distant future. Postmodern theory sees theatre as a quaint and marginalized activity in a wired world, and Philip Auslander questions whether live theatre even really exists anymore. Some of you may dream of seeing your name up in lights on a theatre marquee, but if you are really looking for fame and fortune shouldn't you be studying film at least, or television arts, or computers? What is it about theatre that remains compelling for you? Is it just because it's there?

Auslander's attack on live theatre arises from a sense of the influence of technology, but deconstruction questions whether actors and audience are ever really present under any circumstances. Deconstruction has compelling arguments for saying this, but it does seem rather counter-intuitive. If we buy this argument, does it further undermine a traditional notion of what is special and important about theatre? Also, what are we to do with theoretical arguments that, compelling as they may be, run counter to our sense of the way things are? Does this counter-intuitiveness make theory more or less interesting, more or less compelling?

The theories in this book have been presented in blocks: first I told you about semiotics, then about phenomenology, etc. The theories seem to stand as independent, self-contained entities. On the other hand, I have mentioned that most theoretical work now proceeds by combining elements from different theories. Few these days are orthodox Freudians or Marxists or even deconstructionists. But is there really much intellectual integrity and honesty in picking and choosing whatever suits you from whatever theories you like? Don't Freud's individual notions only really make sense when they are seen as part of a whole? On the other hand, if you can't become a disciple of the whole system, does that mean that you have to reject perfectly useful ideas that system may contain?

We've asked about the future of theatre. We could ask similar questions about the place of theory in the new century. As the old century has drawn to a close it is easier to see broad theoretical outlines than it might have been ten or fifteen years ago. But we still don't know what happens next. On the one hand, it might seem that not much new is happening in theory. The big ideas have all been stated. Have we seen the last of any big new movements? Have we come to a temporary end of theory or exhaustion of theory, analogous to the 'end of history' which has come with the global triumph of capitalism? Is it time for theory to settle down for a while? Perhaps, but theory may just as easily be seen to have so penetrated our intellectual life that, even if it is not making any big new noises, it is as widespread as ever. But it is also just as likely that something new and unexpected is already on its way. If so, I leave you to make your own introductions.

GLOSSARY

Agency, agent   Agency is the ability to act effectively; an agent is someone or something that has agency. Often used in distinction to subject, which implies either a naive sense of freedom and power or a sense of subjection and powerlessness. Agency, on the other hand, implies a degree of, but not unlimited, freedom to act.

Apparatus   In the work of Michel Foucault, an apparatus is an institution broadly conceived, which activates and controls our way of being in society. Schools, for instance, with their buildings, teachers, discipline, books, equipment, degrees, discourses, etc., are apparatuses that mould the way students think and behave.

Arche-writing   In the work of Jacques Derrida, arche-writing is the primal condition of everything that can be taken as having the condition of writing: all human expression and thought. The characteristics of arche-writing are such things as lack of origin, lack of presence, free play over intention, iterability – basically, qualities which separate human expression and thought from a unity of identity and intention, so that thought and expression are always different from what we expect them to be.

Base/superstructure   In Marxist thought, a model for the relation between the economic reality (base) and cultural life (superstructure), which implies that economics is the foundation on which culture is made, and that economic reality determines culture, and that culture is an expression of economic reality.

Binary oppositions   In deconstruction and feminism, binary oppositions, such as truth/falsehood, male/female, good/bad, are hierarchical patterns used by western patriarchal society to structure attitudes in such a way as to privilege one side (for example, male) at the expense of the other (female). The work of deconstruction or feminism becomes to critique and expose these binary oppositions as untenable or unjust.

Border pedagogy   In post-colonial thought, which is often concerned with new ways of teaching and thereby liberating the victims of colonization, border pedagogy is concerned with teaching people to move back and forth between adjoining but different systems, for example mainstream and minority cultures in a large city. Border pedagogy also allows one to reflect on different systems by seeing them from within, from an outside perspective, and in relation to each other.

Bracketing   In phenomenology, bracketing is the act of suspending consideration of something so that another train of thought can be followed without interference.

Canon   The group of works that are treated as central to a culture, that are often the focus of study, production and praise in a society. The works of Shakespeare, for example, are obviously at the centre of the literary, dramatic and theatrical canons of western culture. The canon also often promotes a set of attitudes and patterns of judgement. The canon also excludes and ignores; and many interesting and valuable works, especially those not the product of white men, are outside the canon. Feminism and post-colonial studies, for instance, are therefore concerned to critique the canon and either dismantle it or open it up to works it has so far excluded.

Carnivalesque   In the work of Mikhail Bakhtin, the carnivalesque describes the quality of peasant, popular culture as bawdy, irreverent and open to allowing oppressed voices to speak back to authority.

Commodification   In Marxist and postmodern thought, commodification is the way that capitalism reduces everything to monetary value, to something that can be bought and sold.

Condensation   For Sigmund Freud, condensation is one of the two basic tricks (the other is displacement) whereby the unconscious and dreams express our hidden thoughts in a disguised manner. Condensation is the process whereby one word or image expresses more than one idea.

Cultural code   In Roland Barthes, the cultural code is that aspect of meaning which comes from general cultural knowledge. For example, someone who wears a dress is usually female. A short red dress means something different in western culture than a long, demure dress.

Cultural materialism   Jonathan Dollimore and Alan Sinfield call their politically engaged leftist criticism, derived from Marxism, feminism and other progressive schools, cultural materialism. It seeks to situate cultural works within a social and political order in order to understand them and effect political change.

Death drive   In the work of Sigmund Freud, the death drive is that instinct in living organisms that seeks stasis and quietude. For Freud this is the ultimate instinct, stronger and deeper even than the pleasure principle, which makes human beings seek out sensual and psychological gratification.

Desemiotics For François Lyotard, desemiotics is an interest in that aspect of signs which is purely visceral and sensual and doesn't try to convey meaning.

Diachronic In the work of Ferdinand de Saussure, the diachronic consists of those aspects of language which change over time, the history of language. For example, a word may change its spelling, pronunciation or meaning over time.

Dialogic In Mikhail Bakhtin, the dialogic is that aspect of carnivalesque culture which allows for exchange and dialogue between different voices and positions.

Diaspora In post-colonial theory, diaspora refers to the migration, often forced, of peoples from one part of the world to another. The slave trade, for instance, enacted a black diaspora as people were taken from Africa to the Americas.

Différance In the work of Jacques Derrida, *différance*, which is not actually a word, combines notions of difference and deferral, which are basic aspects of the way writing works: writing is always different than what it was meant to be, and its meaning is always indefinitely deferred.

Difference A widely used idea, which in Ferdinand de Saussure describes the relation between signs (a sign is defined by being different from other signs) and in feminism and post-colonialism refers to the way women and non-Europeans have always been thought of as different from the white, male norm – a difference which has been used to the detriment of women and non-Europeans, but which feminism and post-colonialism wish to celebrate. In Jacques Lacan, difference also describes the way that our unconscious is not identical with our conscious sense of our selves.

Displacement For Sigmund Freud, displacement is one of the two basic tricks (the other is condensation) whereby the unconscious and dreams express our hidden thoughts in a disguised manner. Displacement is the way a word or image refers to something other than itself, something associated with itself.

Dominant, residual, emergent In Raymond Williams, dominant, residual and emergent are three aspects of a culture. The dominant are those forces that are strongest at any time (in our time, the forces of capitalism); the residual are older forces that have not yet completely died out (more communal, rural forces in our time); the emergent are forces that are still developing (feminism, for instance, has been emergent for thirty years or so).

Drama The literary, textual aspect of theatre, for example, the drama texts of Shakespeare.

Écriture feminine In Hélène Cixous, *écriture feminine* refers to the quality of women's writing (also achievable by some men) which makes it flowing, playful and in touch with the rhythms of the female body.

Ego In Sigmund Freud, the conscious part of ourselves, the 'I' we think of when we consider who we are. The ego is really a small and weak part of the self at the mercy of the unconscious forces that really drive us and the parental superego which tries to keep us under control.

Embodiment In phenomenology, embodiment refers to the way we exist in living bodies through which we experience the world. Feminism and other approaches are also very concerned with how our bodies come into contact with the world.

Gestus In Bertolt Brecht's notion of theatre, a *gestus* is a socially significant gesture, one which reveals the power relations between the person who makes the *gestus* and others. Imagine, for instance, the way a peasant removes his hat and stoops before an aristocrat.

Grammatology In Jacques Derrida, grammatology is the study of writing, or rather of arche-writing, which for Derrida is the basic character of all human thought and expression.

Hegemony In materialist thought, hegemony refers to the dominant attitudes, relations, and practices of a political order. In our world, for example, capitalism can be taken as hegemonic.

Hermeneutic code In the work of Roland Barthes, the hermeneutic code is that aspect of cultural works which poses a question for us to pursue. For example, all mysteries and detective stories drive us to answer the question, 'Who dunnit?'

Hommosexuality For Teresa de Lauretis, hommosexuality describes the sexual dynamics among men (not necessarily homosexual) which keep power and recognition circulating with them and away from women

Homoerotic For queer theory, the homoerotic are sexualized but not fully homosexual relations between men.

Homosocial   For queer theory, the homosocial are social, but not necessarily sexual, relations between men: sports teams, old boys' networks, etc.

Hybridity   For Edward Said, hybridity describes more and more the character of identity in the post-colonial world: people have parents from different cultures; they may have been raised in one place and live in another. People, therefore, do not have a simple ethnic identity but identify with two or more cultures.

Hyperreality   For Jean Baudrillard, hyperreality describes the postmodern situation in which we have replaced nature with fabrications of our own, so that we no longer live in a natural reality, but in an artificial hyperreality.

Icon   For Charles Peirce, an icon is the kind of sign that resembles the thing it is a sign for. A realist portrait or a photograph of someone is, for example, an icon.

Id   In the work of Sigmund Freud, the id (Latin for 'it') is the unconscious, that part of our selves which we don't consciously know, but which carries the drives and instincts which motivate us at the deepest level.

Ideological state apparatuses   For Louis Althusser, ideological state apparatuses ('ISAs' for short) are such things as schools, the media, jobs, which make us take part in the established (capitalist) order, not by physically forcing us (no one arrives at your home to take you to work each morning) but by bringing us to identify with our role in the established order.

Ideology   In materialist thought, ideology is the accepted way of looking at the world, a way of looking that various forces instil in us so that we will not question the status quo, but will support it and take up our part in it. Some aspects of capitalist ideology are that individual acquisitiveness is good for everybody, that economic inequality is inevitable or good, that those who don't succeed have only themselves to blame. For materialist thinkers, ideology is false and hides the truth about the world we live in.

Imaginary   For Jacques Lacan, the imaginary is a stage in our relationship to the real characterized by inflexibility and an inability to respond to the complexities of the world around us. Young children and paranoid and psychotic adults have an imaginary relation to the real.

Immasculation   For Judith Fetterley, immasculation describes the process whereby traditionally women have been brought to read culture like men, accepting male attitudes and understandings as their own. In opposition to immasculation, feminism posits a 'resisting reader' who would read as a woman against male norms and prejudices.

Implied reader   For Wolfgang Iser, reading entails taking up the position of the implied reader, the reader a text has set up for itself, one who reads the text as it suggests it should be read.

Index   For Charles Peirce, an index is that kind of sign that points towards the thing it represents. For example, an arrow indicates movement in a certain direction.

Interculturalism   The practice whereby theatre or other cultural forms mix together elements from different cultures. Interculturalism is often practised by western artists and it is sometimes criticized as a form of one-sided western appropriation of non-western art forms.

Interpellation   In the work of Louis Althusser, interpellation is the process whereby we are 'hailed' by ideology, in which we recognize ourselves as the one being addressed by ideological imperatives. In the morning, for instance, I recognize myself as the one being called to by my alarm clock and I get up and freely enter into the ideologically informed act of going to my job.

Interpretive communities   In the work of Stanley Fish, interpretive communities – liberal arts faculties in universities, for instance – are responsible for what a work of art means. Rather than the intentions of the author or the impressionistic responses of the sensitive observer, interpretive communities dictate, allowing or disallowing, what an acceptable or unacceptable reading will be.

Interrogative text   For Catherine Belsey, an interrogative text is one that doesn't provide answers or suggest a settled way of looking at things but rather leaves the reader with uncertainty and questions, so that any answers will have to be formulated by further thinking by the reader.

Iterability   For Jacques Derrida, iterability is that characteristic of writing and texts whereby they arise in ever new contexts in which their meaning and significance will be different from what the writer intended in the original circumstances of writing or from other contexts that have arisen since.

Jouissance   For Roland Barthes, *jouissance* is a playful, orgasmic pleasure that comes from writing or reading texts free of the constraints and rules of appropriate and inappropriate, right or wrong.

Langue In the work of Ferdinand de Saussure, *langue* is language in the sense of rules and abstract patterns that govern a language system such as English. *Langue* is the structure of a given language.

Latent content For Freud, the latent content is the hidden meaning, the psychic truth buried in expressions of the unconscious such as dreams and works of art.

Logocentrism For Jacques Derrida, logocentrism is the misguided western faith in language, especially the spoken word (logos), and its ability to speak truth in a bond with the conscious intentions of the speaker. For Derrida, the connection of all speech and language with writing, or arche-writing, gives the lie to this faith.

Manifest content For Sigmund Freud, the manifest content of expressions of the unconscious such as dreams and works of art is the surface meaning, which appears innocuous or nonsensical but which hides the latent content, the dark unconscious truth. For Freud, the task of interpretation is to read through the manifest content to the latent content.

Méconnaissance For Jacques Lacan, *méconnaissance*, or misrecognition, is the inevitable relation of human understanding to reality. We have no direct knowledge of reality, only of the forms it takes in our psyches, which inevitably distort under the influence of our drives and needs.

Metaphor For Roman Jakobson, metaphor is the function of language that allows one word to be substituted for another: 'the cat in the hat' can become 'the rat in the hat'. Metaphorical substitution is one of the two basic transformations that allow linguistic expression to be generated (the other is metonymy). Jacques Lacan makes a connection between metaphor and condensation, Freud's term for one of the two modes of transformation in dream thought, to argue that the unconscious works essentially like a language.

Metonymy For Roman Jakobson, metonymy is the function of language that allows one word to be connected to another: 'the cat sat on the hat' connects a subject with a verb and a prepositional phrase. Metonymical connection is one of the two basic transformations that allow linguistic expression to be generated (the other is metaphor). Jacques Lacan makes a connection between metonymy and displacement, Freud's term for one of the two modes of transformation in dream thought, to argue that the unconscious works essentially like a language

Mirror stage   For Jacques Lacan, the mirror stage is that period in infancy when we come to recognize our image in a mirror. We develop a fixed, unified sense of our selves, but one that is not particularly complex, sophisticated or open to change. Lacan calls the outlook we have on the world in this stage the imaginary, an immature outlook we need to outgrow if we are to interact more fully with the world.

Mode of production   In Marxist thought, the mode of production is the basic set of economic relations in a society. The two basic elements are the relation of workers to the means of production and the relation of workers to the objects of production. In capitalism, for instance, workers are alienated from both the means of production (they don't own the tools, offices, factories where they work and they have neither job security nor the right to work to their own schedule) and the objects of production (they don't own what they make or share in the profits they generate).

Myth   For Roland Barthes, a myth is an aspect of ideology conveyed through signs and images. A photograph of a smiling factory owner with his arms around a smiling worker presents the myth that the two are part of one big happy family and not in an alienating and exploitive relation of capitalist and worker.

New historicism   Following Stephen Greenblatt, new historicism is a form of American materialist analysis that analyses the connections between literary and non-literary texts and a particular historical situation. This study has also been called 'cultural poetics'. It has tended to see all resistance and subversion of the status quo as ultimately subject to containment by the powers that be.

Oedipus complex   For Sigmund Freud, the Oedipus complex (which he saw at work in *Oedipus Rex* and *Hamlet*) defines the relationship between a child and his (or her) parents. In the case of a boy, for instance (Freud's dominant example), the child begins with an undifferentiated ability to receive pleasure from both parents. Soon the mother becomes the object of pleasure and the father becomes the stern character who blocks the boy from having the mother all to himself. The child wants to eradicate the father so that he can enjoy the mother. But the father is a powerful and threatening force, and the boy has to suppress his desires and submit to the father's will. In maturing, the child buries and forgets the attachment to the mother and hostility to the father and replaces them with desire for a girl like his mother and an identification with the father. He thus takes up a traditional role in the family and society.

Orientalism For Edward Said, orientalism is the ideology the West has imposed on the East. Through empire and colonization the world has come to be seen in a series of related oppositions: West/East; white/black; good/bad; rational/irrational; strong/weak; competent/incompetent; dominant/submissive.

Other For Jacques Lacan, the Other is that part of the self, associated with the mother and the language of the unconscious, which we don't identify with and which seems to us not to be who we are but rather something coming from elsewhere. Feminism and post-colonialism have taken up the identification of women and non-Europeans as other than white and male in order to present an identity which resists and offers an alternative to white male domination.

Overdetermination For Sigmund Freud, the meaning of dreams is overdetermined because there is so much association going on that it is impossible to pin things down to one simple meaning. For Louis Althusser, the relations between economics and culture are overdetermined inasmuch as it is simplistic to see a simple cause-and-effect relationship between, say, a particular mode of production and the works of art it produces.

Parole In the work of Ferdinand de Saussure, *parole* is a particular linguistic utterance, an example of a linguistic system in action.

Pastiche For Fredric Jameson, pastiche is what becomes of parody and satire in the postmodern world. Pastiche is a mixing and matching of elements and styles from different eras and cultures without any overarching point or political purpose.

Patriarchy For feminist thought, patriarchy is the traditional domination of society and oppression of women by men, especially in their role as fathers.

Performance In recent theatre theory, performance is a term with a number of meanings. It can mean performance art, a certain kind of para-theatrical activity we see in the work of such artists as Carolee Schneeman and Coco Fusco; it can mean that aspect of theatre involved in actually putting on a show; it can mean the entire theatrical experience; it can expand to include other theatre-like activities such as sporting events and religious rituals; it can mean just about any activity, including private acts such as getting dressed or walking down the street.

Phallocentrism   For feminist thought, phallocentrism designates the centrality of the penis or phallus in patriarchal culture and therefore the association of the penis or phallus with social privilege and power.

Phallus   For Jacques Lacan, the phallus is the symbolic rather than the actual penis, associated with but not identical to the male sex organ. It is associated with the power of the father in the human psyche and society.

Pleasure principle   In the work of Sigmund Freud, the pleasure principle refers to the way our unconscious, instinctive drives toward pleasure and gratification are at the root of our motivations. Food, sex, power – not altruism, morality, love – are what lie behind all our actions.

Polyphonic   In the work of Mikhail Bakhtin, the polyphonic indicates that aspect of carnivalesque culture which allows different voices and perspectives to be expressed without being dominated by one official point of view.

Readerly text   In the work of Roland Barthes, a readerly text is one that doesn't allow or call for an open-ended, creative reading, but instead leads the reader by the nose and makes all the interpretive decisions on his or her behalf.

Real   For Jacques Lacan, the real is what actually exists, but we have no way of experiencing or comprehending that. We can only come into contact with the real as perceived by our structures of perception, including language and the psyche.

Semiotic   For Julia Kristeva, the semiotic is the state of the infant's attachment to the mother, a pre-linguistic state of impulses and rhythms existing before law, reason and patriarchy.

Sign   For semiotics and semiology, the sign is a perceivable object which represents something else. For Ferdinand de Saussure, it is made up of the signifier and the signified.

Signifier/signified   For Ferdinand de Saussure, the sign has two components: the signifier is the thing we perceive; the signified is the idea being conveyed.

Simulacrum   For Jean Baudrillard, a simulacrum is an artificial version of something real, a simulation, which comes to replace the real thing that it duplicates. Few people, for instance, eat real crab meat any more; artificial crab meat has replaced it in most instances. This process of simulation replacing reality is, for Baudrillard, characteristic of postmodernism.

Structuralism　From the structural semiotics of Ferdinand de Saussure to the structural anthropology of Claude Lévi-Strauss, structuralism has proceeded by scientific principles to find the abstract patterns behind all cultural activity, thereby seeing past idiosyncrasies to the way that many cultural activities are, in the abstract, the same.

Structuration　As opposed to the grand, abstract pattern-finding of structuralism, in the work of Roland Barthes structuration means the particular and changing patterns of a specific work or cultural activity.

Subaltern　In the work of Gayatri Spivak, the subaltern is the subject position of the colonized, a subject position that doesn't allow for a full, independent identity involving full and autonomous self-expression.

Subject-in-process　In the work of Julia Kristeva, the subject-in-process refers to the way human beings change back and forth from being thetic subjects, with a sure and firm sense of rational identity, to subjects disrupted by primal semiotic impulses that undermine their rational sense of self. The subject-in-process is the pattern that emerges from the continuous making, disruption and remaking of identity.

Subjectivity, subject　In materialist thought, subjectivity is the process whereby the human being is made into a functioning individual, a subject. Unlike in liberal political theory, where the subject is seen as free and autonomous, materialism sees subjectivity as producing ideologically moulded individuals who are not free but rather the product of their social and economic environment.

Sublimation　In the work of Sigmund Freud, sublimation is the process whereby we repress our basic drives in the face of familial and social constraint and they re-emerge in more acceptable, elevated endeavours, such as art, philosophy and religion. These elevated endeavours, therefore, are essentially the product of basic drives for sexual and other kinds of gratification.

Superego　For Sigmund Freud, the superego comprises the forces of parental and social restraint that we internalize as part of our selves and that forbids us from doing socially unacceptable things we are driven to do by our basic unconscious drives.

Symbol　For Charles Peirce, a symbol is a kind of sign in which there is no inherent relation between the sign we perceive and what it represents. Most words are symbols: there is only an arbitrary relation between the word 'tree' and an actual tree, for example.

Symbolic   For Jacques Lacan, the symbolic is a normalized relation between an individual and the real, one in which we are flexible in our attitudes and approaches to things. For Julia Kristeva, the symbolic order is the realm of reason, law, language and the father that a child enters when it leaves the earlier maternal, semiotic order of the infant.

Synchronic   For Ferdinand de Saussure, the synchronic refers to the structural aspect of language and its rules at any point in time. It is static rather than subject to historical change.

Thetic subject   For Julia Kristeva, the thetic subject is the subject position given us by the symbolic order: rational, unified, rule-oriented. It is regularly disrupted by the return of earlier semiotic drives and rhythms.

Thickness   For phenomenology, thickness describes the complex, sensuous reality of the world as we perceive it, as opposed to the bloodless and two-dimensional perceptions of abstract thought.

Trauerspiel   In the work of Walter Benjamin, *trauerspiel* is a form of allegorical drama in which signification is rich and overflowing, as opposed to the clear and ordered meanings of traditional realist drama.

Unconcealing   For phenomenology, especially in the work of Martin Heidegger, unconcealing is the process whereby we strip away limiting habits from our perceptions of the world, habits that hide the richness of the world, in order to reveal the world in all its freshness to perception and understanding.

Unconscious   In psychoanalysis, the unconscious is that powerful part of ourselves which we are not directly aware of and that expresses the basic drives that motivate all our actions. We only become aware of the unconscious indirectly, through its expression in dreams, for instance.

Writerly text   In the work of Roland Barthes, a writerly text is one that induces or supports an open-ended, playful reading, one that doesn't try to pin down our interpretation to an acceptable reading suggested by the text itself.

FURTHER READING

There is a common academic practice in which a writer points out the failings in all previous literature on the topic at hand in order to argue that only his or her own new and improved work will do. I want to end on a different tack. This book of mine has only introduced you to theory. If you want to take theory seriously, you will need many more books in order to deepen your knowledge. I want to end, therefore, not by criticizing or dismissing other works but by emphasizing their importance and the way they do things this book has not done.

PRIMARY TEXTS

The primary texts in theory upon which the study of theory and theatre is based are, of course, indispensable. They not only provide access to concepts and arguments in their fuller context but also in many cases force an engagement with the complexity of thinking and expression which often goes hand in hand with theory, but is often obscured by introductory guides. Key texts by the authors discussed in the book appear in the bibliography.

ANTHOLOGIES AND READERS

Anthologies of key selections in the texts of theory are the next best thing to an extensive reading of complete theoretical works. One of the most recent and wide-ranging collections is *The Norton Anthology of Theory and Criticism* edited by Vincent B. Leitch, which goes from Ancient Greece to the present. David Lodge's *Modern Criticism and Theory: A Reader* or Dan Latimer's *Contemporary Critical Theory* provide ready access to influential and representative essays by many major theorists; a collection such as Grossberg, Nelson and Treichler's *Cultural Studies* presents more recent work. More specific anthologies exist for almost all areas of theoretical thought from postmodernism to post-colonialism and gay and lesbian and queer theory. See, for instance, Paul A. Bové's *Early Postmodernism: Foundational Essays*, Joseph Natoli and Linda Hutcheon's *A Postmodern Reader*, Thomas Docherty's *Postmodernism: A Reader*, Bill Ashcroft, Gareth Griffiths and Helen Tiffin's *The Post-Colonial Studies Reader*, Gregory Castle's *Postcolonial Discourses: An Anthology*, Henry Abelove, Michèle Aina Barale and David M. Halperin's *The Lesbian and Gay Studies Reader*.

INTRODUCTIONS TO THEORY

There are many very good introductions to theory. Fredric Jameson's *The Prison House of Language*, Jonathan Culler's *Structuralist Poetics*, Terence Hawkes's *Structuralism and Semiotics*, and Terry Eagleton's *Literary Theory: An Introduction* were among the first. These works helpfully provide a wide range of theoretical work digested by one mind and presented in one voice; often this voice speaks explicitly and bracingly from one theoretical or political position – Marxist, for instance, in the cases of Jameson and Eagleton. Among more rudimentary introductions are Charles E. Bressler's *Literary Criticism: An Introduction to Theory and Practice*, Peter Barry's *Beginning Theory* and Stephen Bonnycastle's *In Search of Authority*. Also, there are many introductions to specific aspects of theory: the New Accents series, published by Routledge, includes Robert C. Holub's *Reception Theory*, Christopher Norris's *Deconstruction: Theory and Practice*, and Toril Moi's *Sexual/Textual Politics*.

ENCYCLOPEDIAS OF THEORY

In a recent consolidation, two very large encyclopedias of 'literary' theory have appeared: Irena R. Makaryk's *Encyclopedia of Contemporary Literary Theory* and Groden and Kreisworth's *Johns Hopkins Guide to Literary Theory and Criticism*. These works attempt to deal with the explosions in theoretical variety of the last 100 years and have the virtues of broad coverage and a wide range of contributors' outlooks (although Makaryk's book is already behind the times, in neglecting gay and lesbian and queer studies). One or both are important companions to any study of theory.

INTRODUCTIONS TO THEATRE THEORY

There is a large body of literature concerned with theories specifically related to the theatre. Bernard F. Dukore's *Dramatic Theory and Criticism: Greeks to Grotowski* is a useful anthology, covering important figures from the distant past, such as Aristotle, Sir Philip Sidney and John Dryden, although it stops somewhat short of the present. Marvin Carlson's *Theories of the Theatre: A Historical and Critical Survey, from the Greeks to the Present*, first published in 1984, expanded in 1993, maps to a dizzying degree the range of western theorization about theatre. Theorists not generally associated with the theatre – Freud, Barthes, Derrida – are represented inasmuch as they have produced essays on theatrical topics.

Dukore and Carlson are not specifically concerned with the relations of theory from outside theatre to theatre; however, other writers have taken up aspects of these relations: Mohammad Kowsar has produced essays on Deleuze and Lacan; Gerald Rabkin and Elinor Fuchs have written essays on deconstruction and theatre; Keir Elam's *The Semiotics of Theatre and Drama* is an overview of semiotic analysis related to plays; Sue-Ellen Case, Jill Dolan, Elaine Aston and Gayle Austin have each written a book which introduces feminist theory to the study of theatre and drama. These are just a few examples of such works.

Other writers have attempted to engage with the broadest possible spectrum of theoretical concerns. Herbert Blau, in a series of complex and difficult books, has taken up ideas from Marxism, psychoanalysis, feminism, deconstruction and phenomenology, and from thinkers ranging from Marx and Freud to Benjamin, Lacan, Kristeva, Derrida, Foucault, Deleuze and Baudrillard. All of these theories are sent spinning through Blau's particular perspectives towards a complex and contradictory vision. Blau is not for beginners. A different approach is taken by Janelle G. Reinelt and Joseph R. Roach's collection *Critical Theory and Performance*, which presents essays by different writers grouped under specific theoretical perspectives: cultural studies; semiotics and deconstruction; Marxism; feminism(s); theatre historiography; hermeneutics and phenomenology; psychoanalysis. Each area is given a general introduction, but each section of the collection then proceeds into disparate and very particular applications of theoretical concerns.

BIBLIOGRAPHY

Abelove, H., M.A. Barale and D.M. Halperin (eds) (1993) *The Lesbian and Gay Studies Reader*, New York: Routledge.

Adorno, T. (1984) *Aesthetic Theory*, London: Routledge.

Aeschylus (1999) *The Oresteia*, T. Hughes (trans.), London: Faber and Faber.

Alter, J. (1990) *A Sociosemiotic Theory of Theatre*, Philadelphia: University of Pennsylvania Press.

Althusser, L. (1969) *For Marx*, London: Verso.

—— (1971) 'Ideology and Ideological State Apparatuses (Notes towards an investigation)', in *Lenin and Philosophy and Other Essays*, London: NLB, pp. 123–73.

Aristotle (1965) *On the Art of Poetry*, in *Classical Literary Criticism*, London: Penguin, pp. 29–75.

Arrell, D. (1999) Review of *Acts of Intervention*, *Modern Drama* 42, 3 (Fall): 460–2.

Artaud, A. (1958) *Theatre and its Double*, New York: Grove Press.

—— (1988) *Selected Writings*, Berkeley: University of California Press.

Ashcroft, B., G. Griffiths and H. Tiffin (1989) *The Empire Writes Back: Theory and Practice in Post-Colonial Literatures*, London: Routledge.

—— (eds) (1995) *The Post-Colonial Studies Reader*, London: Routledge.

Aston, E. (1995) *An Introduction to Feminism and Theatre*, London: Routledge.

—— and G. Savona (1981) *Theatre as Sign-System: A Semiotics of Text and Performance*, London: Routledge.

Auslander, P. (1992) *Presence and Resistance: Postmodernism and Cultural Politics in Contemporary American Performance*, Ann Arbor: University of Michigan Press.

—— (1999) *Liveness: Performance in a Mediatized Culture*, London: Routledge.

Austin, G. (1990) *Feminist Theories for Dramatic Research*, Ann Arbor: University of Michigan Press.

Bakhtin, M. (1968) *Rabelais and His World*, Cambridge, MA: MIT Press.

—— (1984) *Problems of Dostoevsky's Poetics*, Minneapolis: University of Minnesota Press.

Barba, E. (1995) *The Paper Canoe: A Guide to Theatre Anthropology*, London: Routledge.

Barry, P. (1995) *Beginning Theory: An Introduction to Literary and Cultural Theory*, Manchester: Manchester University Press.

Barthes, R. (1972a) *Critical Essays*, Evanston, IL: Northwestern University Press.

—— (1972b) *Mythologies*, London: Jonathan Cape.

—— (1974) *S/Z: An Essay*, New York: Hill and Wang.

—— (1978) *A Lover's Discourse: Fragments*, New York: Hill and Wang.

—— (1979) 'From Work to Text', in *Textual-Strategies: Perspectives in Post-Structuralist Criticism*, J.V. Harari (ed.), Ithaca, NY: Cornell University Press, pp. 73–81.

—— (1982) *A Barthes Reader*, New York: Hill and Wang.

—— (1983) *The Fashion System*, New York: Hill and Wang.

—— (1985a) *The Grain of the Voice: Interviews 1962–1980*, New York: Hill and Wang.

—— (1985b) *The Responsibility of Forms: Critical Essays on Music, Art, and Representation*, New York: Hill and Wang.

—— (1988) 'The Death of the Author', in *Modern Criticism and Theory*, D. Lodge (ed.), London: Longman, pp. 167–72.

Bassi, K. (1998) *Acting Like Men: Gender, Drama, and Nostalgia in Ancient Greece*, Ann Arbor: University of Michigan Press.

Battock, G. and R. Nickas (eds) (1984) *The Art of Performance: A Critical Anthology*, New York: Dutton.

Baudrillard, J. (1975) *The Mirror of Production*, St Louis, MI: Telos.

—— (1981) *For a Critique of the Political Economy of the Sign*, St Louis, MI: Telos.

—— (1983) *Simulations*, New York: Semiotext(e).

—— (1987) *Forget Foucault*, New York: Semiotext(e).

Beckett, S. (1984) *Collected Shorter Plays*, New York: Grove.

Behn, A. (1994) *The Rover or The Banished Cavaliers*, A. Russell (ed.), Peterborough, Ontario: Broadview Press.

Belsey, C. (1980) *Critical Practice*, London: Routledge.

Bene, C. (1977) 'L'Énergie sans cesse renouvelée de l'utopie', *Travail Théâtral* 27: 61–89.

—— and G. Deleuze (1979) *Superposition*, Paris: Les Éditions de Minuit.

Benjamin, W. (1969) *Illuminations*, New York: Schocken.

—— (1977) *The Origin of German Tragic Drama*, London: NLB.

—— (1989) 'N [RE THE THEORY OF KNOWLEDGE, THEORY OF PROGRESS]', in *Benjamin: Philosophy, History, Aesthetics*, G. Smith (ed.), Chicago, IL: University of Chicago Press, pp. 43–83.

Bennett, S. (1990) *Theatre Audiences: A Theory of Production and Reception*, London: Routledge.

Bennett, T. (1977) *Formalism and Marxism*, London: Methuen.

Berry, R. (1977) *On Directing Shakespeare: Interviews with Contemporary Directors*, London: Croom Helm.

Bhabha, H.K. (1986) 'The Other Question: Difference, Discrimination and the Discourse of Colonialism', in *Literature, Politics, Theory: Papers from the Essex Conference 1976–84*, F. Barker, P. Hulme, M. Iversen and D. Loxley (eds), London: Methuen, pp. 148–72.

—— (1992) 'Postcolonial Authority and Postmodern Guilt', in *Cultural Studies*, L. Grossberg, C. Nelson and P.A. Treichler (eds), New York: Routledge, pp. 56–68.

Bharucha, R. (1993) *Theatre and the World: Performance and the Politics of Culture*, London: Routledge.

Birringer, J. (1991) *Theatre, Theory, Postmodernism*, Bloomington: Indiana University Press.

Blau, H. (1981) 'Elsinore: An Analytic Scenario', *Cream City Review* 6, 2: 57–99.

—— (1982a) *Blooded Thought: Occasions of Theatre*, New York: Performing Arts Journal Publications.

—— (1982b) *Take Up the Bodies: Theater at the Vanishing Point*, Urbana: University of Illinois Press.

—— (1983) 'Ideology and Performance', *Theatre Journal* 35, 4 (December): 441–60.

—— (1987a) 'The Audition of Dream and Events', *Drama Review* 31, 3 (Fall): 59–73.

—— (1987b) *The Eye of Prey: Subversions of the Postmodern*, Bloomington: Indiana University Press.

—— (1990) *The Audience*, Baltimore, MD: Johns Hopkins University Press.

—— (n.d.) *Crooked Eclipses: A Theatrical Essay on Shakespeare's Sonnets*, unpublished play.

Boal, A. (1985) *Theatre of the Oppressed*, New York: Theatre Communications Group.

—— (1998) *Legislative Theatre: Using Performance to Make Politics*, London: Routledge.

Bond, E. (1983) *Lear*, London: Methuen.

Bonnycastle, S. (1996) *In Search of Authority: An Introductory Guide to Literary Theory*, 2nd edition, Peterborough, Ontario: Broadview Press.

Bové, P.A. (ed.) (1995) *Early Postmodernism: Foundational Essays*, Durham, NC: Duke University Press.

Brecht, B. (1964) *Brecht on Theatre: The Development of an Aesthetic*, New York: Hill and Wang.

—— (1972) *Collected Plays*, vol. 9, New York: Pantheon Books.

Bressler, C.E. (1999) *Literary Criticism: An Introduction to Theory and Practice*, 2nd edition, Upper Saddle River, New Jersey: Prentice-Hall.

Brook, P. (1968) *The Empty Space*, New York: Atheneum.

—— (1987) *The Shifting Point*, New York: Harper and Row.

Butler, J. (1990) 'Performative Acts and Gender Constitution: An Essay in Phenomenology and Feminist Theory', in *Performing Feminisms: Feminist Critical Theory and Theatre*, S.-E. Case (ed.), Baltimore, MD: Johns Hopkins University Press, pp. 270–82.

Campbell, P. (ed.) (1996) *Analysing Performance: A Critical Reader*, Manchester: Manchester University Press.

Carlson, M. (1990) *Theatre Semiotics: Signs of Life*, Bloomington: Indiana University Press.

—— (1993) *Theories of the Theatre: A Historical and Critical Survey from the Greeks to the Present*, expanded edition, Ithaca, NY: Cornell University Press.

—— (1996) *Performance: A Critical Introduction*, London: Routledge.

Carlson, S. (1995) 'Cannibalizing and Carnivalizing: Reviving Aphra Behn's *The Rover*', *Theatre Journal* 47, 4 (December): 517–39.

Case, S.-E. (1988) *Feminism and Theatre*, New York: Routledge.

Castle, G. (ed.) (2001) *Postcolonial Discourses: An Anthology*, Oxford: Blackwell.

Cerasano, S.P. and M. Wynne-Davies (eds) (1996) *Renaissance Drama by Women: Texts and Documents*, London: Routledge.

Césaire, A. (1985) *A Tempest*, New York: Ubu Repertory Theater Publications.

Chekhov, A. (1982) *Five Major Plays*, New York: Bantam.

Christian, B. (1988) 'The Race for Theory', *Feminist Studies* 14 (Spring): 67–79.

Churchill, C. (1985) *Cloud Nine*, in *Plays: One*, London: Methuen, pp. 243–320.

Cixous, H. (1976) *Portrait of Dora*, in *Benmussa Directs: Portrait of Dora and The Singular Life of Albert Nobbs*, London: John Calder.

—— (1986) 'Sorties: Out and Out: Attacks/Ways Out/Forays', in *The Newly Born Woman*, H. Cixous and C. Clément, Minneapolis: University of Minnesota Press, pp. 63–132.

—— (1994) *The Name of Oedipus: Song of the Forbidden Body*, in *Plays by French and Francophone Women: A Critical Anthology*, C.P. Makward and J.G. Miller (eds), Ann Arbor: University of Michigan Press, pp. 247–326.

Cohen, W. (1985) *Drama of a Nation: Public Theater in Renaissance England and Spain*, Ithaca, NY: Cornell University Press.

Constantinidis, S.E. (1993) *Theatre under Deconstruction: A Question of Approach*, New York: Garland.

Counsell, C. (1996) *Signs of Performance: An Introduction to Twentieth-Century Theatre*, London: Routledge.

Croyden, M. (1990) 'After the Revolution', *Village Voice* (12 June): 97–8, 106.

Culler, J. (1975) *Structuralist Poetics: Structuralism, Linguistics, and the Study of Literature*, Ithaca, NY: Cornell University Press.

Davies, I. (1995) *Cultural Studies and Beyond: Fragments of Empire*, London: Routledge.

de Lauretis, T. (1990) 'Sexual Indifference and Lesbian Representation', in *Performing Feminisms: Feminist Critical Theory and Theatre*, S.-E. Case (ed.), Baltimore, MD: Johns Hopkins University Press, pp. 17–39.

de Man, P. (1979) *Allegories of Reading: Figural Language in Rousseau, Nietzsche, Rilke, and Proust*, New Haven, CT: Yale University Press.

—— (1984) *The Rhetoric of Romanticism*, New York: Columbia University Press.

—— (1986) *The Resistance to Theory*, Minneapolis: University of Minnesota Press.

de Marinis, M. (1993) *The Semiotics of Performance*, Bloomington: Indiana University Press.

Deleuze, G. and F. Guattari (1983) *Anti-Oedipus*, vol. 1 of *Capitalism and Schizophrenia*, Minneapolis: University of Minnesota Press.

—— (1987) *A Thousand Plateaus*, vol. 2 of *Capitalism and Schizophrenia*, Minneapolis: University of Minnesota Press.

Derrida, J. (1976) *Of Grammatology*, Baltimore, MD: Johns Hopkins University Press.

—— (1978) *Writing and Difference*, Chicago, IL: University of Chicago Press.

—— (1980a) 'An Interview with Jacques Derrida', J. Kearns and K. Newton, *The Literary Review* 14 (18 April–1 May): 21–2.

—— (1980b) 'The Law of Genre', *Glyph* 7 (Spring): 202–32.

—— (1985) *The Ear of the Other: Otobiography, Transference, Translation*, New York: Schocken.

—— (1986) 'But Beyond ... (Open Letter To Anne McClintock and Rob Nixon)', *Critical Inquiry* 13, 1 (Autumn): 155–70.

—— (1988) 'Signature Event Context', in *Limited Inc*, Evanston, IL: Northwestern University Press, pp. 1–23.

—— (1991) ' "Eating Well", or the Calculation of the Subject: An Interview with Jacques Derrida', in *Who Comes After the Subject?*, E. Cadava, P. Connor and J.-L. Nancy (eds), New York: Routledge, pp. 96–119.

—— (1992) 'Différance', in *A Critical and Cultural Theory Reader*, A. Easthope and K. McGowan (eds), Toronto: University of Toronto Press, pp. 108–32.

—— (1994) *Specters of Marx: The State of the Debt, the Work of Mourning, and the New International*, Routledge: New York.

Docherty, T. (ed.) (1993) *Postmodernism: A Reader*, Hemel Hempstead: Harvester Wheatsheaf.

Dolan, J. (1988) *The Feminist Spectator as Critic*, Ann Arbor, MI: UMI Research Press.

—— (1992) 'Practicing Cultural Disruptions: Gay and Lesbian Representation and Sexuality', in *Critical Theory and Performance*, J.G. Reinelt and J.R. Roach (eds), Ann Arbor: University of Michigan Press, pp. 263–75.

Dollimore, J. (1984) *Radical Tragedy: Religion, Ideology and Power in the Drama of Shakespeare and his Contemporaries*, Chicago, IL: University of Chicago Press.

—— and A. Sinfield (eds) (1985) *Political Shakespeare: New Essays in Cultural Materialism*, Ithaca, NY: Cornell University Press.

Drainie, B. (1994) '*Oleanna*'s Popularity is Deeply Disturbing', in Toronto *Globe and Mail* (17 November): E5.

D'Souza, D. (1991) *Illiberal Education: The Politics of Race and Sex on Campus*, New York: The Free Press.

Dukore, B.F. (1974) *Dramatic Theory and Criticism: Greeks to Grotowski*, New York: Holt, Rinehart and Winston.

Eagleton, T. (1981) *Walter Benjamin, or Towards a Revolutionary Criticism*, London: Verso.

—— (1983) *Literary Theory: An Introduction*, Minneapolis: University of Minnesota Press.

—— (1991) *Ideology: An Introduction*, London: Verso.

Easthope, A. and K. McGowan (eds) (1993) *A Critical and Cultural Theory Reader*, Toronto: University of Toronto Press.

Elam, K. (1980) *The Semiotics of Theatre and Drama*, London: Routledge.

Ensler, E. (1998) *The Vagina Monologues*, New York: Villard.

Fanon, F. (1965) *The Wretched of the Earth*, London: MacGibbon and Kee.

Feltes, N.N. (1986) *Modes of Production of Victorian Novels*, Chicago, IL: University of Chicago Press.

Ferguson, M.W. (1991) 'The Spectre of Resistance: *The Tragedy of Mariam* (1613)', in *Staging the Renaissance: Reinterpretations of Elizabethan and Jacobean Drama*, D.S. Kastan and P. Stallybrass (eds), New York: Routledge, pp. 235–50.

Filewod, A. (1994) 'Receiving Aboriginality: Tomson Highway and the Crisis of Cultural Authenticity', *Theatre Journal* 46, 3 (October): 363–73.

Fischer-Lichte, E. (1992) *The Semiotics of Theater*, Bloomington: Indiana University Press.

Fish, S. (1980) *Is There a Text in This Class? The Authority of Interpretive Communities*, Cambridge, MA: Harvard University Press.

Foucault, M. (1973) *The Order of Things: An Archeology of the Human Sciences*, New York: Pantheon.

—— (1977) *Language, Counter-Memory, Practice: Selected Essays and Interviews*, Ithaca, NY: Cornell University Press.

—— (1980a) *History of Sexuality*, New York: Pantheon.

—— (1980b) *Power/Knowledge: Selected Interviews and Other Writings 1972–1977*, New York: Pantheon.

—— (1985) *The Use of Pleasure*, New York: Random House.

—— (1986) 'Of Other Spaces', *Diacritics* 16, 1 (Spring): 22–7.

Freire, P. (1970) *Pedagogy of the Oppressed*, New York: Seabury.

—— (1994) *Pedagogy of Hope: Reliving Pedagogy of the Oppressed*, New York: Continuum.

Freud, S. (1953–66) *The Standard Edition of the Complete Psychological Works*, 23 vols, London: Hogarth Press.

—— (1974) 'On Oedipus and Hamlet', in *Dramatic Theory and Criticism: Greeks to Grotowski*, B.F. Dukore (ed.), New York: Holt, Rinehart and Winston, pp. 827–31.

Frye, N. (1969) 'Introduction' to *The Tempest*, in W. Shakespeare, *The Complete Works*, A. Harbage (ed.), London: Penguin, pp. 1369–72.

—— (1986) *Northrop Frye on Shakespeare*, Markham, Ontario: Fitzhenry and Whiteside.

—— (1990) *Words with Power: Being a Second Study of 'The Bible and Literature'*, San Diego, CA: Harcourt Brace.

Fuchs, E. (1985) 'Presence and the Revenge of Writing: Re-thinking Theatre after Derrida', *Performing Arts Journal* 26/7: 163–73.

Fusco, C. (1994) 'The Other History of Intercultural Performance', *The Drama Review* 38, 1 (Spring): 143–67.

—— (ed.) (2000) *Corpus Delecti: Performance Art of the Americas*, London: Routledge.

Gainor, J.E. (ed.) (1995) *Imperialism and Theatre: Essays on World Theatre, Drama, and Performance*, London: Routledge.

Garber, M. (1992) *Vested Interests: Cross Dressing and Cultural Anxiety*, New York: Routledge.

Garner Jr, S.B. (1994) *Bodied Spaces: Phenomenology and Performance in Contemporary Drama*, Ithaca, NY: Cornell University Press.

—— (2000) 'Framing the Classroom: Pedagogy, Power, *Oleanna*', *Theatre Topics* 10, 1 (March): 39–52.

Gilbert, H. and J. Tompkins (1996) *Post-Colonial Drama: Theory, Practice, Politics*, London: Routledge.

Goldberg, J. (ed.) (1994) *Queering the Renaissance*, Durham, NC: Duke University Press.

Goldie, T. (1989) *Fear and Temptation: The Image of the Indigene in Canadian, Australian, and New Zealand Literatures*, Kingston, Ontario: McGill-Queen's University Press.

Gómez-Peña, G. (1994) 'The New World Border: Prophecies for the End of the Century', *The Drama Review* 38, 1 (Spring): 119–42.

Goodman, L. (1998) *The Routledge Reader in Gender and Performance*, New York: Routledge.

Gray, S. (1988) *Swimming to Cambodia*, New York: Theatre Communications Group.

—— (1992a) *Impossible Vacation*, New York: Knopf.

—— (1992b) *Monster in a Box*, New York: Vintage.

Greenblatt, S. (1988) *Shakespearean Negotiations: The Circulation of Social Energy in Renaissance England*, Berkeley: University of California Press.

Groden, M. and M. Kreisworth (eds) (1994) *The Johns Hopkins Guide to Literary Theory and Criticism*, Baltimore, MD: Johns Hopkins University Press.

Grossberg, L., C. Nelson and P.A. Treichler (eds) (1992) *Cultural Studies*, New York: Routledge.

Grotowski, J. (1975) *Towards a Poor Theatre*, London: Methuen.

Gurr, A. (1987) *Playgoing in Shakespeare's London*, Cambridge: Cambridge University Press.

Habermas, J. (1979) *Communication and the Evolution of Society*, London: Heinemann.

Haraway, D.J. (1991) *Simians, Cyborgs, and Women: The Reinvention of Nature*, New York: Routledge.

Hawkes, T. (1977) *Structuralism and Semiotics*, Berkeley: University of California Press.

Heidegger, M. (1975) *Poetry, Language, and Truth*, New York: Harper and Row.

—— (1977) *The Question Concerning Technology and Other Essays*, New York: Harper and Row.

Highway, T. (1988) *The Rez Sisters*, Saskatoon: Fifth House.

—— (1989) *Dry Lips Oughta Move to Kapuskasing*, Saskatoon: Fifth House.

Höfele, A. (1992) 'A Theatre of Exhaustion? "*Posthistoire*" in Recent German Shakespeare Productions', *Shakespeare Quarterly* 43, 1: 80–6.

Holderness, G. (ed.) (1988) *The Shakespeare Myth*, Manchester: Manchester University Press.

Holub, R.C. (1984) *Reception Theory: A Critical Introduction*, London: Routledge.

hooks, b. (1992) 'Representing Whiteness in the Black Imagination', in *Cultural Studies*, L. Grossberg, C. Nelson and P.A. Treichler (eds), New York: Routledge, pp. 338–46.

—— (1993) 'bell hooks Speaking about Paulo Freire – The Man, His Work', in *Paulo Freire: A Critical Encounter*, P. MacLaren and P. Leonard (eds), London: Routledge, pp. 146–54.

Howard, J.E. and S.C. Shershow (eds) (2001) *Marxist Shakespeares*, London: Routledge.

Huffman, K. (1994) '*Oleanna* and *Disclosure* Attack Sexual Harassment in the Work Place', in University of Toronto *Varsity* (8 December): 15.

Husserl, E. (1964) *The Idea of Phenomenology*, The Hague: Martinus Nijhoff.

Hutcheon, L. (1988) *A Poetics of Postmodernism: History, Theory, Fiction*, New York: Routledge.

Hwang, D.H. (1989) *M. Butterfly*, New York: Plume.

Ibsen, H. (1965) *A Doll's House*, in *A Doll's House and Other Plays*, London: Penguin.

Iser, W. (1978) *The Act of Reading: A Theory of Aesthetic Response*, Baltimore, MD: Johns Hopkins University Press.

Jameson, F. (1972) *The Prison House of Language: A Critical Account of Structuralism and Russian Formalism*, Princeton, NJ: Princeton University Press.

—— (1981) *The Political Unconscious: Narrative as a Socially Symbolic Act*, Ithaca, NY: Cornell University Press.

—— (1991) *Postmodernism, or, the Cultural Logic of Late Capitalism*, Durham, NC: Duke University Press.

Janmohamed, A.R. (1994) 'Some Implications of Paulo Freire's Border Pedagogy', in *Between Borders: Pedagogy and the Politics of Cultural Studies*, H.A. Giroux and P. McLaren (eds), New York: Routledge, pp. 242–52.

Jauss, H.R. (1982) *Toward an Aesthetic of Reception*, Minneapolis: University of Minnesota Press.

Jones, H. (1989) 'Feminism and Nationalism in Domestic Melodrama: Gender, Genre, and Canadian Identity', *Essays in Theatre* 8, 1 (November): 5–14.

Jonson, B. (1988) *Five Plays*, Oxford: Oxford University Press.

Kaye, N. (1994) *Postmodernism and Performance*, Basingstoke: Macmillan.

Knowles, R.P. (1994a) 'From Nationalist to Multinational: The Stratford Festival, Free Trade, and the Discourses of Intercultural Tourism', unpublished paper.

—— (1994b) 'Shakespeare, 1993, and the Discourses of the Stratford Festival, Ontario', *Shakespeare Quarterly* 45, 2 (Summer): 211–25.

Kowsar, M. (1986) 'Deleuze on Theatre: A Case Study of Carmelo Bene's Richard III', *Theatre Journal* 38, 1 (March): 19–33.

—— (1992) 'Lacan's Antigone: A Case Study in Psychoanalytic Ethics', in *Critical Theory and Performance*, J.G. Reinelt and J.R. Roach (eds), Ann Arbor: University of Michigan Press, pp. 399–412.

Kristeva, J. (1981) 'Women's Time', *Signs* 7, 1: 12–35.

—— (1984) *Revolution in Poetic Language*, New York: Columbia University Press.

Kushner, T. (1993) *Angels in America, Part One: Millennium Approaches*, New York: Theatre Communications Group.

—— (1994) *Angels in America, Part Two: Perestroika*, New York: Theatre Communications Group.

Lacan, J. (1970) 'Of Structure as an Inmixing of an Otherness Prerequisite to Any Subject Whatever', in *The Languages of Criticism and the Sciences of Man: The Structuralist Controversy*, R. Macksey and E. Donato (eds), Baltimore, MD: Johns Hopkins University Press, pp. 186–200.

—— (1972) 'Seminar on "The Purloined Letter"', *Yale French Studies* 48: 39–72.

—— (1977a) 'Desire and the Interpretation of Desire in *Hamlet*', *Yale French Studies* 55/6: 11–52.

—— (1977b) *Écrits: A Selection*, New York: Norton.

—— (1978) *The Four Fundamental Concepts of Psycho-Analysis*, New York: Norton.

—— and the *école freudienne* (1982) *Feminine Sexuality*, J. Mitchell and J. Rose (eds), New York: Norton.

Laclau, E. (1988) 'Politics and the Limits of Modernity', in *Universal Abandon? The Politics of Postmodernism*, A. Ross (ed.), Minneapolis: University of Minnesota Press, pp. 63–82.

Landy, R.J. (1993) *Persona and Performance: The Meaning of Role in Drama, Therapy, and Everyday Life*, London: Jessica Kingsley Publishers.

Laris, K. (1995) Review of *As You Like It*, *Theatre Journal* 47, 2 (May): 300–2.

Latimer, D. (ed.) (1988) *Contemporary Critical Theory*, San Diego, CA: Harcourt.

Leitch, V.B. (ed.) (2001) *The Norton Anthology of Theory and Criticism*, New York: W.W. Norton.

Lewis, B. (1995) 'Back Over the Rainbow', *American Theatre* 12, 7 (September): 6.

Lodge, D. (ed.) (1988) *Modern Criticism and Theory: A Reader*, London: Longman.

Loney, G. (ed.) (1974) *Peter Brook's Production of* A Midsummer Night's Dream *for the Royal Shakespeare Company: The Complete and Authorized Acting Edition*, Stratford: Royal Shakespeare Company.

Lyons, C.R. and J. Lyons (1994) 'Anna Deavere Smith: Perspectives on her Performance within the Context of Critical Theory', *Journal of Dramatic Theory and Criticism* 9, 1 (Fall): 43–66.

Lyotard, J.-F. (1984) *The Postmodern Condition: A Report on Knowledge*, Minneapolis: University of Minnesota Press.

McClellan, K. (1978) *Whatever Happened to Shakespeare?*, London: Vision.

MacDonald, A.-M. (1990) *Goodnight Desdemona (Good Morning Juliet)*, Toronto: Coach House Press.

Macherey, P. (1978) *A Theory of Literary Production*, London: Routledge.

McLuhan, M. (1964) *Understanding Media: The Extensions of Man*, New York: Signet.

McNulty, C. (1993) 'The Queer as Drama Critic', *Theater* 24, 2: 12–20.

MacPherson, L. (1994) '*Oleanna* Highlights Political Correctness as Next Big Threat', in University of Toronto *Varsity* (20 October): 5.

Magarshack, D. (1992) 'Stanislavsky', in *The Theory of the Modern Stage*, E. Bentley (ed.), Harmondsworth: Penguin.

Makaryk, I.R. (ed.) (1993) *Encyclopedia of Contemporary Literary Theory: Approaches, Scholars, Terms*, Toronto: University of Toronto Press.

Mamet, D. (1992) *Oleanna*, New York: Pantheon.

Marranca, B. (1995) 'Theatre and the University at the End of the Twentieth Century', *Performing Arts Journal* 17, 2/3 (May/September): 55–71.

—— and G. Dasgupta (eds) (1999) *Conversations on Art and Performance*, Baltimore, MD: Johns Hopkins University Press.

Marx, K. (1977) *Capital*, vol. 1, New York: Vintage.

Merleau-Ponty, M. (1962) *Phenomenology of Perception*, London: Routledge.

Minh-Ha, T.T. (1989) *Woman, Native, Other: Writing Postcoloniality and Feminism*, Bloomington: Indiana University Press.

—— (1992) *Framer Framed*, New York: Routledge.

Moi, T. (1985) *Sexual/Textual Politics: Feminist Literary Theory*, London: Routledge.

Morton, D. (1995) 'Birth of the Cyberqueer', *PMLA* 110, 3 (May): 369–81.

Mouffe, C. (1988) 'Radical Democracy: Modern or Postmodern?', in *Universal Abandon? The Politics of Postmodernism*, A. Ross (ed.), Minneapolis: University of Minnesota Press, pp. 31–45.

Mufson, D. (1993) 'The Critical Eye: Sexual Perversity in Viragos', *Theater* 24, 1: 111–13.

Müller, H. (1979) 'Reflections on Post-Modernism', *New German Critique* 16 (Winter): 55–7.

—— (1982) 'The Walls of History', *Semiotext(e)* 4, 2: 36–76.

—— (1984) *Hamletmachine and Other Texts for the Stage*, New York: Performing Arts Journal Publications.

Mulvey, L. (1975) 'Visual Pleasure and Narrative Cinema', *Screen* 16, 3 (Autumn): 6–18.

Natoli, J. and L. Hutcheon (eds) (1993) *A Postmodern Reader*, Albany: State University of New York Press.

Nietzsche, F. (1964) *The Genealogy of Morals: A Polemic*, New York: Russell and Russell.

—— (1966) *Beyond Good and Evil: Prelude to a Philosophy of the Future*, New York: Random House.

—— (1967) *The Birth of Tragedy* and *The Case of Wagner*, New York: Vintage.

Norris, C. (1982) *Deconstruction: Theory and Practice*, London: Routledge.

Osinski, Z. (1986) *Grotowski and his Laboratory*, New York: PAJ Publications.

Pavis, P. (1981) 'The Interplay Between Avant-Garde Theatre and Semiology', *Performing Arts Journal* 15: 75–85.

—— (1982) *Languages of the Stage: Essays in the Semiology of Theatre*, New York: PAJ Publications.

—— (1987) 'Problems of Translation for the Stage: Interculturalism and Post-modern Theatre', in *The Play Out of Context: Transferring Plays from Culture to Culture*, H. Scolnikov and P. Holland (eds), Cambridge: Cambridge University Press, pp. 25–44.

—— (ed.) (1996) *The Intercultural Performance Reader*, London: Routledge.

Peirce, C. (1991) *Peirce on Signs*, J. Hoopes (ed.), Chapel Hill: University of North Carolina Press.

Performance Group (1970) *Dionysus in 69*, R. Schechner (ed.), New York: Farrar, Strauss and Giroux.

Pound, E. (1971) *Personae*, New York: New Directions.

Pyle, F. (1995) *The Ideology of Imagination: Subject and Society in the Discourse of Romanticism*, Stanford, CA: Stanford University Press.

Rabkin, G. (1983) 'The Play of Misreading: Text/Theatre/Deconstruction', *Performing Arts Journal* 19: 44–60.

—— (1985) 'Is There a Text on This Stage? Theatre/Authorship/Interpretation', *Performing Arts Journal* 26/7: 142–59.

Rayner, A. (1994) *To Act, To Do, To Perform: Drama and the Phenomenology of Action*, Ann Arbor: University of Michigan Press.

—— (1995) 'Improper Conjunctions: Metaphor, Performance, and Text', *Essays in Theatre* 14, 1 (November): 3–14.

Reinelt, J.G. and J.R. Roach (eds) (1992) *Critical Theory and Performance*, Ann Arbor: University of Michigan Press.

Rich, A. (1980) 'Compulsory Heterosexuality and Lesbian Experience', *Signs* 5: 631–60.

Ricouer, P. (1970) *Freud and Philosophy: An Essay on Interpretation*, New Haven, CT: Yale University Press.

Roman, D. (1998) *Acts of Intervention: Performance, Gay Culture and Aids*, Bloomington: Indiana University Press.

Said, E. (1978) *Orientalism*, New York: Pantheon.

—— (1993) *Culture and Imperialism*, New York: Knopf.

Sartre, J.-P. (1966) *Being and Nothingness: An Essay on Phenomenological Ontology*, New York: Washington Square Press.

—— (1989) *No Exit and Three Other Plays*, New York: Vintage International.

Savran, D. (1995a) 'Ambivalence, Utopia, and a Queer Sort of Materialism: How *Angels in America* Reconstructs the Nation', *Theatre Journal* 47, 2 (May): 207–27.

—— (1995b) 'The Theatre of the Fabulous: An Interview with Tony Kushner', in *Essays on Kushner's Angels*, P. Brask (ed.), Winnipeg: Blizzard Publishing, pp. 127–54.

Saussure, F. de (1974) *Course in General Linguistics*, New York: Fontana/Collins.

Schechner, R. (1988) *Performance Theory*, revised edition, New York, London: Methuen.

Schneeman, C. (1997) *More than Meat Joy: Performance Works and Selected Writings*, Kingston, NY: McPherson and Company.

Scholes, R. (1974) *Structuralism in Literature: An Introduction*, New Haven, CT: Yale University Press.

Sedgwick, E.K. (1990) *The Epistemology of the Closet*, Berkeley: University of California Press.

Selbourne, D. (1982) *The Making of A MIDSUMMER NIGHT'S DREAM: An Eye-witness Account of Peter Brook's Production from First Rehearsal to Opening Night*, London: Methuen.

Senelick, L. (ed.) (1999) *Lovesick: Modernist plays of Same-Sex Love 1894–1925*, London: Routledge.

Shakespeare, W. (1974) *The Riverside Shakespeare*, G.B. Evans (ed.), Boston, MA: Houghton Mifflin.

Shange, N. (1992) *for colored girls who have considered suicide / when the rainbow is enuf*, in *Plays: One*, London: Methuen, pp. 3–64.

Shaw, G.B. (1997) *Pygmalion*, in *The Bedford Introduction to Drama*, 3rd edition, L.A. Jacobus (ed.), Boston, MA: Bedford Books, pp. 822–71.

Shiach, M. (1991) *Hélène Cixous: A Politics of Writing*, London: Routledge.

Silverstein, M. (1994) ' "Make Us the Women We Can't Be": *Cloud Nine* and the Female Imaginary', *Journal of Dramatic Theory and Criticism* 8, 2 (Spring): 7–22.

Sim, S. (ed.) (1998) *The Icon Critical Dictionary of Postmodern Thought*, Cambridge: Icon Books.

Sinfield, A. (1999) *Out on Stage: Lesbian and Gay Theatre in the Twentieth Century*, New Haven, CT: Yale University Press.

Smith, A.D. (1992) *Twilight: Los Angeles, 1992*, New York: Anchor Books.

Smith, P. (1988) *Discerning the Subject*, Minneapolis: University of Minnesota Press.

Soyinka, W. (1974) *Collected Plays 2*, London: Oxford University Press.

—— (1996) 'Theatre in African Traditional Cultures: Survival Patterns', in *The Twentieth-Century Performance Reader*, M. Huxley and N. Witts (eds), London: Routledge, pp. 241–56.

Spivak, G.C. (1987) *In Other Worlds: Essays in Cultural Politics*, New York: Methuen.

—— (1988) 'Can the Subaltern Speak?', in *Marxism and the Interpretation of Culture*, C. Nelson and L. Grossberg (eds), Urbana: University of Illinois Press, pp. 271–313.

—— (1995) 'Ghostwriting', *Diacritics* 25/2 (Summer): 65–84.

—— (1999) *Critique of Postcolonial Reason*, Cambridge, MA: Harvard University Press.

Stanislavski, C. (1948) *My Life in Art*, New York: Theatre Arts Books.

States, B.O. (1985) *Great Reckonings in Little Rooms: On the Phenomenology of Theater*, Berkeley: University of California Press.

—— (1992) 'The Phenomenological Attitude', in *Critical Theory and Performance*, J.G. Reinelt and J.R. Roach (eds), Ann Arbor: University of Michigan Press, pp. 369–79.

Stoppard, T. (1983) *The Real Thing*, London: Faber.

Taylor, G. (1989) *Reinventing Shakespeare: A Cultural History from the Restoration to the Present*, New York: Weidenfeld and Nicolson.

Taylor, K. (2000) 'The Lost Art of Listening', in Toronto *Globe and Mail* (12 October): R1, 5.

Van Nortwick, T. (1998) *Oedipus: The Meaning of a Masculine Life*, Norman: University of Oklahoma Press.

Vattimo, G. (1988) *The End of Modernity: Nihilism and Hermeneutics in Postmodern Culture*, Baltimore, MD: Johns Hopkins University Press.

Wallace, M. (1992) 'Negative Images: Towards a Black Feminist Cultural Criticism', in *Cultural Studies*, L. Grossberg, C. Nelson and P.A. Treichler (eds), New York: Routledge.

Wallace, R. (1990) *Producing Marginality: Theatre and Criticism in Canada*, Saskatoon: Fifth House.

—— (1994) 'Towards a Poetics of Gay Male Theatre', *Essays on Canadian Writing* 54 (Winter): 212–36.

Weber, C. (1991) 'German Theatre between the Past and the Future', *Performing Arts Journal* 37 (January): 43–59.

Weeks, J. (1995) *Invented Moralities: Sexual Values in an Age of Uncertainty*, New York: Columbia University Press.

Weimann, R. (1978) *Shakespeare and the Popular Tradition in the Theater: Studies in the Social Dimension of Dramatic Form and Function*, Baltimore, MD: Johns Hopkins University Press.

Whitmore, J. (1994) *Directing Postmodern Theater: Shaping Signification in Performance*, Ann Arbor: University of Michigan Press.

Wiles, D. (1987) *Shakespeare's Clown: Actor and Text in the Elizabethan Playhouse*, Cambridge: Cambridge University Press.

Wiley, C. (1991) Review of *for colored girls who have considered suicide / when the rainbow is enuf*, *Theatre Journal* 43: 381–2.

Williams, P. and L. Chrisman (eds) (1994) *Colonial Discourse and Post-Colonial Theory: A Reader*, New York: Columbia University Press.

Williams, R. (1977) *Marxism and Literature*, Oxford: Oxford University Press.

—— (1983) *Towards 2000*, London: Chatto and Windus.

Woolf, V. (1977) *A Room of One's Own*, London: Grafton.

Wright, E. (1998) *Psychoanalytic Criticism: A Reappraisal*, 2nd edition, New York: Routledge.

Žižek, S. (1989) *The Sublime Object of Ideology*, London: Verso.

—— (1991) *Looking Awry: An Introduction to Jacques Lacan through Popular Culture*, Cambridge, MA: MIT Press.

—— (1992) *Enjoy Your Symptom! Jacques Lacan in Hollywood and Out*, New York: Routledge.

INDEX